# Workshop on Semantic Evaluations: Recent Achievements and Future Directions 2009

# (SEW 2009)



**Held at NAACL HLT 2009**

## Boulder, Colorado, USA
## 4 June 2009

**ISBN: 978-1-61738-565-0**

**Printed from e-media with permission by:**

Curran Associates, Inc.
57 Morehouse Lane
Red Hook, NY 12571

**Some format issues inherent in the e-media version may also appear in this print version.**



Printed by Curran Associates, Inc. (2010)

For permission requests, please contact the Association for Computational Linguistics at the address below.

Association for Computational Linguistics
209 N. Eighth Street
Stroudsburg, Pennsylvania 18360

Phone: 1-570-476-8006
Fax: 1-570-476-0860

acl@aclweb.org

**Additional copies of this publication are available from:**

Curran Associates, Inc.
57 Morehouse Lane
Red Hook, NY 12571 USA
Phone: 845-758-0400
Fax: 845-758-2634
Email: curran@proceedings.com
Web: www.proceedings.com

# Introduction

This volume contains papers accepted for presentation at the SEW-2009 Workshop on "Semantic Evaluations: Recent Achievements and Future Directions". This event takes place on June 4, 2009 in Boulder, Colorado, USA, and immediately follows the North American Chapter of the Association for Computational Linguistics - Human Language Technologies (NAACL HLT) 2009 conference.

The main purpose of the workshop is to review, analyze and discuss the latest developments in semantic analysis of text. The fact that the workshop occurs between the last Semantic Evaluation exercise (SemEval-2007) and the preparation for the next SemEval in 2010, presents an exciting opportunity to discuss practical and foundational aspects of semantic processing of text. The workshop targets papers describing both semantic processing systems and evaluation exercises, with special attention to foundational issues in both lexical and propositional semantics, including semantic representation and semantic corpus construction problems.

We issued calls for both regular and short papers, where the latter included papers on semantic evaluation tasks (especially those planned for SemEval-2010) and papers describing ongoing work, possibly with preliminary results. The worskhop received thirty-one submissions. Of these, based on the careful reviews of our program committee, the workshop accepted eight regular papers, four short papers for ongoing work, and ten SemEval-2010 task description papers. We are indebted to all program committee members for their high quality, elaborate and thoughtful reviews. The papers in this proceedings have surely benefited from this feedback.

Having a prominent researcher as an invited speaker greatly contributes to the quality of the workshop. We thank Diana McCarthy for her invited talk. We are also indebted to Katrin Erk and Carlo Strapparava, as well as the panel members, for providing discussion and insights of the future directions for semantic evaluations.

We are grateful to the NAACL HLT 2009 conference organizers for local organization and the forum. We most gratefully acknowledge the support of our sponsors, the ACL Special Interest Group on the Lexicon (SIGLEX), the ACL Special Interest Group on Computational Semantics (SIGSEM), and the ACL Special Interest Group for Annotation (SIGANN).

Welcome to SEW-2009!

Eneko Agirre, Lluís Màrquez, and Richard Wicentowski
June 2009

**Organizers:**

Eneko Agirre, University of the Basque Country (UPV/EHU), Basque Country
Lluís Màrquez, Technical University of Catalonia (UPC), Catalonia
Richard Wicentowski, Swarthmore College, USA

**Program Committee:**

Timothy Baldwin, University of Melbourne
Nicoletta Calzolari, Istituto di Linguistica Computazionale "Antonio Zampolli"
Xavier Carreras, Massachusetts Institute of Technology
Walter Daelemans, University of Antwerp
Katrin Erk, University of Texas at Austin
Roxana Girju, University of Illinois at Urbana-Champaign
Veronique Hoste, Hogeschool Gent
Eduard Hovy, Information Sciences Institute
Nancy Ide, Vassar College
Kenneth Litkowski, CL Research
Bernardo Magnini, ITC-irst
Katja Markert, University of Leeds
David Martínez, University of Melbourne
Diana McCarthy, University of Sussex
Rada Mihalcea, University of North Texas
Roberto Navigli, Universita di Roma "Sapienza"
Hwee Tou Ng, National University of Singapore
Martha Palmer, University of Colorado at Boulder
Ted Pedersen, University of Minnesota at Duluth
German Rigau, University of the Basque Country
Mark Stevenson, University of Sheffield
Carlo Strapparava, Fondazione Bruno Kessler
Mihai Surdeanu, Stanford University
Stan Szpakowicz, University of Ottawa
Dekai Wu, Hong Kong University of Science and Technology
Deniz Yuret, Ko c University

**Additional Reviewers:**

Ravi Sinha, University of North Texas

**Invited Speaker:**

Diana McCarthy, University of Sussex

# Table of Contents

# Conference Program

**Thursday, June 4, 2009**

9:00–9:10 Opening Remarks

9:10–10:05 Invited Talk: *Alternative Annotations of Word Usage*
Diana McCarthy

10:05–10:30 *Making Sense of Word Sense Variation*
Rebecca Passoneau, Ansaf Salleb-Aouissi and Nancy Ide

10:30–11:00 Break

11:00–11:25 *Refining the most frequent sense baseline*
Judita Preiss, Jon Dehdari, Josh King and Dennis Mehay

11:25–11:50 *One Translation Per Discourse*
Marine Carpuat

11:50–12:15 *Using Web Selectors for the Disambiguation of All Words*
Hansen A. Schwartz and Fernando Gomez

12:15–12:40 *Large-scale Semantic Networks: Annotation and Evaluation*
Vaclav Novak, Sven Hartrumpf and Keith Hall

12:40–14:00 Lunch

14:00–15:30 Poster Session

*Making Semantic Topicality Robust Through Term Abstraction*
Paul M. Heider and Rohini K. Srihari

*Meeting TempEval-2: Shallow Approach for Temporal Tagger*
Oleksandr Kolomiyets and Marie-Francine Moens

*Using Lexical Patterns in the Google Web 1T Corpus to Deduce Semantic Relations Between Nouns*
Paul Nulty and Fintan Costello

**Thursday, June 4, 2009 (continued)**

| | |
|---|---|
| | *Improvements To Monolingual English Word Sense Disambiguation*<br>Weiwei Guo and Mona Diab |
| | *SemEval-2010 Task 1: Coreference Resolution in Multiple Languages*<br>Marta Recasens, Toni Martí, Mariona Taulé, Lluís Màrquez and Emili Sapena |
| | *SemEval-2010 Task 2: Cross-Lingual Lexical Substitution*<br>Ravi Sinha, Diana McCarthy and Rada Mihalcea |
| | *SemEval-2010 Task 3: Cross-lingual Word Sense Disambiguation*<br>Els Lefever and Veronique Hoste |
| | *SemEval-2010 Task 7: Argument Selection and Coercion*<br>James Pustejovsky and Anna Rumshisky |
| | *SemEval-2010 Task 8: Multi-Way Classification of Semantic Relations Between Pairs of Nominals*<br>Iris Hendrickx, Su Nam Kim, Zornitsa Kozareva, Preslav Nakov, Diarmuid Ó Séaghdha, Sebastian Padó, Marco Pennacchiotti, Lorenza Romano and Stan Szpakowicz |
| | *SemEval-2010 Task 9: The Interpretation of Noun Compounds Using Paraphrasing Verbs and Prepositions*<br>Cristina Butnariu, Su Nam Kim, Preslav Nakov, Diarmuid Ó Séaghdha, Stan Szpakowicz and Tony Veale |
| | *SemEval-2010 Task 10: Linking Events and Their Participants in Discourse*<br>Josef Ruppenhofer, Caroline Sporleder, Roser Morante, Collin Baker and Martha Palmer |
| | *SemEval-2010 Task 13: Evaluating Events, Time Expressions, and Temporal Relations (TempEval-2)*<br>James Pustejovsky and Marc Verhagen |
| | *SemEval-2010 Task 14: Evaluation Setting for Word Sense Induction & Disambiguation Systems*<br>Suresh Manandhar and Ioannis Klapaftis |
| | *SemEval-2010 Task 17: All-words Word Sense Disambiguation on a Specific Domain*<br>Eneko Agirre, Oier Lopez de Lacalle, Christiane Fellbaum, Andrea Marchetti, Antonio Toral and Piek Vossen |
| 15:30–16:00 | Break |
| 16:00–16:25 | *Relation detection between named entities: report of a shared task*<br>Cláudia Freitas, Diana Santos, Cristina Mota, Hugo Gonçalo Oliveira and Paula Carvalho |

**Thursday, June 4, 2009 (continued)**

16:25–16:50 *Error Analysis of the TempEval Temporal Relation Identification Task*
Chong Min Lee and Graham Katz

16:50–17:15 *Automatic Recognition of Logical Relations for English, Chinese and Japanese in the GLARF Framework*
Adam Meyers, Michiko Kosaka, Nianwen Xue, Heng Ji, Ang Sun, Shasha Liao and Wei Xu

17:15–18:00 Panel on SemEval-2010

18:00–18:05 Closing

# Alternative Annotations of Word Usage

Diana McCarthy,
Department of Informatics,
University of Sussex
Falmer BN1 9QJ, UK
dianam@sussex.ac.uk

**Abstract**

Right from Senseval's inception there have been questions over the choice of sense inventory for word sense disambiguation (Kilgarriff, 1998). While researchers usually acknowledge the issues with predefined listings produced by lexicographers, such lexical resources have been a major catalyst to work on annotating words with meaning. As well as the heavy reliance on manually produced sense inventories, the work on word sense disambiguation has focused on the task of selecting the single best sense from the predefined inventory for each given token instance. There is little evidence that the state-of-the-art level of success is sufficient to benefit applications. We also have no evidence that the systems we build are interpreting words in context in the way that humans do. One direction that has been explored for practical reasons is that of finding a level of granularity where annotators and systems can do the task with a high level of agreement (Navigli et al., 2007; Hovy et al., 2006). In this talk I will discuss some alternative annotations using synonyms (McCarthy and Navigli, 2007), translations (Sinha et al., 2009) and WordNet senses with graded judgments (Erk et al., to appear) which are not proposed as a panacea to the issue of semantic representation but will allow us to look at word usages in a more graded fashion and which are arguably better placed to reflect the phenomena we wish to capture than the 'winner takes all' strategy.

## References

Katrin Erk, Diana McCarthy, and Nick Gaylord. Investigations on word senses and word usages. In Proceedings of ACL-IJCNLP 2009, to appear.

Eduard Hovy, Mitch Marcus, Martha Palmer, Lance Ramshaw, and Ralph Weischedel. Ontonotes: The 90% solution. In *Proceedings of the HLT-NAACL 2006 workshop on Learning word meaning from non-linguistic data*, New York City, USA, 2006. Association for Computational Linguistics.

Adam Kilgarriff. Gold standard datasets for evaluating word sense disambiguation programs. *Computer Speech and Language*, 12(3):453–472, 1998.

Diana McCarthy and Roberto Navigli. SemEval-2007 task 10: English lexical substitution task. In *Proceedings of (SemEval-2007)*, pages 48–53, Prague, Czech Republic, 2007.

Roberto Navigli, Kenneth C. Litkowski, and Orin Hargraves. SemEval-2007 task 7: Coarse-grained English all-words task˙ In *Proceedings of the 4th International Workshop on Semantic Evaluations (SemEval-2007)*, pages 30–35, Prague, Czech Republic, 2007.

Ravi Sinha, Diana McCarthy, and Rada Mihalcea. Semeval-2010 task 2: Cross-lingual lexical substitution. In *Proceedings of the NAACL-HLT Workshop SEW-2009*, Boulder, Colorado, USA, 2009.



*Proceedings of the NAACL HLT Workshop on Semantic Evaluations: Recent Achievements and Future Directions*, page 1,
Boulder, Colorado, June 2009. 

# Making Sense of Word Sense Variation

**Rebecca J. Passonneau** *and* **Ansaf Salleb-Aouissi**
Center for Computational Learning Systems
Columbia University
New York, NY, USA
(becky@cs|ansaf@ccls).columbia.edu

**Nancy Ide**
Department of Computer Science
Vassar College
Poughkeepsie, NY, USA
ide@cs.vassar.edu

## Abstract

We present a pilot study of word-sense annotation using multiple annotators, relatively polysemous words, and a heterogenous corpus. Annotators selected senses for words in context, using an annotation interface that presented WordNet senses. Interannotator agreement (IA) results show that annotators agree well or not, depending primarily on the individual words and their general usage properties. Our focus is on identifying systematic differences across words and annotators that can account for IA variation. We identify three lexical use factors: semantic specificity of the context, sense concreteness, and similarity of senses. We discuss systematic differences in sense selection across annotators, and present the use of association rules to mine the data for systematic differences across annotators.

## 1 Introduction

Our goal is to grapple seriously with the natural sense variation arising from individual differences in word usage. It has been widely observed that usage features such as vocabulary and syntax vary across corpora of different genres and registers (Biber, 1995), and that serve different functions (Kittredge et al., 1991). Still, we are far from able to predict specific morphosyntactic and lexical variations across corpora (Kilgarriff, 2001), much less quantify them in a way that makes it possible to apply the same analysis tools (taggers, parsers) without retraining. In comparison to morphosyntactic properties of language, word and phrasal meaning is fluid, and to some degree, generative (Pustejovsky, 1991; Nunberg, 1979). Based on our initial observations from a word sense annotation task for relatively polysemous words, carried out by multiple annotators on a heterogeneous corpus, we hypothesize that different words lead to greater or lesser interannotator agreement (IA) for reasons that in the long run should be explicitly modelled in order for Natural Language Processing (NLP) applications to handle usage differences more robustly. This pilot study is a step in that direction.

We present related work in the next section, then describe the annotation task in the following one. In Section 4, we present examples of variation in agreement on a matched subset of words. In Section 5 we discuss why we believe the observed variation depends on the words and present three lexical use factors we hypothesize to lead to greater or lesser IA. In Section 6, we use association rules to mine our data for systematic differences among annotators, thus to explain the variations in IA. We conclude with a summary of our findings goals.

## 2 Related Work

There has been a decade-long community-wide effort to evaluate word sense disambiguation (WSD) systems across languages in the four Senseval efforts (1998, 2001, 2004, and 2007, cf. (Kilgarriff, 1998; Pedersen, 2002a; Pedersen, 2002b; Palmer et al., 2005)), with a corollary effort to investigate the issues pertaining to preparation of manually annotated gold standard corpora tagged for word senses (Palmer et al., 2005). Differences in IA and system performance across part-of-speech have been examined, as in (Ng et al., 1999; Palmer et al.,



*Proceedings of the NAACL HLT Workshop on Semantic Evaluations: Recent Achievements and Future Directions*, pages 2–9,
Boulder, Colorado, June 2009. 

| Word | POS | No. senses | No. occurrences |
|---|---|---|---|
| fair | Adj | 10 | 463 |
| long | Adj | 9 | 2706 |
| quiet | Adj | 6 | 244 |
| land | Noun | 11 | 1288 |
| time | Noun | 10 | 21790 |
| work | Noun | 7 | 5780 |
| know | Verb | 11 | 10334 |
| say | Verb | 11 | 20372 |
| show | Verb | 12 | 11877 |
| tell | Verb | 8 | 4799 |

Table 1: Ten Words

2005). Pedersen (Pedersen, 2002a) examines variation across individual words in evaluating WSD systems, but does not attempt to explain it.

Factors that have been proposed as affecting human or system sense disambiguation include whether annotators are allowed to assign multilabels (Veronis, 1998; Ide et al., 2002; Passonneau et al., 2006), the number or granularity of senses (Ng et al., 1999), merging of related senses (Snow et al., 2007), sense similarity (Chugur et al., 2002), sense perplexity (Diab, 2004), entropy (Diab, 2004; Palmer et al., 2005), and in psycholinguistic experiments, reactions times required to distinguish senses (Klein and Murphy, 2002; Ide and Wilks, 2006).

With respect to using multiple annotators, Snow et al. included disambiguation of the word *president*–a relatively non-polysemous word with three senses–in a set of tasks given to Amazon Mechanical Turkers, aimed at determining how to combine data from multiple non-experts for machine learning tasks. The word sense task comprised 177 sentences taken from the SemEval Word Sense Disambiguation Lexical Sample task. Majority voting among three annotators achieve 99% accuracy.

## 3 The Annotation Task

The Manually Annotated Sub-Corpus (MASC) project is creating a small, representative corpus of American English written and spoken texts drawn from the Open American National Corpus (OANC).[1] The MASC corpus includes hand-validated or manually produced annotations for a variety of linguistic phenomena. One of the goals of

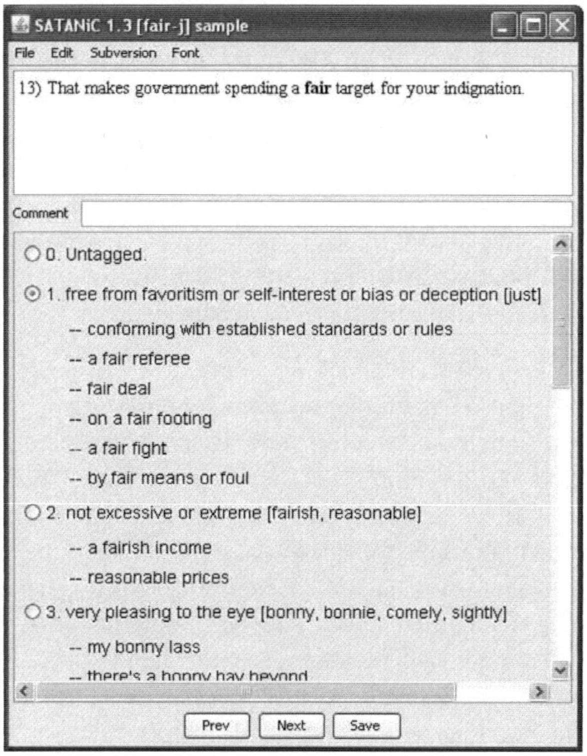


Figure 1: MASC word sense annotation tool

the project is to support efforts to harmonize WordNet (Miller et al., 1993) and FrameNet (Ruppenhofer et al., 2006), in order to bring the sense distinctions each makes into better alignment. As a starting sample, we chose ten fairly frequent, moderately polysemous words for sense tagging, targeting in particular words that do not yet exist in FrameNet, as well as words with different numbers of senses in the two resources. The ten words with part of speech, number of senses, and occurrences in the OANC are shown in Table 1. One thousand occurrences of each word , including all occurrences appearing in the MASC subset and others semi-randomly[2] chosen from the remainder of the 15 million word OANC, were annotated by at least one annotator of six undergraduate annotators at Vassar College and Columbia University.

Fifty occurrences of each word in context were sense-tagged by all six annotators for the in-depth study of inter-annotator agreement (IA) reported here. We have just finished collecting annotations of fifty new occurrences. All annotations are pro-

[1]http://www.anc.org

[2]The occurrences were drawn equally from each of the genre-specific portions of the OANC.

duced using the custom-built interface to WordNet shown in Figure 1: the sentence context is at the top with the word in boldface (**fair**), a comment region below that allows the annotator to keep notes, and a scrollable area below that shows three of the ten WordNet senses for "*fair*."

## 4 Observation: Varying Agreement, depending on Lexical Items

We expected to find varying levels of interannotator agreement (IA) among all six annotators, depending on obvious grouping factors such as the part of speech, or the number of senses per word. We do find widely varying levels of agreement, but as described here, most of the variation does not depend on these a priori factors. Inherent usage properties of the words themselves, and systematic patterns of variation across annotators, seem to be the primary factors, with a secondary effect of part of speech.

In previous work (Passonneau, 2004), we have discussed why we use Krippendorff's $\alpha$ (Krippendorff, 1980), and for purposes of comparison we also report Cohen's $\kappa$; note the similarity in values[3]. As with the various agreement coefficients that factor out the agreement that would occur by chance, values range from 1 for perfect agreement and -1 for perfect opposition, to 0 for chance agreement. While there are no hard and fast criteria for what constitutes good IA, Landis and Koch (Landis and Koch, 1977) consider values between 0.40 and 0.60 to represent moderately good agreement, and values above 0.60 as quite good; Krippendorff (Krippendorff, 1980) considers values above 0.67 moderately good, and values above 0.80 as quite good. (cf. (Artstein and Poesio, 2008) for discussion of agreement measurement for computational linguistic tasks.)

Table 2 shows IA for a pair of adjectives, nouns and verbs from our sample for which the IA scores are at the extremes (high and low) in each pair: the average delta is 0.24. Note that the agreement decreases as part-of-speech varies from adjectives to nouns to verbs, but for all three parts-of-speech, there is a wide spread of values. It is striking, given that the same annotators did all words, that one in each pair has relatively better agreement.

[3] $\alpha$ handles multiple annotators; Arstein and Poesio (Artstein and Poesio, 2008) propose an extension of $\kappa$ ($\kappa^3$) we use here.

| POS | Word | $\alpha$ | $\kappa$ | No. senses | Used |
|---|---|---|---|---|---|
| adj | long | 0.6664 | 0.6665 | 9 | 8 |
| | fair | 0.3546 | 0.3593 | 10 | 5 |
| noun | work | 0.5359 | 0.5358 | 7 | 7 |
| | land | 0.2627 | 0.2671 | 11 | 8 |
| verb | tell | 0.4152 | 0.4165 | 8 | 8 |
| | show | 0.2636 | 0.2696 | 12 | 11 |

Table 2: Varying interannotator agreement across words

The average of the agreement values shown in Table 2 ($\overline{\alpha}$=0.4164; $\overline{\kappa}$=0.4191) is somewhat higher than the average 0.317 found for 191 words annotated for WordNet senses in (Ng et al., 1999), but lower than their recomputed $\kappa$ of 0.85 for verbs, after they reanalyzed the data to merge senses for 42 of the verbs. It is widely recognized that achieving high $\kappa$ scores (or percent agreement between annotators, cf. (Palmer et al., 2005)) is difficult for word sense annotation.

Given that the same annotators have higher IA on some words, and lower on others, we hypothesize that it is the word usages themselves that lead to the high deltas in IA for each part-of-speech pair. We discuss the impact of three factors on the observed variations in agreement:

1. Greater specificity in the contexts of use leads to higher agreement
2. More concrete senses give rise to higher agreement
3. A sense inventory with closely related senses (e.g., relatively lower average inter-sense similarity scores) gives rise to lower agreement

## 5 Explanatory Factors

First we list factors that can not explain the variation in Table 2. Then we turn to examples illustrating factors that can, based on a manual search for examples of two types: examples where most annotators agreed on a single sense, and examples where two or three senses were agreed upon by multiple annotators. Later we how how we use association rules to detect these two types of cases automatically. For these examples, the WordNet sense number is shown (e.g., WN S1) with an abbreviated gloss, followed by the number of annotators who chose it.

### 5.1 Ruled Out Factors

It appears that neither annotator expertise, a word's part of speech, the number of senses in WordNet, the number of senses annotators find in the corpus, nor the nature of the distribution across senses, can account for the variation in IA in Table 2. All six annotators used the same annotation tool, the same guidelines, and had already become experienced in the word sense annotation task.

The six annotators all exhibit roughly the same performance. We measure an individual annotator's performance by computing the average pairwise IA ($\overline{IA_2}$). For every annotator $A_i$, we first compute the pairwise agreement of $A_i$ with every other annotator, then average. This gives us a measure for comparing individual annotators with each other: annotators that have a higher $\overline{IA_2}$ have more agreement, on average, with other annotators. Note that we get the same ranking of individuals when for each annotator, we calculate how much the agreement among the five remaining annotators improves over the agreement among all six annotators. If agreement improves relatively more when annotator $A_i$ is dropped, then $A_i$ agrees less well with the other five annotators. While both approaches give the same ranking among annotators, $\overline{IA_2}$ also provides a number that has an interpretable value.

On a word-by-word basis, some annotators do better than others. For example, for *long*, the best annotator (A) has $\overline{IA_2}$=0.79, and the worst (F) has 0.44. However, across ten words annotated by all six, the average of their $\overline{IA_2}$ is 0.39 with a standard deviation of 0.037. F at 0.32 is an outlier; apart from F, annotators have similar $\overline{IA}$ across words.

Table 2 lists the distribution of available senses in WordNet for the four words (column 4), and the number of senses used (column 5). The words *work* and *tell* have relatively fewer senses (seven and eigith) compared with nine through twelve for the other words. However, neither the number (or proportion) of senses used by annotators, nor the distribution across senses, has a significant correlation with IA, as given by Pearson's correlation test.

### 5.2 Lexical Use Factors

Underspecified contexts lead to ambiguous word meanings, a factor that has been recognized as being associated with polysemous contexts (Palmer et al., 2005). We find that the converse is also true: relatively specific contexts reduce ambiguity.

The word *long* seems to engender the greatest IA primarily because the contexts are concrete and specific, with a secondary effect that adjectives have higher IA overall than the other parts of speech. Sentences such as (1.), where a specific unit of temporal or spatial measurement is mentioned (*months*), restrict the sense to extent in space or time.

1. For 18 long months Michael could not find a job.
   WN S1. temporal extent [N=6 of 6]

In the few cases where annotators disagree on *long*, the context is less specific or less concrete. In example (2.), *long* is predicated of the word *chapter*, which has non-concrete senses that exemplify a certain type of productive polysemy (Pustejovsky, 1991). It can be taken to refer to a physical object (a specific set of pages in an actual book), or a conceptual object (the abstract literary work). The adjective inherits this polysemy. The three annotators who agree on sense two (spatial extent) might have the physical object sense in mind; the two who select sense one (temporal extent) possibly took the point of view of the reader who requires a long time to read the chapter.

2. After I had submitted the manuscript my editor at Simon Schuster had suggested a number of cuts to streamline what was already a long and involved chapter on Brians ideas.
   WN S2.spatial extent [N=3 of 6],
   WN S1.temporal extent [N=2 of 6],
   WN S9.more than normal or necessary [N=1 of 6]

Several of the senses of *work* are concrete, and quite distinct: sense seven, "an artist's or writer's output"; sense three, "the occupation you are paid for"; sense five, "unit of force in physics"; sense six, "the place where one works." These are the senses most often selected by a majority of annotators. Senses one and two, which are closely related, are the two senses most often selected by different annotators for the same instance. They also represent examples of productive polysemy, here between an activity sense (sense one) and a product-of-the-activity sense (sense two). Example (3) shows a sentence where the verb *perform* restricts the meaning to the *activity* sense, which all annotators selected.

3. The work performed by Rustom and colleagues suggests that cell protrusions are a general mechanism for cell-to-cell communication and that information exchange is occurring through the direct membrane continuity of connected cells independently of exo- and endocytosis.
   WN S1.activity of making something [N=6 of 6]

In sentence (4.), four annotators selected sense one (activity) and two selected sense two (result):

4. A close friend is a plastic surgeon who did some minor OK semi-major facial work on me in the past.
   WN S1.activity directed toward making something [N=4 of 6],
   WN S2.product of the effort of a person or thing [N=2 of 6]

For the word *fair*, if five or six annotators agree, often they have selected sense one–"free of favoritism or bias"–as in example (5). However, this sense is often selected along with sense two–"not excessive or extreme"as in example (6). Both senses are relatively abstract.

5. By insisting that everything Microsoft has done is fair competition they risk the possibility that the public if it accepts the judges finding to the contrary will conclude that Microsoft doesn't know the difference.
   WN S1.free of favoritism/bias [N=6 of 6]

6. I I think that's true I can remember times my parents would say well what do you think would be a fair punishment.
   WN S1.free of favoritism/bias [N=3 of 6],
   WN S2.not excessive or extreme [N=3 of 6]

Example (7) illustrates a case where all annotators agreed on a sense for *land*. The named entity *India* restricts the meaning to sense five, "territory occupied by a nation." Apart from a few such cases of high consensus, *land* seems to have low agreement due to senses being so closely related they can be merged. Senses one and seven both have to do with property (cf. example (8))., senses three and five with geopolitical senses, and senses two and four with the earth's surface or soil. If these three pairs of senses are merged into three senses, the IA goes up from 0.2627 to 0.3677.

7. India is exhilarating exhausting and infuriating a land where you'll find the practicalities of daily life overlay the mysteries that popular myth attaches to India.
   WN S5.territory occupied by a nation [N=6 of 6]

8. uh the Seattle area we lived outside outside of the city in the country and uh we have five acres of land up against a hillside where i grew up and so we did have a garden about a one a half acre garden
   WN S4.solid part of the earth's surface [N=1 of 6],
   WN S1.location of real estate [N=2 of 6],
   WN S7.extensive landed property [N=3 of 6]

Examples for *tell* and *show* exhibit the same trend in which agreement is greater when the sense is more specific or concrete, which we illustrate briefly with *show*. Example (9) describes a specific work of art, an El Greco painting, and agreement is universal among the six annotators on sense 5. In contrast, example (10) shows a fifty-fifty split among annotators for a sentence with a very specific context, an experiment regarding delivery of a DNA solution, but where the sense is abstract rather than concrete: the argument of *show* is an abstract proposition, namely a conclusion is drawn regarding what the experiment demonstrates, rather than a concrete result such as a specific measurement, or statistical outcome. Sense two in fact contains the word "experiment" that occurs in (9), which presumably biases the choice of sense two. Impressionistically, senses two and three appear to be quite similar.

9. El Greco shows St. Augustine and St. Stephen, in splendid ecclesiastical garb, lifting the count's body.
   WN S5.show in, or as in, a picture, N=6 of 6

10. These experiments show that low-volume jet injection specifically targeted delivery of a DNA solution to the skin and that the injection paths did not reach into the underlying tissue.
    WN S2.establish the validity of something, as by an example, explanation or experiment, N=3 of 6
    WN S3.provide evidence for, N=3 of 6

### 5.3 Quantifying Sense Similarity

Application of an inter-sense similarity measure (ISM) proposed in (Ide, 2006) to the sense inventories for each of the six words supports the observation that words with very similar senses have lower IA scores. ISM is computed for each pair in a given word's sense inventory, using a variant of the lesk measure (Banerjee and Pedersen, 2002). Agglomerative clustering may then be applied to the resulting similarity matrix to reveal the overall pattern of inter-sense relations.

ISMs for senses pairs of *long, fair, work, land, tell,* and *show* range from 0 to 1.44.[4] We compute a *confusion threshhold CT* based on the ISMs for all 250 sense pairs as

$$CT = \mu_{\mathrm{A}} + 2\sigma_{\mathrm{A}}$$

where $A$ is the sum of the ISMs for the six words' 250 sense pairs.

Table 3 shows the ISM statistics for the six words. The values show that the ISMs for *work* and *long* are significantly lower than for *land* and *fair*. The ISMs for the two verbs in the study, *show* and *tell*, are distributed across nearly the same range (0 - 1.38 and 0 - 1.22, respectively), despite substantially lower IA scores for *show*. However, the ISMs for three of *show*'s sense pairs are well above $CT$, vs. one for *tell*, suggesting that in addition to the range of ISMs for a given word's senses, the number of sense pairs with high similarity contributes to low IA. Overall, the correlation between the percentage of ISMs above $CT$ for the words in this study and their IA scores is .8, which supports this claim.

| POS | Word | Max | Mean | Std. Dev | > CT |
|---|---|---|---|---|---|
| adj | long | .71 | .28 | .18 | 0 |
| | fair | 1.25 | .28 | .34 | 5 |
| noun | work | .63 | .22 | .16 | 0 |
| | land | 1.44 | .17 | .29 | 3 |
| verb | tell | 1.22 | .15 | .25 | 1 |
| | show | 1.38 | .18 | .27 | 3 |

Table 3: ISM statistics

## 6 Association Rules

Association rules express relations among instances based on their attributes. Here the attributes of interest are the annotators who choose one sense versus those who choose another. Mining association rules to find strong relations has been studied in many domains (see for instance (Agrawal et al., 1993; Zaki et al., 1997; Salleb-Aouissi et al., 2007)). Here we illustrate how association rules can be used to mine relations such as systematic differences in word sense choices across annotators.

An association rule is an expression $\mathcal{C}_1 \Rightarrow \mathcal{C}_2$, where $\mathcal{C}_1$ and $\mathcal{C}_2$ express conditions on features describing the instances in a dataset. The strength of the rules is usually evaluated by means of measures such as *Support (Supp)* and *Confidence (Conf)*. Where $\mathcal{C}$, $\mathcal{C}_1$ and $\mathcal{C}_2$ express conditions on attributes:

- Supp($\mathcal{C}$) is the fraction of instances satisfying $\mathcal{C}$
- Supp($\mathcal{C}_1 \Rightarrow \mathcal{C}_2$) = Supp($\mathcal{C}_1 \wedge \mathcal{C}_2$)
- Conf($\mathcal{C}_1 \Rightarrow \mathcal{C}_2$) = Supp($\mathcal{C}_1 \wedge \mathcal{C}_2$)/Supp($\mathcal{C}_1$)

Given two thresholds MinSupp (for minimum support) and MinConf (for minimum confidence), a rule is *strong* when its support is greater than MinSupp and its confidence greater than MinConf. Discovering strong rules is usually a two-step process of retrieving instances above MinSupp, then from these retrieving instances above MinConf.

The types of association rules to mine can include any attributes in either the left hand side or the right hand side of rules. In our data, the attributes consist of the word sense assigned by annotators, the annotators, and the instances (words). In order to find rules that relate annotators to each other, the dataset must be pre-processed to produce flat (two-dimensional) tables. Here we focus on annotators to get a flat table in which each line corresponds to an annotator/sense combination: $Annotator\_Sense$. We denote the six annotators as A1 through A6, and word senses by WordNet sense number.

Here are 15 unique pairs of annotators, so one way to look at where agreements occur is to determine how many of these pairs choose the same sense with non-negligible support and confidence. *Tell* has much better IA than *show*, but less than *long* and *work*. We would expect association rules among many pairs of annotators for some but not all of its senses. We find 11 pairs of rules of the form $A_i\_Tell{:}Sense1 \rightarrow A_j\_Tell{:}Sense1$, $A_j\_Tell{:}Sense1 \rightarrow A_i\_Tell{:}Sense1$, indicating a bi-directional relationship between pairs of annotators choosing the same sense, with support ranging from 14% to 44% and confidence ranging from 37% to 96%. This indicates good support and confidence for many possible pairs

Our interest here is primarily in mining for systematic disagreements thus we now turn to pairs of rules where in one rule, an attribute $Annotator\_Sense_i$ occurs in the left hand side, and a distinct attribute $Annotator\_Sense_j$ occurs in the right. Again, we are especially interested in

[4] Note that because the scores are based on overlaps among WordNet relations, glosses, examples, etc., there is no predefined ceiling value for the ISMs. For the words in this study, we compute a ceiling value by taking the maximum of the ISMs for each of the 57 senses with itself, 4.85 in this case.

| i | j | Supp(%) | $\text{Conf}_i$(%) | $\text{Conf}_j$(%) |
|---|---|---|---|---|
| | | $A_i\_fair.S1 \leftrightarrow A_j\_fair.S2$ | | |
| A3 | A6 | 20 | 100 | 32.3 |
| A5 | A6 | 20 | 100 | 31.2 |
| A1 | A2 | 16 | 80 | 40 |
| | | $A_i\_show.S2 \leftrightarrow A_j\_show.S3$ | | |
| A1 | A3 | 32 | 84.2 | 69.6 |
| A5 | A3 | 24 | 63.2 | 80.0 |
| A4 | A3 | 22 | 91.7 | 57.9 |
| A4 | A6 | 14 | 58.3 | 46.7 |
| A4 | A2 | 12 | 60.0 | 50.0 |
| A5 | A2 | 12 | 60.0 | 40.0 |
| | | $A_i\_show.S5 \leftrightarrow A_j\_show.S10$ | | |
| A1 | A6 | 12 | 85.7 | 40.0 |
| A5 | A2 | 10 | 83.3 | 50.0 |
| A4 | A2 | 10 | 83.3 | 30.5 |
| A4 | A6 | 10 | 71.4 | 38.5 |
| A3 | A2 | 8 | 66.7 | 40.0 |
| A3 | A6 | 8 | 57.1 | 40.0 |
| A5 | A6 | 8 | 57.1 | 40.0 |

Table 4: Association Rules for Systematic Disagreements

bi-directional cases where there is a corresponding rule with the left and right hand clauses reversed. Table 4 shows some general classes of disagreement rules using a compact representation with a bidirectional arrow, along with a table of variables for the different pairs of annotators associated with different levels of support and confidence.

For *fair*, Table 4 summarizes three pairs of rules with good support (16-20% of all instances) in which one annotator chooses sense 1 of *fair* and another chooses sense 2: A3 and A5 choose sense 1 where A6 chooses sense 2, and A1 chooses sense 1 where A2 chooses sense 2. The confidence varies for each rule, thus in 100% of cases where A6 selects sense 2 of *fair*, A3 selects sense 1, but in only 32.3% of cases is the converse true. Example (6) where half the annotators picked sense 1 of *fair* and half picked sense 2 falls into the set of instances covered by these rules. The rules indicate this is not isolated, but rather part of a systematic pattern of usage.

The word *land* had the lowest interannotator agreement among the six annotators, with eight of eleven senses were used overall (cf. Table 2). Here we did not find pairs of rules in which distinct $Annotator\_Sense$ attributes that occur in the left and right sides of one rule occur in the right and left sides of another rule. For *show*,

Table 4 illustrates two systematic divisions among groups of annotators. With rather good support ranging from 12% to 32%, senses 2 and 3 exhibit a systematic difference: annotators A1, A4 and A5 select sense 2 where annotators A3, A3 and A6 select sense 3. Similarly, senses 5 and 10 exhibit a systematic difference: with a more modest support of 8% to 12%, annotators A1, A3, A4 and A5 select sense 5 where annotators A2 and A6 select sense 10.

## 7 Conclusion

We have performed a sense assignment experiment among multiple annotators for word occurrences drawn from a broad range of genres, rather than the domain-specific data utilized in many studies. The selected words were all moderately polysemous. Based on the results, we identify several factors that distinguish words with high vs. low interannotator agreement scores. We also show the use of association rules to mine the data for systematic annotator differences. Where relevant, the results can be used to merge senses, as done in much previous work, or to identify internal structure within a set of senses, such as a word-based sense-hierarchy. In our future work, we want to develop the use of association rules in several ways. First, we hope to fully automated the process of finding systematic patterns of difference across annotators. Second, we hope to extend their use to mining associations among the representations of instances in order to further investigate the lexical use factors discussed here.

## Acknowledgments

This work was supported in part by National Science Foundation grant CRI-0708952.

## References

Rakesh Agrawal, Tomasz Imielinski, and Arun N. Swami. 1993. Mining association rules between sets of items in large databases. In Peter Buneman and Sushil Jajodia, editors, *Proceedings of the 1993 ACM SIGMOD International Conference on Management of Data, Washington, D.C., May 26-28, 1993*, pages 207–216. ACM Press.

Ron Artstein and Massimo Poesio. 2008. Inter-coder agreement for computational linguistics. *Computational Linguistics*, 34(4):555–596.

Satanjeev Banerjee and Ted Pedersen. 2002. An adapted Lesk algorithm for word sense disambiguation using WordNet. In *Proceedings of the third International Conference on Intelligent Text Processing and Computational Linguistics (CICLing-2002)*, pages 136–45, Mexico City, Mexico.

Douglas Biber. 1995. *Dimensions of register variation : a cross-linguistic comparison*. Cambridge University Press, Cambridge.

Irina Chugur, Julio Gonzalo, and Felisa Verdejo. 2002. Polysemy and sense proximity in the senseval-2 test suite. In *Proceedings of the SIGLEX/SENSEVAL Workshop on Word Sense Disambiguation: Recent Successes and Future Directions*, pages 32–39, Philadelphia.

Mona Diab. 2004. Relieving the data acquisition bottleneck in word sense disambiguation. In *Proceedings of the 42nd Annual Meeting on Association for Computational Linguistics*, pages 303–311.

Nancy Ide and Yorick Wilks. 2006. Making sense about sense. In E. Agirre and P. Edmonds, editors, *Word Sense Disambiguation: Algorithms and Applications*, pages 47–74, Dordrecht, The Netherlands. Springer.

Nancy Ide, Tomaz Erjavec, and Dan Tufis. 2002. Sense discrimination with parallel corpora. In *Proceedings of ACL'02 Workshop on Word Sense Disambiguation: Recent Successes and Future Directions*, pages 54–60, Philadelphia.

Nancy Ide. 2006. Making senses: Bootstrapping sense-tagged lists of semantically-related words. In Alexander Gelbukh, editor, *Computational Linguistics and Intelligent Text*, pages 13–27, Dordrecht, The Netherlands. Springer.

Adam Kilgarriff. 1998. SENSEVAL: An exercise in evaluating word sense disambiguation programs. In *Proceedings of the First International Conference on Language Resources and Evaluation (LREC)*, pages 581–588, Granada.

Adam Kilgarriff. 2001. Comparing corpora. *International Journal of Corpus Linguistics*, 6:1–37.

Richard Kittredge, Tanya Korelsky, and Owen Rambow. 1991. On the need for domain communication knowledge. *Computational Intelligence*, 7(4):305–314.

Devra Klein and Gregory Murphy. 2002. Paper has been my ruin: Conceptual relations of polysemous words. *Journal of Memory and Language*, 47:548–70.

Klaus Krippendorff. 1980. *Content analysis: An introduction to its methodology*. Sage Publications, Beverly Hills, CA.

J. Richard Landis and Gary G. Koch. 1977. The measurement of observer agreement for categorical data. *Biometrics*, 33(1):159–174.

George A. Miller, Richard Beckwith, Christiane Fellbaum, Derek Gross, and Katherine Miller. 1993. Introduction to WordNet: An on-line lexical database (revised). Technical Report Cognitive Science Laboratory (CSL) Report 43, Princeton University, Princeton. Revised March 1993.

Hwee Tou Ng, Chung Yong Lim, and Shou King Foo. 1999. A case study on inter-annotator agreement for word sense disambiguation. In *SIGLEX Workshop On Standardizing Lexical Resources*.

Geoffrey Nunberg. 1979. The non-uniqueness of semantic solutions: Polysemy. *Linguistics and Philosophy*, 3:143–184.

Martha Palmer, Hoa Trang Dang, and Christiane Fellbaum. 2005. Making fin-egrained and coarse-grained sense distinctions. *Journal of Natural Language Engineering*, 13.2:137–163.

Rebecca J. Passonneau, Nizar Habash, and Owen Rambow. 2006. Inter-annotator agreement on a multilingual semantic annotation task. In *Proceedings of the International Conference on Language Resources and Evaluation (LREC)*, pages 1951–1956, Genoa, Italy.

Rebecca J. Passonneau. 2004. Computing reliability for coreference annotation. In *Proceedings of the International Conference on Language Resources and Evaluation (LREC)*, Portugal.

Ted Pedersen. 2002a. Assessing system agreement and instance difficulty in the lexical sample tasks of Senseval-2. In *Proceedings of the ACL-02 Workshop on Word Sense Disambiguation: Recent Successes and Future Directions*, pages 40–46.

Ted Pedersen. 2002b. Evaluating the effectiveness of ensembles of decision trees in disambiguating SENSEVAL lexical samples. In *Proceedings of the ACL-02 Workshop on Word Sense Disambiguation: Recent Successes and Future Directions*, pages 81–87.

James Pustejovsky. 1991. The generative lexicon. *Computational Linguitics*, 17(4):409–441.

Josef Ruppenhofer, Michael Ellsworth, Miriam R. L. Petruck, Christopher R. Johnson, and Jan Scheffczyk. 2006. Framenet ii: Extended theory and practice. Available from http://framenet.icsi.berkeley.edu/index.php.

Ansaf Salleb-Aouissi, Christel Vrain, and Cyril Nortet. 2007. Quantminer: A genetic algorithm for mining quantitative association rules. In *IJCAI*, pages 1035–1040.

Rion Snow, Daniel Jurafsky, and Andrew Y. Ng. 2007. Learning to merge word senses. In *Proceedings of the 2007 Joint Conference on Empirical Methods in Natural Language Processing and Computational Natural Language Learning*, pages 1005–1014, Prague.

Jean Veronis. 1998. A study of polysemy judgements and inter-annotator agreement. In *SENSEVAL Workshop*, pages Sussex, England.

Mohammed Javeed Zaki, Srinivasan Parthasarathy, Mitsunori Ogihara, and Wei Li. 1997. New algorithms for fast discovery of association rules. In *KDD*, pages 283–286.

# Refining the most frequent sense baseline

**Judita Preiss**
Department of Linguistics
The Ohio State University
judita@ling.ohio-state.edu

**Jon Dehdari**
Department of Linguistics
The Ohio State University
jonsafari@ling.ohio-state.edu

**Josh King**
Computer Science and Engineering
The Ohio State University
kingjo@cse.ohio-state.edu

**Dennis Mehay**
Department of Linguistics
The Ohio State University
mehay@ling.ohio-state.edu

## Abstract

We refine the most frequent sense baseline for word sense disambiguation using a number of novel word sense disambiguation techniques. Evaluating on the SENSEVAL-3 English all words task, our combined system focuses on improving every stage of word sense disambiguation: starting with the lemmatization and part of speech tags used, through the accuracy of the most frequent sense baseline, to highly targeted individual systems. Our supervised systems include a ranking algorithm and a Wikipedia similarity measure.

## 1 Introduction

The difficulty of outperforming the most frequent sense baseline, the assignment of the sense which appears most often in a given annotated corpus, in word sense disambiguation (WSD) has been brought to light by the recent SENSEVAL WSD system evaluation exercises. In this work, we present a combination system, which, rather than designing a single approach to all words, enriches the most frequent sense baseline when there is high confidence for an alternative sense to be chosen.

WSD, the task of assigning a sense to a given word from a sense inventory is clearly necessary for other natural language processing tasks. For example, when performing machine translation, it is necessary to distinguish between word senses in the original language if the different senses have different possible translations in the target language (Yngve, 1955). A number of different approaches to WSD have been explored in recent years, with two distinct approaches: techniques which require annotated training data (supervised techniques) and techniques which do not (unsupervised methods).

It has long been believed that supervised systems, which can be tuned to a word's context, greatly outperform unsupervised systems. This theory was supported in the SENSEVAL WSD system evaluation exercises, where the performance gap between the best supervised system and the best unsupervised system is large. Unsupervised systems were found to never outperform the most frequent sense (MFS) baseline (a sense assignment made on the basis of the most frequent sense in an annotated corpus), while supervised systems occasionally perform better than the MFS baseline, though rarely by more than 5%. However, recent work by McCarthy et al. (2007) shows that acquiring a predominant sense from an unannotated corpus can outperform many supervised systems, and under certain conditions will also outperform the MFS baseline.

Rather than proposing a new algorithm which will tackle all words, we focus on improving upon the MFS baseline system when an alternative system proposes a high confidence answer. An MFS refining system can therefore benefit from answers suggested by a very low recall (but high precision) WSD system. We propose a number of novel approaches to WSD, but also demonstrate the importance of a highly accurate lemmatizer and part of speech tagger to the English all words task of SENSEVAL-3.[1]

We present our enriched most frequent sense

[1] Unless specified otherwise, we use WordNet 1.7.1 (Miller et al., 1990) and the associated sense annotated SemCor corpus (Miller et al., 1993) (translated to WordNet 1.7.1 by Rada Mihalcea).



*Proceedings of the NAACL HLT Workshop on Semantic Evaluations: Recent Achievements and Future Directions*, pages 10–18,
Boulder, Colorado, June 2009. 

baseline in Section 2, which motivates the lemmatizer and part of speech tagger refinements presented in Section 3. Our novel high precision WSD algorithms include a reranking algorithm (Section 4), and a Wikipedia-based similarity measure (Section 5). The individual systems are combined in Section 6, and we close with our conclusions in Section 7.

## 2 Most frequent sense baseline

The most frequent sense (MFS) baseline assumes a sense annotated corpus from which the frequencies of individual senses are learnt. For each target word, a part of speech tagger is used to determine the word's part of speech, and the MFS for that part of speech is selected. Although this is a fairly naive baseline, it has been shown to be difficult to beat, with only 5 systems of the 26 submitted to the SENSEVAL-3 English all words task outperforming the reported 62.5% MFS baseline. The success of the MFS baseline is mainly due to the frequency distribution of senses, with the shape of the sense rank versus frequency graph being a Zipfian curve (i.e., the top-ranked sense being much more likely than any other sense).

However, two different MFS baseline performance results are reported in Snyder and Palmer (2004), with further implementations being different still. The differences in performance of the MFS baseline can be attributed to a number of factors: the English all words task is run on natural text and therefore performance greatly depends on the accuracy of the lemmatizer and the part of speech tagger employed.[2] If the lemmatizer incorrectly identifies the stem of the word, the MFS will be looked up for the wrong word and the resulting sense assignment will be incorrect. The performance of the MFS given the correct lemma and part of speech information is 66%, while the performance of the MFS with a Port Stemmer without any POS information is 32%. With a TreeTagger (Schmidt, 1994), and a sophisticated lemma back-off strategy, the performance increases to 56%. It is this difference in performance which motivates refining the most frequent sense baseline, and our work on improving the underlying lemmatizer and part of speech tagger presented in Section 3.

Our initial investigation refines the SemCor based MFS baseline using the automatic method of determining the predominant sense presented in McCarthy et al. (2007).

1. For nouns and adjectives which appear in SemCor fewer than 5 times, we employ the automatically determined predominant sense.

2. For verbs which appear in SemCor fewer than 5 times, we employ subcategorization frame similarity rather than Lesk similarity to give us a verb's predominant sense.

### 2.1 Predominant sense

McCarthy et al. (2007) demonstrate that it is possible to acquire the predominant sense for a word in a corpus without having access to annotated data. They employ an automatically created thesaurus (Lin, 1998), and a sense–word similarity metric to assign to each sense $s_i$ of a word $w$ a score corresponding to

$$\sum_{n_j \in N_w} dss(w, n_j) * \frac{sss(s_i, n_j)}{\sum_{s'_i \in senses(w)} sss(s'_i, n_j)}$$

where $dss(w, n_j)$ reflects the distributional similarity of word $w$ to $n_j$, $w$'s thesaural neighbour, and $sss(s_i, n_j) = \max_{s_x \in senses(n_j)} sss'(s_i, s_x)$ is the maximum similarity[3] between $w$'s sense $s_i$ and a sense $s_x$ of $w$'s thesaural neighbour $n_j$. The authors show that although this method does not always outperform the MFS baseline based on SemCor, it does outperform it when the word's SemCor frequency is below 5. We therefore switch our MFS baseline to this value for such words. This result is represented as 'McCarthy' in Table 1, which contains the results of the techniques presented in this Section evaluated on the SENSEVAL-3 English all words task.

### 2.2 Verb predominant sense

McCarthy et al. (2007) observe that their predominant sense method is not performing as well for

[2] Other possible factors include: 1) The sense distribution in the corpus which the MFS baseline is drawn from, 2) If SemCor is used as the underlying sense annotated corpus, the accuracy of the mapping from WordNet 1.6 (with which SemCor was initially annotated) to WordNet 1.7.1 could also have an effect on the performance).

[3] We use the Lesk (overlap) similarity as implemented by the WordNet::similarity package (Pedersen et al., 2004).

| System | Precision | Recall | $F$-measure |
|---|---|---|---|
| MFS | 58.4% | 58.4% | 58.4% |
| McCarthy | 58.5% | 58.5% | 58.5% |
| Verbs | 58.5% | 58.5% | 58.5% |
| All | 58.6% | 58.6% | 58.6% |

Table 1: Refining the MFS baseline with predominant sense

verbs as it does for nouns and adjectives. We hypothesize that this is due to the thesaural neighbours obtained from Lin's thesaurus, and we group verbs according to the subcategorization frame (SCF) distributions they present in the VALEX (Korhonen et al., 2006) lexicon. A word $w_1$ is grouped with word $w_2$ if the Bhattacharyya coefficient

$$BC(w_1, w_2) = \sum_{x \in X} \sqrt{p(x)q(x)}$$

where $p(x)$ and $q(x)$ represent the probability values for subcategorization class $x$, is above a certain threshold. The $BC$ coefficient then replaces the $dss$ value in the original formula and the predominant senses are obtained. Again, this system is only used for words with frequency lower than 5 in SemCor. The great advantage of the Bhattacharyya coefficient over various entropy based similarity measures which are usually used to compare SCF distributions (Korhonen and Krymolowski, 2002), is that it is guaranteed to lie between 0 and 1, unlike the entropy based measures which are not easily comparable between different word pairs. This result is represented by 'Verbs' in Table 1.

Table 1 displays the results for the MFS, the MFS combined with the two approaches described above, and the MFS combining MFS with verbs and McCarthy.

## 3 Lemmatization and Part of Speech Tagging

We made use of several lemmatizers and part-of-speech taggers, in order to give the other WSD components the best starting point possible.

### 3.1 Lemmatization

Lemmatization, the process of obtaining the canonical form of a word, was the first step for us to ultimately identify the correct WordNet sense of a given word in the English all words task. We found that without any lemmatizing of the test input, the maximum $f$-score possible was in the mid-50's. Conversely, we found that a basic most-frequent-sense system that had a perfectly-lemmatized input achieved an $f$-score in the mid-60's. This large difference in the ceiling of a non-lemmatized system and the floor of a perfectly-lemmatized system motivated us to focus on this task.

We looked at three different lemmatizers: the lemmatizing backend of the XTAG project (XTAG Research Group, 2001)[4]; Celex (Baayen et al., 1995), and the lemmatizing component of an enhanced TBL tagger (Brill, 1992).[5] We then employed a voting system on these three components, taking the lemma from the most individual lemmatizers. If all three differ, we take the lemma from the most accurate individual system, namely the TBL tagger.

#### 3.1.1 Lemmatizer Evaluation

We evaluated the lemmatizers against the lemmas found in the SENSEVAL-3 gold standard.[6] Even the lowest performing system improved accuracy by 31.74% over the baseline, which baseline simply equates the given token with the lemma. Table 2 shows the results of evaluating the lemmatizers against the EAW key.

While the simple voting system performed better than any of the individual lemmatizers, hyphenated words proved problematic for all of the systems. Some hyphenated words in the test set remained hyphenated in the gold standard, and some others were separated. However, evaluation results show that splitting hyphenated words increases lemmatizing accuracy by 0.9% .

### 3.2 Part of Speech Tagging

We also investigated the contribution of part of speech taggers to the task of word sense disambiguation. We considered three taggers: the Elworthy bigram tagger (Elworthy, 1994) within the RASP parser (Briscoe et al., 2006), an enhanced

[4] `http://www.cis.upenn.edu/~xtag`

[5] `http://gposttl.sourceforge.net`

[6] We removed those lines from both the test input and the gold standard which were marked U (= unknown, 34 lines), and we removed the 40 lines from the test input that were missing from the gold standard. This gave us 2007 words in both the test set and the gold standard.

| Lemmatizer | Accuracy |
|---|---|
| Baseline | 57.50% |
| XTAG | 89.24% |
| Celex | 91.58% |
| TBL | 92.38% |
| Voting {XTAG,Celex,TBL} | 93.77% |
| Voting, no hyphen {XTAG,Celex,TBL} | **94.67%** |

Table 2: Accuracy of several lemmatizers on <head> words of EAW task.

| POS Tagger | Accuracy |
|---|---|
| Baseline | 84.10% |
| TBL | 90.48% |
| Elworthy | 90.58% |
| TnT | 91.13% |
| Voting {TBL,Elw.,TnT} | **91.88%** |

Table 3: Accuracy of several POS taggers on <head> words of EAW task.

TBL tagger (Brill, 1992)[7] and a TnT-style trigram tagger (Halácsy et al., 2007).[8] The baseline was a unigram tagger which selects the most frequently-occurring tag of singletons when dealing with unseen words.

All three of the main taggers performed comparably, although only the Elworthy tagger provides probabilities associated with tags, rather than getting a single tag as output. This additional information can be useful, since we can employ different strategies for a word with one single tag with a probability of 1, versus a word with multiple tags, the most probable of which might only have a probability of 0.3 for example. For comparative purposes, we mapped the various instantiations of tags for nouns, verbs, adjectives, and adverbs to these four basic tags, and evaluated the taggers' results against the EAW key. Table 3 shows the results of this evaluation.

The performance of these taggers on the EAW <head>-words is lower than results reported on other datasets. This can explained by the lack of frequently-occurring function words, which are easy to tag and raise overall accuracy. Also, the words in the test set are often highly ambiguous not only with respect to their word sense, but also their part of speech.

## 4 Supervised Learning of Sparse Category Indices for WSD

In this component of our refinement of the baseline, we train a supervised system that performs higher-precision classification, only returning an answer when a predictive feature that strongly predicts a particular sense is observed. To achieve this, we implemented a "feature focus" classifier (sparse weighted index) as described in (Madani and Connor, 2008, henceforth, MC08). MC08's methods for restricting and pruning the number of feature-to-class associations are useful for finding and retaining only strong predictive features. Moreover, this allowed us to use a rich feature set (more than 1.6 million features) without an unwieldy explosion in the number of parameters, as feature-class associations that are not strong enough are simply dropped.

### 4.1 Sparse Category Indices

MC08 describe a space and time efficient method for learning discriminative classifiers that rank large numbers of output classes using potentially millions of features for many instances in potentially tera-scale data sets. The authors describe a method for learning 'category indices' — i.e., weighted bipartite graphs $G \subseteq F \times W \times C$, where $F$ is the set of features, $C$ is the set of output classes and all weights (or 'associations') $w \in W$ between features and the output classes they predict are real-valued and in [0.0, 1.0]. The space and time efficiency of MC08's approach stems chiefly from three (parameterisable) restrictions on category indices and how they are updated. First, at any time in the learning process, only those edges $(f_i, w_j, c_k) \in G$ whose associations $w_j$ are a large enough proportion of the sum of all class associations for $f_i$ are retained: that is, only retain $w_j$ s.t. $w_j \geq$ **wmin**.[9] Second, by setting an upper bound **dmax** on the number of associations that a feature $f_i$ is allowed to have, only the largest feature associations are retained. Setting **dmax** to a low number ($\leq 25$) makes each feature a high-precision, low-recall predictor of output classes. Further, the **dmax** and **wmin** restrictions on parameter reten-

[7] http://gposttl.sourceforge.net

[8] http://code.google.com/p/hunpos

[9] Recall that $w_j \in W$ are all between 0.0 and 1.0 and sum to 1.0.

tion allow efficient retrieval and update of feature weights, as only a small number of feature weights need be consulted for predicting output classes or learning from prediction mistakes in an online learning setting.[10] Finally, in the online learning algorithm,[11] in addition to the small number of features that need be consulted or updated, an error margin **marg** can be set so that parameter update only occurs when the $\mathbf{score}(c) - \mathbf{score}(c^*) \leq \mathbf{marg}$, where $c$ is the correct output class and $c^* \neq c$ is the most confident incorrect prediction of the classifier. Setting $\mathbf{marg} = 0.0$ leads to purely error-driven learning, while $\mathbf{marg} = 1.0$ always updates on every learning instance. Values of $\mathbf{marg} \in (0.0, 1.0)$ will bias the category index learner to update at different levels of separation of the correct class from the most confident incorrect class, ranging from almost always error driven (near 0.0) to almost error-insensitive learning (near 1.0).

### 4.2 Integration into the WSD Task

Using both the Semcor-3 and English Lexical Sample training data sets (a total of ≈45,000 sentences, each with one or more labeled instances), we trained a sparse category index classifier as in MC08 with the following features: using words, lemmas and parts of speech (POSs) as tokens, we define features for (1) preceding and following unigrams and bigrams over tokens, as well as (2) the conjunction of the preceding unigrams (i.e., a 3-word window minus the current token) and (3) the conjunction of the preceding and following bigrams (5-word window minus the current token). Finally all surrounding lemmas in the sentence are treated as left- or right-oriented slot-independent features with an exponentially decaying level of activation $\mathbf{act}(l_i) = 0.5 \cdot \exp\big(0.5 \cdot - \mathbf{dist}(l_i, \mathbf{targ\_wd})\big)$ — where $\mathbf{dist}(l_i, \mathbf{targ\_wd})$ is simply the word distance from the target word to the contextual lemma $l_i$.[12] Although WSD is not a many-class, large-scale classification task,[13] we nevertheless found MC08's pruning mechanisms useful for removing weak feature-word associations. Due to the aggressive pruning of feature-class associations, our model only has ≈1.9M parameters out of a potential $1,600,000 \times 200,000 = 320$ billion (the number of features times the number of WordNet 3.0 senses).

### 4.3 Individual System Results

To integrate the predictions of the classifier into the EAW task, we looked up all senses for each lemma-POS pairing, backing off to looking up the words themselves by the same POS, and finally resorting to splitting hyphenated words and rejoining multiword units (as marked up in the EAW test set). Being high precision, the classifier does not return a valid answer for every lemma, so we report results with and without backing off to the most frequent sense baseline to fill in these gaps.

Individual system scores are listed in Table 4. The classifier on its own returns very few answers (with a coverage — as distinct from recall — of only 10.4% of the test set items). Although the classifier-only performance does not have broad enough coverage for stand-alone use, its predictions are nonetheless useful in combination with the baseline. Further, we expect coverage to grow when trained over a larger corpus (such as the very large web-extracted corpus of Agirre et al. (2004), which this learning method is well suited for).

## 5 Wikipedia for Word Sense Disambiguation

Wikipedia, an online, user-created encyclopedia, can be considered a collection of articles which link to each other. While much information exists within the textual content of Wikipedia that may assist in WSD, the approach presented here instead uses the article names and link structure within Wikipedia to find articles which are most related to a WordNet sense or context. We use the Green method to find a relatedness metric for articles from Wikipedia[14] (Ol-

[10] **dmax** bounds the number of feature-class associations (parameters) must be consulted in prediction and updating, but, because of the **wmin** restriction, MC08 found that, on average, many fewer feature associations — ≤ 16 — were ever touched per training or testing instance in their classification experiments. See Madani and Connor (2008) for more details.

[11] Again, see Madani and Connor (2008) for more details.

[12] The value 0.5 is also a parameter that we have fixed, but it could in principle be tuned to a particular data set. In the interest of simplicity, we have not done this.

[13] Large-scale data sets are available, but this does not change the level of polysemy in WordNet, which is not in the thousands for any given lemma.

[14] Computations were performed using a January 3rd 2008 download of the English Wikipedia.

| Back-off | Precision | Recall | Prec. (n-best) | Rec. (n-best) |
|---|---|---|---|---|
| YES | 0.592 | 0.589 | 0.594 | 0.589 |
| No | 0.622 | 0.065 | 0.694 | 0.070 |

Table 4: Precision and recall of sparse category index classifier — both "soft" scores of standard Senseval script and scores where any correct answer in list returned by the classifier is counted as a correct answer ('n-best'). 'Back-off' signals whether the system backs off to the most frequent sense baseline.

livier and Senellart, 2007) based on each sense or context of interest.

Advantages of this method over alternative methods that attempt to incorporate Wikipedia into WSD is that our system is unsupervised and that no manual mapping needs to take place between WordNet and Wikipedia. Mihalcea (2007) demonstrates that manual mappings can be created for a small number of words with relative ease, but for a very large number of words the effort involved in mapping would approach presented involves no be considerable. The approach presented here involves no mapping between WordNet and Wikipedia but human effort in mapping between WordNet and Wikipedia, but instead initializes the Green method with a vector based only on the article names (as described in Section 5.2).

### 5.1 Green Method

The Green method (Ollivier and Senellart, 2007) is used to determine the importance of one node in a directed graph with respect to other nodes.[15] In the context of Wikipedia the method finds the articles which are most likely to be frequented if a random walk were used to traverse the articles, starting with a specific article and returning to that article if the random walk either strays too far off topic or to an article which is generally popular even without the context of the initial article. One of the features of the Green method is that it does not simply reproduce the global PageRank (Brin and Page, 1998), instead determining the related pages nearby due to relevance to the initial node.

The probability that the random walker of Wikipedia will transfer to an article is defined as a uniform distribution over the outlinks of the page where the random walker is currently located. As an approximation to the method described by Ollivier and Senellart (2007), we create a subgraph of Wikipedia for every computation, comprised of the articles within a distance of 2 outlink traversals from the initial articles. Since Wikipedia is very highly connected, this constructed subgraph still contains a large number of articles and performance of the Green method on this subgraph is similar to that on the whole connectivity graph.

### 5.2 Green Method for Contexts

To use the Green method to find Wikipedia articles which correspond to a given word to be disambiguated, articles which may discuss that word and the context surrounding that word are found in Wikipedia as an initial set of locations for the random walker to start. This is done by looking for the word itself as the name of an article. If there is not an article whose name corresponds to the word in question, then articles with the word as a substring of the article name are found.

Since the goal of WSD is to choose the best word sense within the context of other words, we use a given word's context to select a set of Wikipedia articles which may discuss the content of the word in question. The expectation is that the context words will aid in disambiguation and that the context words will together be associated with an appropriate sense of the word being disambiguated. For this method we defined a word's context as the word itself, the content words in the sentence the word occurs in, and those occurring in the sentences before and after that sentence.

### 5.3 Green Method for Senses

Every sense of a word to be disambiguated also needs to be represented as corresponding articles in Wikipedia before using the Green method. The words that we search for in the titles of Wikipedia articles include the word itself, and, for every sense, the content words of the sense's WordNet gloss, as well as the content of the sense's hypernym gloss

[15] In subsequent sections we give a high-level description of using the Green method with Wikipedia, however see Ollivier and Senellart (2007) for a much more detailed explanation.

and the synonyms of the hypernym. Exploring this particular aspect of this module — which information about a sense to extract before using the Green Method — is a point for further exploration.

### 5.4 Interpreting Projections

The Green method as described by Ollivier and Senellart (2007) uses, as the initial set of articles, the vector containing only one article: that article for which related articles are being searched. We use as the initial set of articles the collection of articles in Wikipedia corresponding to either the context for the word to be disambiguated or the sense of a word. The random walker is modeled as starting in any of the articles in this set with uniform probability. Within the context of the Green method, this means that this initial set of articles corresponds to what would be linked to from a *new* Wikipedia article about the sense or context. Each of the content words in this new article (which is not in Wikipedia) would link to one of the articles in the set found by the methods described above. In this way the results of the Green method computation can be interpreted as a relatedness metric for the sense or context itself and the articles which are in Wikipedia.

### 5.5 Analysis

The process of finding the sense of a word to be disambiguated is as follows: the vector output from the Green method (a relatedness measure between the initial seed and each article in Wikipedia) for the context of the word is compared against the vector output from using the Green method on each sense that the word could have. The comparison is done using the cosine of the angle between the two vectors.

To determine for which instances in SENSEVAL this method may perform well, an analysis was performed on a small development set (15 sentences) from SemCor. A simple heuristic was formulated, selecting the sense with the nearest Green method output to the sentence's Green method output when the ratio between the first and second highest ranked senses' cosine angle scores was above a threshold. Applying this heuristic to the EAW task yielded an expectedly low recall of 11% but a precision of 81% on all the words that this heuristic could apply, but only a precision of 25% (recall 0.5%) for non-monosemous words (which were the desired targets of the method). Of 37 instances where this method differs from the MFS baseline in the EAW task, 8 instances are correctly disambiguated by this module.

| | MFS | Rerank | Wiki |
|---|---|---|---|
| MFS | – | 94% | 97% |
| Rerank | 23% | – | 99% |
| Wiki | 45% | 98% | – |

Table 5: Complementarity between modules

## 6 Results

Although the individual systems have fairly low recall, we can calculate pairwise complementarity between systems $s_i$ and $s_j$ by evaluating

$$\left(1 - \frac{|\text{wrong in } s_i \text{ and } s_j|}{|\text{wrong in } s_i|}\right)$$

The results, presented in Table 5, indicate that the systems complement each other well, and suggest that a combination system could have a higher performance than the individual systems.

We investigate a number of techniques to combine the results – while the integration of the lemma / part of speech refinement is done by all modules as a preprocessing step, the method of combination of the resulting modules is less clear. As shown in Florian et al. (2002), a simple voting mechanism achieves comparable performance to a stacking mechanism. We present our results in Table 6, DT gives the result of a 10-fold cross-validation of WEKA stacked decision trees and nearest neighbours built from the individual system results (Witten and Frank, 2000).

Very few decisions are changed with the voting method of combination, and the overall result does not outperform the best MFS baseline (presented in the table as "All MFS"). This combination method may be more useful with a greater number of systems being combined – our system only combines three systems (thus only one non-MFS system has to suggest the MFS for this to be selected), and backs off to the MFS sense in case all three disagree. The degree of complementarity between the Wiki system and the MFS system indicates that these will override the Rerank system in many cases.

Better results are seen with the simple stacking result: in this case, systems are ordered and thus

| System | Precision | Recall | $F$-measure |
|---|---|---|---|
| All MFS | 58.6% | 58.6% | 58.6% |
| Voting | 58.6% | 58.6% | 58.6% |
| Stacking | 58.9% | 58.9% | 58.9% |
| Stacked DT/NN | 58.7% | 58.7% | 58.7% |

Table 6: Resulting refined system (forced-choice)

are not being subjected to overriding by other MFS skewed systems.

## 7 Conclusion

We have presented a refinement of the most frequent sense baseline system, which incorporates a number of novel approaches to word sense disambiguation methods. We demonstrate the need for accurate lemmatization and part of speech tagging, showing that that is probably the area where the biggest boost in performance can currently be obtained. We would also argue that examining the absolute performance in a task where the baseline is so exceedingly variable (ourselves, we have found the baseline to be as low as 56% with restricted lemma backoff, 58.4% with a fairly sophisticated lemma / PoS module, against published baselines of 61.5% in McCarthy et al., 62.5% reported in Snyder, or the upper bound baseline of 66% using correct lemmas and parts of speech), the performance difference between the baseline used and the resulting system is interesting in itself.


### Acknowledgments

We would like to thank DJ Hovermale for his input throughout this project.


## References


Agirre, E., , and de Lacalle Lekuona, O. L. (2004). Publicly Available Topic Signatures for all WordNet Nominal Senses. In *Proceedings of the* $4^{th}$ *International Conference on Languages Resources and Evaluations (LREC)*, Lisbon, Portugal.

Baayen, H., Piepenbrock, R., and Gulikers, L. (1995). The CELEX lexical database (release 2). CD-ROM. Centre for Lexical Information, Max Planck Institute for Psycholinguistics, Nijmegen; Linguistic Data Consortium, University of Pennsylvania.

Brill, E. (1992). A simple rule-based part of speech tagger. In *Proceedings of the Third Conference on Applied Natural Language Processing*, pages 152–155, Trento, Italy.

Brin, S. and Page, L. (1998). The anatomy of a large-scale hypertextual web search engine. In *Computer Networks and ISDN Systems*, pages 107–117.

Briscoe, E., Carroll, J., and Watson, R. (2006). The second release of the RASP system. In *Proceedings of the COLING/ACL 2006 Interactive Presentation Sessions*, Sydney, Australia.

Elworthy, D. (1994). Does Baum-Welch re-estimation help taggers? In *Proceedings of the 4th ACL Conference on Applied NLP*, pages 53–58, Stuttgart, Germany.

Florian, R., Cucerzan, S., Schafer, C., and Yarowsky, D. (2002). Combining classifiers for word sense disambiguation. *Journal of Natural Language Engineering*, 8(4):327–342.

Halácsy, P., Kornai, A., and Oravecz, C. (2007). HunPos – an open source trigram tagger. In *Proceedings of the 45th Annual Meeting of the Association for Computational Linguistics Companion Volume Proceedings of the Demo and Poster Sessions*, pages 209–212, Prague, Czech Republic. Association for Computational Linguistics.

Korhonen, A., Krymolovski, Y., and Briscoe, T. (2006). A large subcategorization lexicon for natural language processing applications. In *Proceedings of the 5th international conference on Language Resources and Evaluation*, pages 1015–1020.

Korhonen, A. and Krymolowski, Y. (2002). On the robustness of entropy-based similarity measures in evaluation of subcategorization acquisition systems. In *Proceedings of the 6th Conference on Natural Language Learning*, pages 91–97.

Lin, D. (1998). Automatic retrieval and clustering of similar words. In *Proceedings of the COLING-ACL'98*, pages 768–773.

Madani, O. and Connor, M. (2008). Large-Scale

Many-Class Learning. In *Proceedins of the SIAM Conference on Data Mining (SDM-08).*

McCarthy, D., Koeling, R., Weeds, J., and Carroll, J. (2007). Unsupervised acquisition of predominant word senses. *Computational Linguistics*, 33(4):553–590.

Mihalcea, R. (2007). Using Wikipedia for automatic word sense disambiguation. In *Human Language Technologies 2007: The Conferece of the North Americ an Chapter of the Association for Computational Linguistics*, Rochester, New York.

Miller, G., Beckwith, R., Felbaum, C., Gross, D., and Miller, K. (1990). Introduction to WordNet: An on-line lexical database. *Journal of Lexicography*, 3(4):235–244.

Miller, G., Leacock, C., Ranee, T., and Bunker, R. (1993). A semantic concordance. In *Proceedings of the 3rd DARPA Workshop on Human Language Technology*, pages 232–235.

Ollivier, Y. and Senellart, P. (2007). Finding related pages using Green measures: An illustration with Wikipedia. In *Association for the Advancement of Artificial Intelligence Conference on Artificial Intelligence (AAAI 2007).*

Pedersen, T., Patwardhan, S., and Michelizzi, J. (2004). Wordnet::similarity - measuring the relatedness of concepts. In *Proceedings of Fifth Annual Meeting of the North American Chapter of the Association for Computational Linguistics*, pages 38–41.

Schmidt, H. (1994). Probabilistic part-of-speech tagging using decision trees. In *Proceedings of the International Conference on New Methods in Language Processing*, pages 44–49.

Snyder, B. and Palmer, M. (2004). The english all-words task. In Mihalcea, R. and Chklowski, T., editors, *Proceedings of SENSEVAL-3: Third International Workshop on Evaluating Word Sense Disambiguating Systems*, pages 41–43.

Witten, I. H. and Frank, E. (2000). *Data mining: Practical Machine Learning Tools and Techniques with Java Implementations*, chapter 8. Morgan Kaufmann Publishers.

XTAG Research Group (2001). A lexicalized tree adjoining grammar for English. Technical Report IRCS-01-03, IRCS, University of Pennsylvania.

Yarowsky, D. (1993). One Sense Per Collocation. In *Proceedings of the Human Language Technology Conference*, Princeton, NJ, USA.

Yngve, V. H. (1955). Syntax and the problem of multiple meaning. In Locke, W. N. and Booth, A. D., editors, *Machine translation of languages*, pages 208–226. John Wiley and Sons, New York.

# One Translation per Discourse

**Marine Carpuat**
Center for Computational Learning Systems
Columbia University
475 Riverside Drive, New York, NY 10115
marine@ccls.columbia.edu

## Abstract

We revisit the one sense per discourse hypothesis of Gale *et al.* in the context of machine translation. Since a given sense can be lexicalized differently in translation, do we observe one translation per discourse? Analysis of manual translations reveals that the hypothesis still holds when using translations in parallel text as sense annotation, thus confirming that translational differences represent useful sense distinctions. Analysis of Statistical Machine Translation (SMT) output showed that despite ignoring document structure, the one translation per discourse hypothesis is strongly supported in part because of the low variability in SMT lexical choice. More interestingly, cases where the hypothesis does not hold can reveal lexical choice errors. A preliminary study showed that enforcing the one translation per discourse constraint in SMT can potentially improve translation quality, and that SMT systems might benefit from translating sentences within their entire document context.

## 1 Introduction

The one sense per discourse hypothesis formulated by Gale *et al.* (1992b) has proved to be a simple yet powerful observation and has been successfully used in word sense disambiguation (WSD) and related tasks (e.g., Yarowsky (1995); Agirre and Rigau (1996)). In this paper, we investigate its potential usefulness in the context of machine translation.

A growing body of work suggests that translational differences represent observable sense distinctions that are useful in applications. In monolingual WSD, word alignments in parallel corpora have been successfully used as learning evidence (Resnik and Yarowsky, 1999; Diab and Resnik, 2002; Ng *et al.*, 2003). In Statistical Machine Translation (SMT), recent work shows that WSD helps translation quality when the WSD system directly uses translation candidates as sense inventories (Carpuat and Wu, 2007; Chan *et al.*, 2007; Giménez and Màrquez, 2007).

In this paper, we revisit the one sense per discourse hypothesis using word translations in parallel text as senses. Our first goal is to empirically evaluate whether the one translation per document hypothesis holds on French-English reference corpora, thus verifying whether translations exhibit the same properties as monolingual senses. Our second goal consists in evaluating whether the one translation per discourse hypothesis has the potential to be as useful to statistical machine translation as the one sense per discourse hypothesis to WSD. Current Statistical Machine Translation (SMT) systems translate one sentence at a time, ignoring any document level information. Implementing a one translation per document constraint might help provide consistency in translation for sentences drawn from the same document.

After briefly discussing related work, we will show that the one translation per discourse hypothesis holds on automatic word alignments of manually translated data. Despite ignoring any information beyond the sentential level, automatic SMT out-

*The author was partially funded by GALE DARPA Contract No. HR0011-06-C-0023. Any opinions, findings and conclusions or recommendations expressed in this material are those of the authors and do not necessarily reflect the views of the Defense Advanced Research Projects Agency.



*Proceedings of the NAACL HLT Workshop on Semantic Evaluations: Recent Achievements and Future Directions*, pages 19–27,
Boulder, Colorado, June 2009. ©2009 Association for Computational Linguistics

put also strongly exhibits the one translation per discourse property. In addition, we will show that having more than one translation per discourse in SMT output often reveals lexical choice errors, and that enforcing the constraint might help improve overall consistency across sentences and translation quality throughout documents.

## 2 Related Work

In the original one sense per discourse study, Gale *et al.* (1992b) considered a sample of 9 polysemous English words. A total of 5 judges were showed pairs of concordance lines for these words taken from Grolier's Encyclopedia and asked to identify whether they shared the same sense. Results strongly support the one sense per discourse hypothesis: 94% of polysemous words drawn from the same document have the same sense. The experiment was replicated with the same conclusion on the Brown corpus. Yarowsky (1995) successfully used this observation as an approximate annotation technique in an unsupervised WSD model.

A subsequent larger scale study of polysemy based on the WordNet sense inventory in the SEMCOR corpus does not support the hypothesis as strongly (Krovetz, 1998). Only 77% of ambiguous words have a single sense per discourse. Analysis revealed that the one sense per discourse hypothesis is only supported for homonymous senses and not for finer-grained sense distinction.

In machine translation, discourse level information has only been indirectly used by adaptation of translation or language models to specific genre or topics (e.g., Foster and Kuhn (2007); Koehn and Schroeder (2007)). While phrase-based SMT models incorporate the one sense per collocation hypothesis by attempting to translate phrases rather than single words (Koehn *et al.*, 2007), the one sense per discourse hypothesis has not been explicitly used in SMT modeling. Even the recent generation of SMT models that explicitly use WSD modeling to perform lexical choice rely on sentence context rather than wider document context and translate sentences in isolation (Carpuat and Wu, 2007; Chan *et al.*, 2007; Giménez and Màrquez, 2007; Stroppa *et al.*, 2007; Specia *et al.*, 2008). Other context-sensitive SMT approaches (Gimpel and Smith, 2008) and global lexical choice models (Bangalore *et al.*, 2007) also translate sentences independently.

## 3 One translation per discourse in reference translations

In this section we investigate whether the one sense per discourse hypothesis holds in translation. Does one sense per discourse mean one translation per discourse?

On the one hand, one translation per discourse might be too strict a constraint to allow for variations in lexicalization of a given sense. While a WSD task produces a set of predefined sense labels, a single sense might be correctly translated in many different ways in a full sentence translation.

On the other hand, if the author of the source language text is assumed to consistently use one sense per word per document, translators might also prefer consistent translations of the same source language word throughout a document. In addition, translated text tends to exhibit more regularities than original text, as shown by machine learning approches to discriminate between "translationese" and original texts (Baroni and Bernardini, 2006) although patterns of syntactic regularity seemed more informative than lexical choice for those experiments.

### 3.1 Manual translation data

We will test the one translation per discourse hypothesis on a corpus of French and English translations, using standard freely available MT data sets and software.

We use a corpus of 90 French-English news articles made available for the WMT evaluations[1]. All development data that contained article boundaries were used. The data is split into two sets of about 27k words each as described in Table 1. The articles cover topics ranging from international and local politics to sports and music. They are drawn from a wide variety of newspapers and magazines originally published in various European languages. As a result, even though only a single English reference translation is available, it was produced by several different interpreters. It would have been interesting to perform this analysis with multiple references, but this is unfortunately not possible with

[1] http://www.statmt.org/wmt09/translation-task.html

| Test set | Language | Sentences | Tokens | Types | Singletons |
|---|---|---|---|---|---|
| no. 1 | French | 1070 | 27440 | 5958 | 3727 |
| | English (ref) | 1070 | 24544 | 5566 | 3342 |
| | English (SMT) | 1070 | 24758 | 5075 | 2932 |
| no. 2 | French | 1080 | 27924 | 6150 | 3839 |
| | English (ref) | 1080 | 24825 | 5686 | 3414 |
| | English (SMT) | 1080 | 25128 | 5240 | 3080 |

Table 1: Data statistics for the bilingual corpus, including the French side, the manually translated English side (ref) and the automatic English translations (SMT)

the French-English data currently available.

Since golden word-alignments are not available, we automatically word align the corpus using standard SMT training techniques. Using IBM-4 alignment models learned on the large WMT training corpus (see Section 4.1 for more details), we align GIZA++(Och and Ney, 2003) to obtain the IBM-4 alignments in both translation directions, expand their intersection with additional links using the grow-diag-final-and heuristic (Koehn *et al.*, 2007). This creates a total of 51660 alignment links, and about 89% of French tokens are aligned to at least one English token. Note that all links involving stopwords are not considered for the rest of the study.

### 3.2 One translation per discourse holds

For every French lemma that occurs more than once in a document, we compute the number of English translations. In order to allow for morphological and syntactic variations, we compute those statistics using English lemmas obtained by running Treetagger (Schmid, 1994) with the standard French and English parameter settings[2]. A higher level of generalization is introduced by conducting the same analysis using stems, which are simply defined as 4-letter prefixes.

We have a total of 2316 different lemma types and 6603 lemma-document pairs. The scale of this empirical evaluation is much larger than in Gale *et al.* (1992a) where only 9 target words were considered and in Krovetz (1998) which used the entire SEMCOR corpus vocabulary.

The resulting distribution of number of English translations per French word-document pair is given in the first half of Table 2. Remarkably, more than 98% of the French lemmas are aligned to no more than 2 English translations and 80% of French lemmas have a single translation per document. While these numbers are not as high as the 94% agreement reported by Gale *et al.* (1992b) in their empirical study, they still strongly support the one translation per discourse hypothesis.

Generalizing from lemmas to stems yields a 4.3 point increase in the percentage of French lemmas with a single translation per document. Note that using stems might yield to false positives since different words can share the same prefix, however, since we only compare words that align to the same French word in a given document, the amount of noise introduced should be small. Manual inspection shows that this increase is often due to variations in the POS of the translation, more specifically variations between noun and verb forms which share the same 4-letter prefix as can be seen in the following examples:

**verb vs. noun** `conclude vs. conclusion, investigate vs. investigation, apply vs. application, inject vs. injection, establish vs. establishment, criticize vs. critism, recruit vs. recruitment, regulate vs. regulation`

### 3.3 Exceptions: one sense but more than one translation per discourse

We investigate what happens in the 15 to 20% of cases where a French word is not consistenly translated throughout a document. Do these translation differences reflect sense ambiguity in French, or are they close variations in English lexical choice? For

[2] http://www.ims.uni-stuttgart.de/projekte/corplex/TreeTagger/

| | reference | | SMT | |
|---|---|---|---|---|
| | **lemmas** | stems | **lemmas** | stems |
| 1 | **80.82%** | 85.14% | **83.03%** | 86.38% |
| 2 | 17.88% | 13.91% | 15.43% | 12.47% |
| 3 | 01.12% | 00.95% | 01.25% | 00.85% |
| 4 | 00.18% | 00.00% | 00.17% | 00.22% |

Table 2: Distribution of number of English translation per document using the word-aligned reference translations and the automatic SMT translations

a given French word, how semantically similar are the various English translations?

We measure semantic similarity using the shortest path length in WordNet (Fellbaum, 1998) as implemented in the WordNet Similarity package (Pedersen *et al.*, 2004). The path length is defined as the number of WordNet nodes or synsets in a path between two words: words that belong to the same synset therefore have a shortest path length of 1, while words that are related via a common synonym, hypernym or hyponym have a shortest path length of 2. Note that this similarity metric is only defined for two WordNet vocabulary words of the same POS.

For 57% of the French lemmas with multiple translations, those translations can be linked by a WordNet path of no more than 4 nodes. In 19% of the cases, the translations belong to the same synset, another 19% are separated by a path of length 2 only. Given that sense distinctions in WordNet are very fine-grained, these numbers show that the translations have very similar meanings. In other words, while the one sense per translation hypothesis does not hold for those 57%, the one sense per discourse hypothesis still holds.

Examples of those synonymous translations are given below:

**synonyms with SPL = 1** `adjust and adapt, earn and gain, movie and film, education and training, holiday and day`

**synonyms with SPL = 2** `travel and circulate, scientist and researcher, investigation and inquiry, leave and abandon, witness and eyewitness`

**synonyms with SPL = 3** `ratio and proportion, quiet and peace, plane and aircraft`

### 3.4 Exceptions: more than one sense per discourse

Among the words with a high WordNet path length or no existing path, we find translations that are not synonyms or semantically similar words, but related words sometimes with different POS. They fall within two categories.

The first category is that of fine-grained sense distinctions for which the one sense per discourse hypothesis has been showed to break for monolingual WordNet sense distinctions Krovetz (1998). However, for those closely related words, it would be possible to write correct English translations that use the same English form throughout a document.

**Nationality translation** `Tibet vs. Tibetan, French vs. France, Paris vs. Parisian, Europe vs. European, French vs. Frenchman`

**Agent/entity** `policeman vs. police, alderman vs. city`

The second category of not identical but related translations is explained by a limitation of our experiment set-up: we are looking at single-word translations while the translation of a longer multiword phrase should be considered as a whole. In the following example, the French word `émission` is aligned to both `emission` and `greenhouse` in the same document, because French does not repeat the long phrase `émission de gaz à effet de serre` throughout the document, while the more concise English translation `greenhouse gas emissions` is used throughout:

**Fr** `après la période de réduction des émissions [...] la Hongrie a pris l'engagement de réduire les émissions de gaz à effet de serre de 6 pour cent [...]`

**En** `[...] to cut greenhouse gas emissions after 2012 [...] Hungary agreed to cut its greenhouse gas emissions by 6 percent [...]`

Finally, there are a few rare instances where the different translations for a French word reflect a sense distinction in French and could not be correctly translated in English with the same English word. These are cases where both the one sense per discourse hypothesis and the one translation per discourse break, and where it is not possible to paraphrase the English sentences to fullfill either constraints. In these instances, the French word is used in two different senses related by metonymy, but the metonymy relation does not translate into English and two non-synonym English words are used as a result. For instance, the French word `bureau` translates to both `office` and `desk` in the same document, while `retraite` translates both to `retirement` and `pension`.

We found a single instance where two homonym senses of the French word `coffre` are in the same sentence. This sentence seems to be a headline, which suggests that the author or translator deliberately used the ambiguous repetition to attract the attention of the reader.

**Fr** `un coffre dans le coffre`

**En** `a trunk in the boot`

## 4 One translation per discourse in SMT

We now turn to empirically testing the one translation per discourse hypothesis on automatically translated text.

While there is an implicit assumption that a well-written document produced by a human writer will not introduce unncessary ambiguities, most SMT systems translate one sentence at a time, without any model of discourse or document. This might suggest that the one translation per discourse hypothesis will not be as strongly supported as by manual translations.

However, this effect might be compensated by the tendency of automatically translated text to exhibit little variety in lexical choice as MT systems tend to produce very literal word for word translations. As can be seen in Table 1 the reference translations use a larger vocabulary than the automatic translations for the same text.

### 4.1 Automatically translated data

We build a standard SMT system and automatically translate the data set described in Section 3.1. We strictly follow the instructions for building a phrase-based SMT system that is close to the state-of-the-art in the WMT evaluations[3], using the large training sets of about 460M words from Europarl and news.

We use the Moses phrase-based statistical machine translation system (Koehn *et al.*, 2007) and follow standard training, tuning and decoding strategies. The translation model consists of a standard Moses phrase-table with lexicalized reordering. Bidirectional GIZA++ word alignments are intersected using the grow-diag-final-and heuristic. Translations of phrases of up to 7 words long are collected and scored with translation probilities and lexical weighting. The English language model is a 4-gram model with Kneser-Ney smoothing, built with the SRI language modeling toolkit (Stolcke, 2002).

The word alignment between French input sentences and English SMT output is easily obtained as a by-product of decoding. We have a total of 56003 alignment links, and 96% of French tokens are linked to a least one English translation.

### 4.2 One translation per discourse holds

We perform the same analysis as for the manual translations. The distribution of the number of translations for a given French word that occurs repeatedly in a document still strongly supports the one translation per document hypothesis (Table 2). In fact, SMT lexical choice seems to be more regular than in manual translations.

### 4.3 Exceptions: where SMT and reference disagree

Again, it is interesting to look at instances where the hypothesis is not verified. We will not focus on the exceptions that fall in the categories previously observed in Section 3. Instead, we take a closer look at cases where the reference consistently uses the same English translation, while SMT selects different translation candidates.

There are cases where the SMT system arbitrarily chooses different synonymous translation candidates for the same word in different sentences. This is not incorrect but will affect translation quality as measured by automatic metrics which compare

[3]http://www.statmt.org/wmt09/baseline.html

| Test set | Decoding Input | METEOR | BLEU | NIST |
|---|---|---|---|---|
| no. 1 | Moses | 49.05 | 20.45 | 6.135 |
| | +postprocess (transprob) | 48.73 | 19.93 | 6.064 |
| | +postprocess (bestmatch) | 50.01 | 20.64 | 6.220 |
| | +decode (transprob) | 49.04 | 20.44 | 6.128 |
| | +decode (bestmatch) | 49.36 | 20.70 | 6.179 |
| no. 2 | Moses | 49.60 | 21.10 | 6.211 |
| | +postprocess (transprob) | 49.20 | 20.43 | 6.128 |
| | +postprocess (bestmatch) | 50.56 | 21.19 | 6.291 |
| | +decode (transprob) | 49.58 | 21.02 | 6.201 |
| | +decode (bestmatch) | 50.60 | 21.21 | 6.243 |

Table 3: Enforcing one translation per discourse can help METEOR, BLEU and NIST scores when using the supervised sense disambiguation technique (bestmatch). Relying on the unsupervised context-independent SMT translation probabilities (transprob) does not help.

matches between SMT output and manually translated references. For instance, in a single document, the French `agents pathogènes` translates to both (1) `pathogens` and (2) `disease-causing agents` while the reference consistently translates to `pathogens`. Similarly, the French phrase `parmi les détenus` is inconsistently translated to `among detainees` and `among those arrested` in the same document.

**Synonym translations** `detainees vs. arrested, apartment vs. flat, good vs. beautiful, unit vs. cell`

However, the majority of differences in translation reflect lexical choice errors. For instance, the French adjective `biologique` is incorrectly disambiguated as `organic` in the phrase `fille biologique` which should be translated as `biological daughter`.

**SMT lexical choice errors** `conseiller: advisor vs. councillor, arrondissement: district vs. rounding-off, bal: ball vs. court, biologique: biological vs. organic, assurance: insurance vs. assurance, franchise: frankness vs. deductible`

While some of those translation distinctions can be explained by differences in topics, all of those French words occur in a large number of documents and cannot be disambiguated by topic alone. This suggests that local sentential context is not sufficient to correctly disambiguate translation candidates.

## 5 Detecting SMT errors

Based on the observations from the previous section, we further evaluate whether breaking the one translation per discourse hypothesis is indicative of a translation error. For this purpose, we attempt to correct the translations provided by the Moses SMT system by enforcing the one translation per discourse constraint and evaluate the impact on translation quality.

### 5.1 Enforcing one translation per discourse

In order to get a sense of the potential impact of the one translation per discourse constraint in SMT, we attempt to enforce it using two simple postprocessing techniques.

First, we select a set of French words which are not consistently translated to a single English words in a given document. We apply a document frequency-based filter to select content words for each document. This yields a set of 595 French target word types occurring in a total of 89 documents.

Second, we propose a single English translation for all the occurrences of the French target in a document. We used two different strategies: (1) the fully unsupervised strategy consists in selecting the translation with highest probability among those produced by the baseline SMT system, and

| | |
|---|---|
| Moses<br><br><br>+postprocess | Young people under 25 years face various drawbacks when a contract with an *assurance* at an accessible price , as can be the low experience in the conduct and seniority of driving licences .<br>young people under 25 years against various drawbacks when a contract with an **insurance** at an accessible price , as can be the small experience in the conduct and seniority of driving licences . |
| Moses<br><br>+postprocess | drivers the most far-sighted can opt for insurance any risk with *frankness* , so that they get *blankets* insurance to any risk but at a price more accessible .<br>drivers the most far-sighted can opt for insurance any risk with *exemption* , so that they get *blankets* insurance to any risk but at a price more accessible . |
| Moses<br><br>+postprocess | " These *ill* are isolated , nurses puts gloves rubber and masks of protection and we have antibiotics adapted to treat them , " said Tibor Nyulasi .<br>" These **patient** are isolated , personnel puts gloves rubber and masks of protection and we have antibiotics appropriate to treat them , " say Tibor Nyulasi . |
| Moses<br><br>+postprocess | according to the Ministry of Defence , they also **served** to make known to the public the real **aims** of the presence of the army abroad .<br>according to the Ministry of Defence , they also *use* to make known to the public the real **purpose** of the presence of the army abroad . |
| Moses<br>+postprocess | the public authorities also **prepare** Christmas .<br>the public authorities also *puritan* Christmas . |

Table 4: Examples of translation improvement (bold) and degradation (italics) by enforcing the one translation per discourse constraint through postprocessing

(2) the supervised strategy picks, among the baseline SMT translations, the one that matches the reference. Note that the supervised strategy does not predict perfect translations, but an approximation of the golden translations: in addition to noise in word alignments due to phrasal translations, the translations selected are lemmas that might not be in the correctly inflected form for use in the full sentence translation.

Third, we integrate the selected translation candidates by (1) postprocessing the baseline SMT output - the translations of the French target word are simply replaced by the recommended translation, and (2) encouraging the SMT system to choose the recommended translations by annotating SMT input using the xml input markup scheme - again, this approach is not optimal as it introduces additional translation candidates without probability scores and forces single word translation to compete with phrasal translation even if they are consistent.

### 5.2 Impact on translation quality

As reported in Table 3, small increases in METEOR (Banerjee and Lavie, 2005), BLEU (Papineni *et al.*, 2002) and NIST scores (Doddington, 2002) suggest that SMT output matches the references better after postprocessing or decoding with the suggested lemma translations. Examples of both improved and degraded lexical choice are given in Table 4.

Since we are modifying translations for a limited set of single-words only, only 10% to 30% of the test set sentences are translated differently. We manually inspected a random sample of 100 of those sentence pairs for two different systems: postprocess (bestmatch) and decode (bestmatch). For each sentence pair, we determined whether the "one sense per discourse" processing improved, degraded or made no difference in translation quality compared to the baseline Moses output. Among the sentence pairs where a real change in translation quality was observed, the postprocessing heuristic yielded improvements in 62.5% (decode) and 64.5% (postprocess) of sentences considered. For 41% (decode) and 57% (postprocess) of the sentences in the sample, changes only consisted of synonym substitution, morphological variations or local reorderings which did not impact translation quality.

Taken together, these results suggest that the "one sense per discourse" constraint should be useful to SMT and that it would be worthwile to integrate it directly into SMT modeling.

## 6 Conclusion

We investigated the one sense per discourse hypothesis (Gale *et al.*, 1992b) in the context of machine translation. Analysis of manual translations showed that the hypothesis still holds when using translations in parallel text as sense annotation, thus confirming that translational differences represent useful sense distinctions. Analysis of SMT output showed that despite ignoring document structure, the one translation per discourse hypothesis is strongly supported in part because of the low variability in SMT lexical choice. More interestingly, cases where the hypothesis does not hold can reveal lexical choice errors in an unsupervised fashion. A preliminary study showed that enforcing the one translation per discourse constraint in SMT can potentially improve translation quality, and that SMT systems might benefit from translating sentences within their entire document context.

In future work, we will (1) evaluate whether one translation per discourse holds for other language pairs such as Arabic-English and Chinese-English, which are not as closely related as French-English and for which multiple reference corpora are available, and (2) directly implement the one translation per discourse constraint within SMT.

## References


Eneko Agirre and German Rigau. Word sense disambiguation using conceptual density. In *Proceedings of COLING'96*, pages 16–22, Copenhagen, Denmark, 1996.

Satanjeev Banerjee and Alon Lavie. METEOR: An automatic metric for MT evaluation with improved correlation with human judgement. In *Proceedings of Workshop on Intrinsic and Extrinsic Evaluation Measures for MT and/or Summarization at the 43th Annual Meeting of the Association of Computational Linguistics (ACL-2005)*, Ann Arbor, Michigan, June 2005.

Srinivas Bangalore, Patrick Haffner, and Stephan Kanthak. Statistical machine translation through global lexical selection and sentence reconstruction. In *Proceedings of the 45th Annual Meeting of the Association of Computational Linguistics*, pages 152–159, Prague, Czech Republic, June 2007. Association for Computational Linguistics.

Marco Baroni and Silvia Bernardini. A new approach to the study of translationese: Machine-learning the difference between original and translated text. *Literary and Linguistic Computing*, 21(3):259–274, 2006.

Marine Carpuat and Dekai Wu. Improving statistical machine translation using word sense disambiguation. In *Proceedings of the 2007 Joint Conference on Empirical Methods in Natural Language Processing and Computational Natural Language Learning (EMNLP-CoNLL 2007)*, pages 61–72, Prague, June 2007.

Yee Seng Chan, Hwee Tou Ng, and David Chiang. Word sense disambiguation improves statistical machine translation. In *45th Annual Meeting of the Association for Computational Linguistics (ACL-07)*, Prague, June 2007.

Mona Diab and Philip Resnik. An unsupervised method for word sense tagging using parallel text. In *Proceedings of the 40th Annual Meeting of the Association for Computational Linguistics*, pages 255–262, Philadelphia, Pennsylvania, July 2002.

George Doddington. Automatic evaluation of machine translation quality using n-gram co-occurrence statistics. In *Proceedings of the Human Language Technology conference (HLT-2002)*, San Diego, CA, 2002.

Christiane Fellbaum, editor. *WordNet: An Electronic Lexical Database*. MIT Press, 1998.

George Foster and Roland Kuhn. Mixture-model adaptation for SMT. In *Proceedings of the Second Workshop on Statistical Machine Translation*, pages 128–135, Prague, Czech Republic, June 2007.

William A. Gale, Kenneth W. Church, and David Yarowsky. A method for disambiguating word senses in a large corpus. *Computers and the Humanities*, 26:415–439, 1992.

William A. Gale, Kenneth W. Church, and David Yarowsky. One sense per discourse. In *Proceedings of the workshop on Speech and Natural Language*, Harriman, NY, February 1992.

Jesús Giménez and Lluís Màrquez. Context-aware discriminative phrase selection for statistical machine translation. In *Workshop on Statistical Machine Translation*, Prague, June 2007.

Kevin Gimpel and Noah Smith. Rich source-side context for statistical machine translation. In *Workshop on Statistical Machine Translation*, Columbus, Ohio, June 2008.

Philipp Koehn and Josh Schroeder. Experiments in domain adaptation for statistical machine translation. In *Workshop on Statistical Machine Translation*, Prague, June 2007.

Philipp Koehn, Hieu Hoang, Alexandra Birch, Chris Callison-Burch, Marcello Federico, Nicola Bertoldi, Brooke Cowan, Wade Shen, Christine Moran, Richard Zens, Chris Dyer, Ondrej Bojar, Alexandra Constantin, and Evan Herbst. Moses: Open source toolkit for statistical machine translation. In *Annual Meeting of the Association for Computational Linguistics (ACL), demonstration session*, Prague, Czech Republic, June 2007.

Robert Krovetz. More than one sense per discourse. In *NEC Princeton NJ Labs., Research Memorandum*, 1998.

Hwee Tou Ng, Bin Wang, and Yee Seng Chan. Exploiting parallel texts for word sense disambiguation: An empirical study. In *Proceedings of ACL-03, Sapporo, Japan*, pages 455–462, 2003.

Franz Josef Och and Hermann Ney. A systematic comparison of various statistical alignment models. *Computational Linguistics*, 29(1):19–52, 2003.

Kishore Papineni, Salim Roukos, Todd Ward, and Wei-Jing Zhu. BLEU: a method for automatic evaluation of machine translation. In *Proceedings of the 40th Annual Meeting of the Association for Computational Linguistics*, 2002.

Ted Pedersen, Siddharth Patwardhan, and Jason Michelizzi. WordNet::Similarity - Measuring the relatedness of concepts. In *Proceedings of Fifth Annual Meeting of the North American Chapter of the Association for Computational Linguistics (NAACL-04)*, pages 38–41, Boston, MA, May 2004.

Philip Resnik and David Yarowsky. Distinguising systems and distinguishing senses: New evaluation methods for word sense disambiguation. *Natural Language Engineering*, 5(2):113–133, 1999.

Helmut Schmid. Probabilistic part–of–speech tagging using decision trees. In *Proceedings of the Conference on New Methods in Language Processin*, pages 44–49, Manchester, UK, 1994.

Lucia Specia, Baskaran Sankaran, and Maria das Graças Volpe Nunes. n-best reranking for the efficient integration of word sense disambiguation and statistical machine translation. In *Proceedings of the Conference on Computational Linguistics and Intelligent Text Processing (CICLing'08)*, Haifa, Israel, February 2008.

Andreas Stolcke. SRILM—an extensible language modeling toolkit. In *International Conference on Spoken Language Processing*, Denver, Colorado, September 2002.

Nicolas Stroppa, Antal van den Bosch, and Andy Way. Exploiting source similarity for smt using context-informed features. In *Proceedings of the 11th Conference on Theoretical and Methodological Issues in Machine Translation (TMI 2007)*, Skovde, Sweden, September 2007.

David Yarowsky. Unsupervised word sense disambiguation rivaling supervised methods. In *Proceedings of the 33rd Annual Meeting of the Association for Computational Linguistics*, pages 189–196, Cambridge, MA, 1995.

# Using Web Selectors for the Disambiguation of All Words

**Hansen A. Schwartz** and **Fernando Gomez**
School of Electrical Engineering and Computer Science
University of Central Florida
Orlando, FL 32816, USA
{hschwartz, gomez}@cs.ucf.edu

## Abstract

This research examines a word sense disambiguation method using selectors acquired from the Web. Selectors describe words which may take the place of another given word within its local context. Work in using Web selectors for noun sense disambiguation is generalized into the disambiguation of verbs, adverbs, and adjectives as well. Additionally, this work incorporates previously ignored adverb context selectors and explores the effectiveness of each type of context selector according to its part of speech. Overall results for verb, adjective, and adverb disambiguation are well above a random baseline and slightly below the most frequent sense baseline, a point which noun sense disambiguation overcomes. Our experiments find that, for noun and verb sense disambiguation tasks, each type of context selector may assist target selectors in disambiguation. Finally, these experiments also help to draw insights about the future direction of similar research.

## 1 Introduction

The great amount of text on the Web has emerged as an unprecedented electronic source of natural language. Recently, word sense disambiguation systems have fostered the size of the Web in order to supplant the issue of limited annotated data availability for supervised systems (Mihalcea, 2002; Agirre and Martinez, 2004). Some unsupervised or minimally supervised methods use the Web more directly in disambiguation algorithms that do not use a training set for the specific target words.

One such minimally supervised method uses selectors acquired from the Web for noun sense disambiguation by comparing the selectors of a given sentence to a target noun within the sentence (Schwartz and Gomez, 2008). Although this work found strong results, many aspects of the use of selectors was left unexplored. For one, the method was only applied to noun sense disambiguation, focusing on the well-developed noun hypernym hierarchy within WordNet (Miller et al., 1993). Additionally, the role of different types of selectors was not extensively explored, and adverb selectors were not used at all. We seek to address those issues.

In this paper, we extend our method of using selectors from the Web for noun sense disambiguation into a more robust method of disambiguating words of all parts of speech. After a brief background on selectors and related work, we explain the acquisition and empirical application of selectors from nouns, verbs, adjectives, pronouns/proper nouns, and adverbs. Finally, results are presented from the SemEval-2007 coarse grained all-words task (Navigli et al., 2007), and we explore the influence of various types of selectors on the algorithm in order to draw insight for future improvement of Web-based methods.

## 2 Background

In this section we describe related research in selectors and solving the problem of word sense disambiguation (WSD). Specifically, two types of WSD research are examined: works that used the Web in direct manner, and works which applied a similarity or relatedness measure.

### 2.1 Selectors

The term selector comes from (Lin, 1997), and refers to a word which can take the place of another given word within the same local context. Although



*Proceedings of the NAACL HLT Workshop on Semantic Evaluations: Recent Achievements and Future Directions*, pages 28–36,
Boulder, Colorado, June 2009. 

Lin searched a dependency relationship database in order to match local context, it is not yet possible to parse dependency relationships of the entire Web. In turn, one must search for text as local context. For example, in the sentence below, the local context for 'strikers' would be composed of "he addressed the" and "at the rally.".

*He addressed the strikers at the rally.*

Previously, we introduced the idea of using selectors of other words in a sentence in addition to selectors of the target, the word being disambiguated (Schwartz and Gomez, 2008). Words taking the place of a target word are referred to as *target selectors* and words which take the place of other words in a sentence are referred to as *context selectors*. *Context selectors* can be classified further based on their part of speech. In our example, if 'striker' was the target word, the *verb context selectors* would be verbs replacing 'addressed' and the *noun context selectors* would be nouns replacing 'rally'.

*Similarity* is used to measure the relationship between a target word and its *target selectors*, while *relatedness* measures the relationship between a target word and *context selectors* from other parts of the sentence. Thus, the use of selectors in disambiguating words relies on a couple assumptions:

1. Concepts which appear in matching syntactic constructions are *similar*.
2. Concepts which appear in the context of a given target word are *related* to the correct sense of the target word.

Note that 'concept' and 'word sense' are used interchangeably throughout this paper. This idea of distinguishing similarity and relatedness has an extensive history (Rada et al., 1989; Resnik, 1999; Patwardhan et al., 2003; Budanitsky and Hirst, 2006), but most algorithms only find a use for one or the other.

### 2.2 Related Word Sense Disambiguation

A key aspect of using selectors for disambiguation is the inclusion of context in the Web search queries. This was done in works by (Martinez et al., 2006) and (Yuret, 2007), which substituted relatives or similar words in place of the target word within a given context. The context, restricted with a window size, helped to limit the results from the Web. These works followed (Mihalcea and Moldovan, 1999; Agirre et al., 2001) in that queries were constructed through the use of a knowledge-base, filling the queries with pre-chosen words. We also use context in the web search, but we acquire words matching a wildcard in the search rather than incorporate a knowledge-base to construct queries with pre-chosen relatives. Consequently, the later half of our algorithm uses a knowledge-base through similarity and relatedness measures.

Some recent works have used similarity or relatedness measures to assist with WSD. Particuarly, (Patwardhan et al., 2003) provide evaluations of various relatedness measures for word sense disambiguation based on words in context. These evaluations helped us choose the similarity and relatedness measures to use in this work. Other works, such as (Sinha and Mihalcea, 2007), use similarity or relatedness measures over graphs connecting words within a sentence. Likewise, (Navigli and Velardi, 2005) analyze the connectivity of concepts in a sentence among Structured Semantic Interconnections (SSI), graphs of relationships based on many knowledge sources. These works do not use selectors or the Web. Additionally, *target selectors* and *context selectors* provide an application for the distinction between *similarity* and *relatedness* not used in these other methods.

Several ideas distinguish this current work from our research described in (Schwartz and Gomez, 2008). The most notable aspect is that we have generalized the overall method of using Web selectors into disambiguating verbs, adverbs, and adjectives in addition to nouns. Another difference is the inclusion of selectors for adverbs. Finally, we also explore the actual impact that each type of selector has on the performance of the disambiguation algorithm.

## 3 Approach

In this section we describe the Web Selector algorithm such that verbs, adjectives, and adverbs are disambiguated in addition to nouns. The algorithm essentially runs in two steps: *acquisition of selectors* and *application of selectors*.

### 3.1 Acquisition of Selectors

Selectors are acquired for all appropriate parts of speech. Whether the selectors are used as *target selectors* or *context selectors* depends on the target word with which they are being applied. Thus, one process can be used to acquire all *noun*, *verb*, *adjective*, and *adverb selectors*. Additionally, noun selectors can be acquired for pronouns and proper nouns (referred to as "pro" selectors). These are regular nouns found to replace a pronoun or proper noun within their local context.

The first step in acquisition is to construct a query with a wildcard in place of the target. In our example, with 'address' as the target, the query is "he * the strikers at the rally." Yahoo! Web Services[1] provides the functionality for searching the web for phrases with wildcards. Selectors are extracted from the samples returned from the web search by matching the words which take the place of the wildcard. All words not found in WordNet under the same part of speech as the target are thrown out as well as phrases longer than 4 words or those containing punctuation.

The system enters a loop where it:

- searches the web with a given query, and
- extracts selectors from the web samples.

The query is truncated and the search is repeated until a goal for the number of selectors was reached or the query becomes too short. This approach, detailed in (Schwartz and Gomez, 2008), removes select punctuation, determiners, and gradually shortens the query one word at a time. Selectors retrieved from a larger query are removed from the results of smaller queries as the smaller queries should subsume the larger query results. Some selectors retrieved for the example, with their corresponding web query are listed in Table 1.

*He addressed the * at the rally*
crowd:1
*He addressed * at the rally*
student:1, supporter:2
*He addressed * at the*
Council:1, Muslim:1, Saturday:1, Ugandan:1, analyst:2, attendee:20, audience:3, class:2, consumer:1, council:1, delegate:64, diplomat:2, employee:2, engineer:1, fan:1, farmer:1, globalization:1, graduate:5, guest:2, hundred:3, investor:1, issue:1, journalist:9, lawmaker:11, legislator:1, member:6, midshipman:1, mourner:1, official:2, parliamentarian:1, participant:17, patient:1, physician:18, reporter:8, sailor:1, secretary:1, soldier:3, staff:3, student:20, supporter:8, thousand:3, today:2, trader:1, troops:2, visitor:1, worker:1
*He * the strikers at the*
treat:2
*He * the strikers at*
get:1, keep:1, price:1, treat:1

Table 1: Lists of selectors for the target words 'striker' and 'address' returned by corresponding web queries.

### 3.2 Similarity and Relatedness

To apply selectors in disambiguation, *similarity* and *relatedness* measures are used to compare the selectors with the target word. We incorporate the use of a few previously defined measures over WordNet (Miller et al., 1993). The WordNet::Similarity package provides a flexible implementation of many of these measures (Pedersen et al., 2004). We configured WordNet::Similarity for WordNet version 2.1, the same version used to annotate our chosen experimental corpus.

A *relatedness* measure was used with *context selectors*, and we chose the adapted Lesk algorithm (Banerjee and Pedersen, 2002). An important characteristic of this measure is that it can handle multiple parts of speech. For *target selectors* we sought to use measures over the WordNet ontology in order to most closely measure *similarity*. An information-content (IC) measure (Resnik, 1999) was used for target selectors of nouns and verbs. However, because IC measures do not work with all parts of speech, we used the adapted Lesk algorithm as an approximation of *similarity* for adjectives and adverbs. Note that finding the best relatedness or similarity measure was outside the scope of this paper.

The following function, based on Resnik's *word similarity* (Resnik, 1999), is used to find the max similarity or relatedness between a concept and a word (specifically between a sense of the target word, $c_t$ and a selector, $w_s$).

$$maxsr(c_t, w_s) = \max_{c_s \in w_s} [meas(c_t, c_s)]$$

where $c_s$ is a sense of the selector and $meas$ is a similarity or relatedness measure.

[1] http://developer.yahoo.com/search/

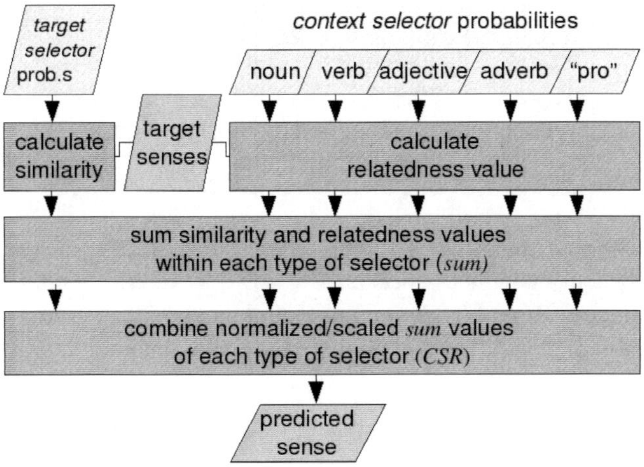


Figure 1: General flow in applying selectors to word sense disambiguation. Note that the target selectors may be any part of speech.

### 3.3 Application of Selectors

Next, we briefly describe the empirical basis for scoring senses of the target word. This step is outlined in Figure 1. The occurrences of selectors can be converted to a probability of a selector, $w_s$ appearing in a web query, $q$:

$$p(w_s, q)$$

The senses of the target word are compared with each selector. For a given sense of the target word, $c_t$, the similarity or relatedness from a selector and query is computed as:

$$SR(c_t, w_s, q) = \frac{p(w_s, q) * maxsr(c_t, w_s)}{senses(w_s)}$$

where $senses(w_s)$ is the number of senses of the selector.

As the queries get shorter, the accuracy of the selectors becomes weaker. In turn, the $SR$ value from selectors is scaled by a ratio of the web query length, $wql$, to the original sentence length, $sl$. This scaling is applied when the *SR* values for one target word sense are summed:

$$sum(c_t, T) = \sum_{q \in qs(T)} \sum_{w_s \in sels(q)} SR(c_t, w_s, q) * \frac{wql}{sl}$$

where $qs(T)$ represents the set of queries for a selector type, $T$, and $w_s$ ranges over all selectors found with $q$, denoted $sels(q)$.

The general approach of disambiguation is to find the sense of a target word which is most similar to all target selectors and most related to all context selectors. This follows our assumptions about selectors given in the background section. Thus, similarity and relatedness values from different selector types (represented as $Types$) must be combined. By aggregating the normalized $sums$ from all types of selectors, we get a combined similarity/relatedness for a given target word sense:

$$CSR(c_t) = \sum_{T \in Types} scale(T) * \frac{sum(c_t, T)}{\max_{c_i \in w_t}[sum(c_i, T)]}$$

where $w_t$ represents the set of all senses belonging to the target word, and $scale(T)$ is a coefficient used to weight each type of selector. This term is important in this work, because our experiments explore the impact of various selector types.

The top sense is then chosen by looking at the $CSR$ of all senses. For some situations, specifically when other senses have a score within 5% of the top $CSR$, the difference between concepts is very small. In these cases, the concept with the lowest sense number in WordNet is chosen from among the top scoring senses.

## 4 Experiments

Our experiments are run over the SemEval2007 Task 7: coarse-grained English all-words. The sense inventory was created by mapping senses in WordNet 2.1 to the Oxford Dictionary of English (Navigli et al., 2007). The corpus was composed of five documents with differing domains resulting in 2269 annotated word instances. Our system runs on fine-grained WordNet senses, but evaluation is done by checking if the predicted fine-grained sense maps to the correct coarse-grained sense. Many issues associated with fine-grained annotation, such as those brought up in (Ide and Wilks, 2006) are avoided through the use of this corpus.

First, we apply the generalized Web selector algorithm in a straight-forward manner to the entire task. Then, we delve into analyzing the acquired selectors and the influence of each type of *context selector* in order to gain insights into future related work.

| $\mathbf{BL}_{Rand}$ | **MED** | ***WS*** | $\mathbf{BL}_{MFS}$ |
|---|---|---|---|
| 53.43 | 70.21 | **76.02** | 78.89 |

Table 2: Results as F1 Values of our system, ***WS***, compared with baselines: random, $\mathbf{BL}_{Rand}$; most frequent sense, $\mathbf{BL}_{MFS}$; median system performance at SemEval07, **MED**.

| **UPV-WSD** | **NUS-PT** | **SSI** |
|---|---|---|
| 78.63 | 82.50 | 83.21 |

Table 3: Results as F1 Values of top performing systems for the SemEval07 Task07 (UPV = (Buscaldi and Rosso, 2007), NUS-PT = (Chan et al., 2007), and SSI = a task organizer's system (Navigli and Velardi, 2005)).

### 4.1 Evaluating All Words

In this section, we seek to apply the algorithm to all instances of the testing corpus in order to compare with baselines and other disambiguation algorithms. Unless stated otherwise, all results are presented as F1 values, where $F1 = 2 * \frac{P*R}{P+R}$. For SemEval2007, all systems performed better than the random baseline of 53.43%, but only 4 of 13 systems achieved an F1 score higher than the MFS baseline of 78.89% (Navigli et al., 2007).

Table 2 lists the results of applying the generalized Web selector algorithm described in this paper in a straight-forward manner, such that all $scale(T)$ are set to 1. We see that this version of the system performs better than the median system in the SemEval07 task, but it is a little below the MFS baseline. A comparison with top systems is seen in Table 3. Our overall results were just below that of the top system not utilizing training data, (UPV-WSD (Buscaldi and Rosso, 2007)), and a little over 6 percentage points below the top supervised system (NUS-PT (Chan et al., 2007)).

The results are broken down by part of speech in Table 4. We see that adjective disambiguation was the furthest above our median point of reference, and noun disambiguation results were above the MFS baseline. On the other hand, our adverb disambiguation results appear weakest compared to the baselines. Note that we previously reported a noun sense disambiguation F1 value of 80.20% on the same corpus (Schwartz and Gomez, 2008). Current results differ because the previous work used

| | **N** | **V** | **A** | **R** |
|---|---|---|---|---|
| **MED** | 70.76 | 62.10 | 71.55 | 74.04 |
| ***WS*** | **78.52** | **68.36** | **81.21** | **75.48** |
| $\mathbf{BL}_{MFS}$ | 77.44 | 75.30 | 84.25 | 87.50 |
| *insts* | 1108 | 591 | 362 | 208 |

Table 4: Results as F1 values (precision = recall) of our system by parts of speech (N = noun, V = verb, A = adjective, R = adverb). *insts* = disambiguation instances of each part of speech. For other keys see Table 2.

different $scale(T)$ values as well as a custom noun similarity measure.

### 4.2 Selector Acquisition Analysis

We examine the occurrences of acquired selectors. Listed as the column headings of Table 5, selectors are acquired for five parts of speech (*pro* is actually a combination of two parts of speech: pronoun and proper noun). The data in Table 5 is based on results from acquiring selectors for our experimental corpus. The information presented includes:

- *insts* — instances which the algorithm attempts to acquire selectors
- *% w/ sels* — percentage of instances for which selectors were acquired
- *sels/inst* — average number of selectors for an instance (over all *insts*)
- *unique/inst* — average number of unique selectors for an instance (over all *insts*)
- *insts/sent* — average instances in a sentence

| | ***noun*** | ***verb*** | ***adj.*** | ***adverb*** | ***pro*** |
|---|---|---|---|---|---|
| *insts* | 1108 | 591 | 362 | 208 | 370 |
| ***% w/ sels*** | 54.5 | 65.8 | 61.0 | 57.2 | 27.0 |
| ***sels/inst*** | 36.5 | 51.2 | 29.5 | 17.7 | 15.9 |
| ***unique/inst*** | 11.6 | 13.1 | 8.4 | 4.1 | 5.6 |
| ***insts/sent*** | 4.5 | 2.4 | 1.5 | 0.8 | 1.5 |

Table 5: Various statistics on the acquired selectors for the SemEval07 Task 7 broken down by part of speech. Row descriptions are in the text.

The selector acquisition data provides useful information. In general, *% w/ sels* was low from being unable to find text on the Web matching local context (even with truncated queries). The lowest *% w/ sels*, found for *pro*, was expected considering only nouns which replace the original words are used (pronouns acquired were thrown out since they are not compatible with the relatedness measures). There was quite a variation in the *sels/inst* depending on the type, and all of these numbers are well below the upper-bound of 200 selectors acquired before the algorithm stops searching. It turned out that only 15.9% of the instances hit this mark. This means that most instances stopped acquiring selectors because they hit the minimum query length (5 words). In fact, the average web query to acquire at least one selector had a length of 6.7 words, and the bulk of selectors came from shorter queries (with less context from shorter queries, the selectors returned are not as strong). We refer to the combination of quantity and quality issues presented above, in general, as the *quality selector sparsity* problem.

Although quality and quantity were not ideal, when one considers data from the sentence level, things are more optimistic. The average sentence had 10.7 instances (of any part of speech listed), so when certain selector types were missing, others were present. As explained previously, the *target selector* and *context selector* distinction is made after the acquisition of selectors. Thus, each instance is used as both (exception: *pro* instances were never used as *target selectors* since they were not disambiguated) . Employing this fact, more information can be discovered. For example, the average noun was disambiguated with 36.5 *target selectors*, 122.9 *verb context selectors* (51.2 *sels/inst* * 2.4 *insts/sent*), 44.3 *adjective context selectors*, 14.2 *adverb context selectors*, and 23.9 *pro context selectors*. Still, with the bulk of those selectors coming from short queries, the reliability of the selectors was not strong.

### 4.3 Exploring the Influence of Selector Types

This section explores the influence of each context selector on the disambiguation algorithm, by changing the value of $scale(T)$ in the previously listed $CSR$ function.

Examining Table 6 reveals precision results when disambiguating instances with *target selectors*, based only on the target word's similarity with target selectors. This serves as a bearing for interpreting results of context selector variation.

We tested how well each type of *context selector* complements the *target selectors*. Accordingly,

| wsd | **prec. %** | *insts.* |
|---|---|---|
| **N** | 64.08 | 348 |
| **V** | 52.86 | 227 |
| **A** | 77.36 | 106 |
| **R** | 58.39 | 56 |

Table 6: Precision when disambiguating with *target selectors* only. All instances contain target selectors and multiple senses in WordNet. (*insts.* = number of instances disambiguated.)

| wsd | ***noun*** | ***verb*** | ***adj.*** | ***adverb*** | ***pro*** |
|---|---|---|---|---|---|
| **N** | 272 | 186 | 120 | 84 | 108 |
| **V** | 211 | 167 | 110 | 80 | 103 |
| **A** | 97 | 78 | 50 | 40 | 34 |
| **R** | 47 | 44 | 30 | 17 | 26 |

Table 7: Instance occurrences used for disambiguation when experimenting with all types of context selectors (listed as columns). The rows represent the four parts of speech disambiguated.

$scale(target)$ was set to 1, and $scale(T)$ for all other context types were set to 0. In order to limit external influences, we did not predict words with only one sense in WordNet or instances where the $CSR$ was zero (indicating no selectors). Additionally, we only tested on examples which had at least one target selector and at least one selector of the specific type being examined. This restriction ensures we are avoiding some of the *quality selector sparsity* problem described in the analysis. Nevertheless, results are expected to be a little lower than our initial tests as we are ignoring other types of selectors and not including monosemous words according to WordNet. Table 7 lists the instance occurrences for each of the four parts of speech that were disambiguated, based on these restrictions.

Figures 2 through 5 show graphs of the precision score while increasing the influence of each context selector type. Each graph corresponds to the disambiguation of a different part of speech, and each line in a graph represents one of the five types of context selectors:

1. *noun context*
2. *verb context*
3. *adjective context*
4. *adverb context*
5. *pro context*

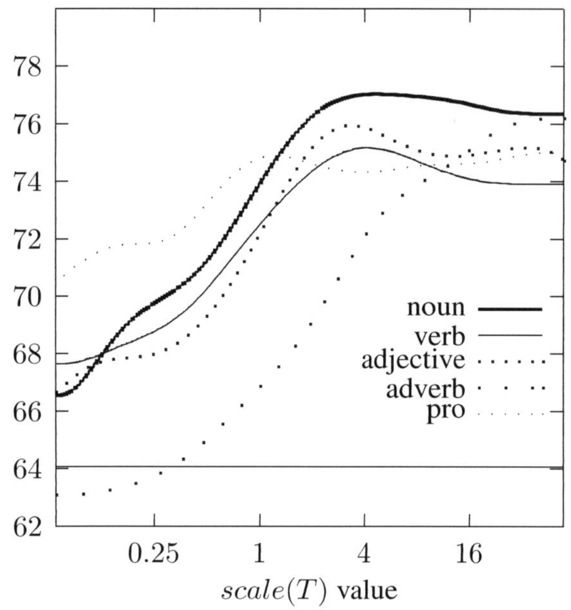


Figure 2: The **noun** sense disambiguation precision when varying the $scale(T)$ value for each type of context selector. $scale(target)$ is always 1.

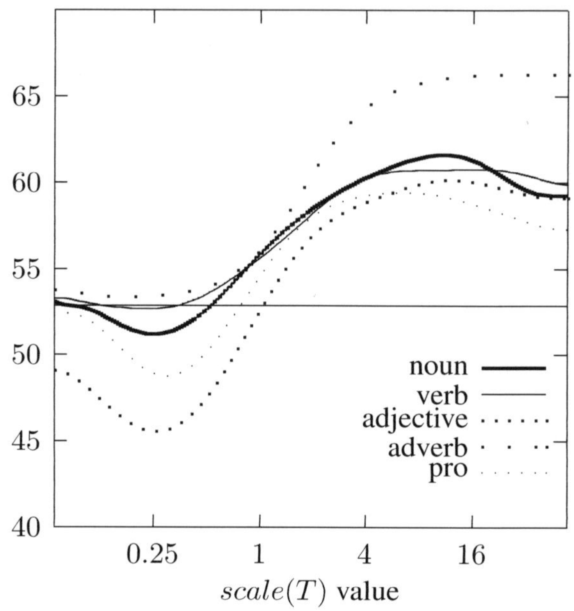


Figure 3: The **verb** sense disambiguation precision when varying the $scale(T)$ value for each type of context selector. $scale(target)$ is 1.

The lines are formed with a Bezier curve algorithm[2] on the precision data. The horizontal line represents the precision of only using the target selectors to disambiguate instances with target selectors. Precision either decreases or remains the same if any graph line was extended past the right-most boundary.

When examining the figures, one should note when the precision increases as the $scale$ value increases. This indicates that increases in influence of the particular type of context selector improved the results. The x-axis increases exponentially, since we would like a ratio of $scale(T)$ to $scale(target)$, and at $x = 1$ the *context selector* has the same influence as the *target selector*.

We see that all types of *context selectors* improve the results for noun and verb sense disambiguation. Thus, our inclusion of adverb context selectors was worthwhile. It is difficult to draw a similar conclusion from the adverb and adjective disambiguation graphs (Figures 4 and 5), although it still appears that the *noun context selectors* are helpful for both and the *pro context selectors* are helpful for the adjective task. We also note that most selector types achieve highest precision above a $scale$ value of 1, indicating that the *context selector* should have more influence than the *target selectors*. This is probably due to the existence of more selectors from context than those from the target word. The results of adverb disambiguation should be taken lightly, because there were not many disambiguation instances that fit the restrictions (see Table 7).

### 4.4 Discussion of Future Work

Based on the results of our analysis and experiments, we list two avenues of future improvement:

1. *Automatic Alternative Query Construction*: This idea is concerned with the quality and quantity of selectors acquired for which there is currently a trade-off. As one shortens the query to receive more quantity, the quality goes down due to a less accurate local context. One may be able to side-step this trade-off by searching with alternative queries which capture just as much local context. For example, the query "He * the strikers at the rally" can be mapped into the passive transformation "the strikers were * at the rally by him". Query

[2] http://www.gnuplot.info/docs/node124.html

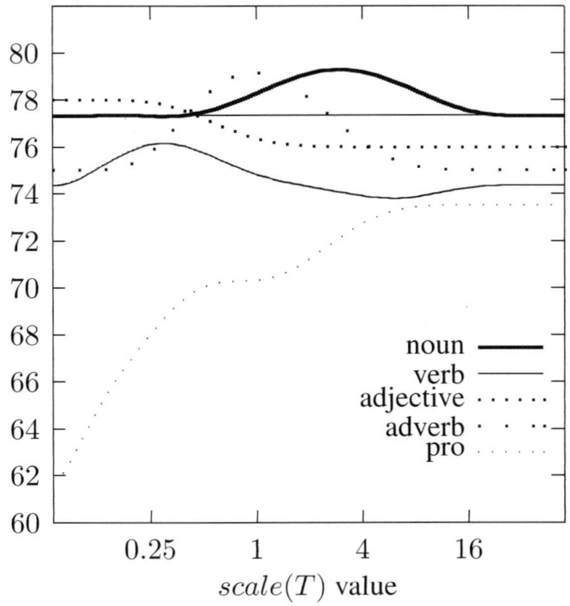


Figure 4: The **adjective** sense disambiguation precision when varying the $scale(T)$ value for each type of context selector. $scale(target)$ is 1.

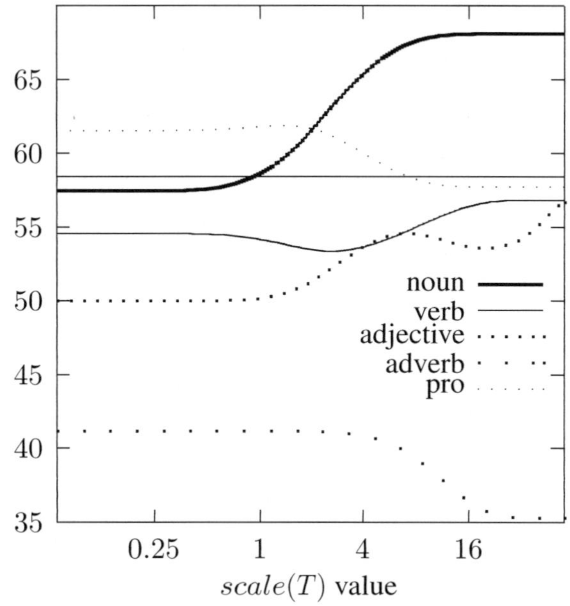


Figure 5: The **adverb** sense disambiguation precision when varying the $scale(T)$ value for each type of context selector. $scale(target)$ is 1.

reconstruction can be accomplished by using a constituent-based parser, which will help to produce syntactic alternations and other transformations such as the dative.

2. *Improving Similarity and Relatedness*: Noun sense disambiguation was the only subtask to pass the MFS baseline. One reason we suspect for this is that work in similarity and relatedness has a longer history over nouns than over other parts of speech (Budanitsky and Hirst, 2006). Additionally, the hypernym (is-a) relationship of the noun ontology of WordNet captures the notion of *similarity* more clearly than the primary relationships of other parts of speech in WordNet. Accordingly, future work should look into specific measures of *similarity* for each part of speech, and further improvement to *relatedness* measures which function accross different parts of speech. A subtle piece of this type of work may find a way to effectively incorporate pronouns in the measures, allowing less selectors to be thrown out.

## 5 Conclusion

We found the use of Web selectors to be a worthwhile approach to the disambiguation of other parts of speech in addition to nouns. However, results for verb, adjective, and adverb disambiguation were slightly below the most frequent sense baseline, a point which noun sense disambiguation overcomes. The use of this type of algorithm is still rich with avenues yet to be taken for improvement.

Future work may address aspects at all levels of the algorithm. To deal with a *quality selector sparsity* problem, a system might automatically form alternative web queries utilizing a syntactic parser. Research may also look into defining *similarity* measures for adjectives and adverbs, and refining the similarity measures for nouns and verbs. Nevertheless, without these promising future extensions the system still performs well, only topped by one other minimally supervised system.

## 6 Acknowledgement

This research was supported by the NASA Engineering and Safety Center under Grant/Cooperative Agreement NNX08AJ98A.

## References


Eneko Agirre and David Martinez. 2004. Unsupervised WSD based on automatically retrieved examples: The importance of bias. In *Proceedings of EMNLP 2004*, pages 25–32, Barcelona, Spain, July.

Eneko Agirre, Olatz Ansa, and David Martinez. 2001. Enriching wordnet concepts with topic signatures. In *In Proceedings of the NAACL workshop on WordNet and Other Lexical Resources: Applications, Extensions and Customizations*, Pittsburg, USA.

Satanjeev Banerjee and Ted Pedersen. 2002. An adapted lesk algorithm for word sense disambiguation using wordnet. In *Proceedings of the Third International Conference on Intelligent Text Processing and Computational Linguistics*. Mexico City, Mexico.

Alexander Budanitsky and Graeme Hirst. 2006. Evaluating wordnet-based measures of lexical semantic relatedness. *Computational Linguistics*, 32(1):13–47.

Davide Buscaldi and Paolo Rosso. 2007. UPV-WSD : Combining different WSD methods by means of fuzzy borda voting. In *Proceedings of SemEval-2007*, pages 434–437, Prague, Czech Republic, June.

Yee Seng Chan, Hwee Tou Ng, and Zhi Zhong. 2007. NUS-PT: Exploiting parallel texts for word sense disambiguation in the english all-words tasks. In *Proceedings of Proceedings of SemEval-2007*, pages 253–256, Prague, Czech Republic, June.

Nancy Ide and Yorick Wilks, 2006. *Word Sense Disambiguation: Algorithms And Applications*, chapter 3: Making Sense About Sense. Springer.

Dekang Lin. 1997. Using syntactic dependency as local context to resolve word sense ambiguity. In *Proceedings of the 35th annual meeting on Association for Computational Linguistics*, pages 64–71.

David Martinez, Eneko Agirre, and Xinglong Wang. 2006. Word relatives in context for word sense disambiguation. In *Proceedings of the 2006 Australasian Language Technology Workshop*, pages 42–50.

Rada Mihalcea and Dan I. Moldovan. 1999. An automatic method for generating sense tagged corpora. In *Proceedings of AAAI-99*, pages 461–466.

Rada Mihalcea. 2002. Bootstrapping large sense tagged corpora. In *Proceedings of the 3rd International Conference on Languages Resources and Evaluations LREC 2002*, Las Palmas, Spain, May.

George Miller, R. Beckwith, Christiane Fellbaum, D. Gross, and K. Miller. 1993. Five papers on wordnet. Technical report, Princeton University.

Roberto Navigli and Paola Velardi. 2005. Structural semantic interconnections: A knowledge-based approach to word sense disambiguation. *IEEE Trans. Pattern Anal. Mach. Intell.*, 27(7):1075–1086.

Roberto Navigli, Kenneth C. Litkowski, and Orin Hargraves. 2007. Semeval-2007 task 07: Coarse-grained english all-words task. In *Proceedings of SemEval-2007*, pages 30–35, Prague, Czech Republic. Association for Computational Linguistics.

Siddharth Patwardhan, S. Banerjee, and T. Pedersen. 2003. Using Measures of Semantic Relatedness for Word Sense Disambiguation. In *Proceedings of the Fourth International Conference on Intelligent Text Processing and Computational Linguistics*, pages 241–257, Mexico City, Mexico, February.

Ted Pedersen, S. Patwardhan, and J. Michelizzi. 2004. WordNet::Similarity - Measuring the Relatedness of Concepts. In *Human Language Technology Conference of the NAACL Demonstrations*, pages 38–41, Boston, MA, May.

R. Rada, H. Mili, E. Bicknell, and M. Blettner. 1989. Development and application of a metric on semantic nets. In *IEEE Transactions on Systems, Man and Cybernetics*, volume 19, pages 17–30.

Philip Resnik. 1999. Semantic similarity in a taxonomy: An information-based measure and its application to problems of ambiguity in natural language. *Journal of Artificial Intelligence Research*, 11:95–130.

Hansen A. Schwartz and Fernando Gomez. 2008. Acquiring knowledge from the web to be used as selectors for noun sense disambiguation. In *CoNLL 2008: Proceedings of the Twelfth Conference on Computational Natural Language Learning*, pages 105–112, Manchester, England, August.

Ravi Sinha and Rada Mihalcea. 2007. Unsupervised graph-based word sense disambiguation using measures of word semantic similarity. Irvine, CA, September.

Deniz Yuret. 2007. KU: Word sense disambiguation by substitution. In *Proceedings of SemEval-2007*, pages 207–214, Prague, Czech Republic, June.

# Large-scale Semantic Networks: Annotation and Evaluation

**Václav Novák**
Institute of Formal and Applied Linguistics
Charles University in Prague, Czech Republic
novak@ufal.mff.cuni.cz

**Sven Hartrumpf**
Computer Science Department
University of Hagen, Germany
Sven.Hartrumpf@FernUni-Hagen.de

**Keith Hall***
Google Research
Zürich, Switzerland
kbhall@google.com

## Abstract

We introduce a large-scale semantic-network annotation effort based on the MutliNet formalism. Annotation is achieved via a process which incorporates several independent tools including a MultiNet graph editing tool, a semantic concept lexicon, a user-editable knowledge-base for semantic concepts, and a MultiNet parser. We present an evaluation metric for these semantic networks, allowing us to determine the quality of annotations in terms of inter-annotator agreement. We use this metric to report the agreement rates for a pilot annotation effort involving three annotators.

## 1 Introduction

In this paper we propose an annotation framework which integrates the MultiNet semantic network formalism (Helbig, 2006) and the syntactico-semantic formalism of the Prague Dependency Treebank (Hajič et al., 2006) (PDT). The primary goal of this task is to increase the interoperability of these two frameworks in order to facilitate efforts to annotate at the semantic level while preserving intra-sentential semantic and syntactic annotations as are found in the PDT.

The task of annotating text with global semantic interactions (e.g., semantic interactions within some discourse) presents a cognitively demanding problem. As with many other annotation formalisms, we propose a technique that builds from cognitively simpler tasks such as syntactic and semantic annotations at the sentence level including rich morphological analysis. Rather than constraining the semantic representations to those compatible with the sentential annotations, our procedure provides the syntacitco-semantic tree as a reference; the annotators are free to select nodes from this tree to create nodes in the network. We do not attempt to measure the influence this procedure has on the types of semantic networks generated. We believe that using a soft-constraint such as the syntactico-semantic tree, allows us to better generate human labeled semantic networks with links to the interpretations of the individual sentence analyses.

In this paper, we present a procedure for computing the annotator agreement rate for MultiNet graphs. Note that a MultiNet graph does not represent the same semantics as a syntactico-semantic dependency tree. The nodes of the MultiNet graph are connected based on a corpus-wide interpretation of the entities referred to in the corpus. These global connections are determined by the intra-sentential interpretation but are not restricted to that interpretation. Therefore, the procedure for computing annotator agreement differs from the standard approaches to evaluating syntactic and semantic dependency treebanks (e.g., dependency link agreement, label agreement, predicate-argument structure agreement).

As noted in (Bos, 2008), *"Even though the design of annotation schemes has been initiated for single semantic phenomena, there exists no annotation scheme (as far as I know) that aims to inte-*

*Part of this work was completed while at the Johns Hopkins University Center for Language and Speech Processing in Baltimore, MD USA.



*Proceedings of the NAACL HLT Workshop on Semantic Evaluations: Recent Achievements and Future Directions*, pages 37–45,
Boulder, Colorado, June 2009. 

*grate a wide range of semantic phenomena all at once. It would be welcome to have such a resource at ones disposal, and ideally a semantic annotation scheme should be multi-layered, where certain semantic phenomena can be properly analysed or left simply unanalysed.*"

In Section 1 we introduce the theoretical background of the frameworks on which our annotation tool is based: MultiNet and the Tectogrammatical Representation (TR) of the PDT. Section 2 describes the annotation process in detail, including an introduction to the encyclopedic tools available to the annotators. In Section 3 we present an evaluation metric for MultiNet/TR labeled data. We also present an evaluation of the data we have had annotated using the proposed procedure. Finally, we conclude with a short discussion of the problems observed during the annotation process and suggest improvements as future work.

### 1.1 MultiNet

The representation of the Multilayered Extended Semantic Networks (MultiNet), which is described in (Helbig, 2006), provides a universal formalism for the treatment of semantic phenomena of natural language. To this end, they offer distinct advantages over the use of the classical predicate calculus and its derivatives. For example, MultiNet provides a rich ontology of *semantic-concept types*. This ontology has been constructed to be language independent. Due to the graphical interpretation of MultiNets, we believe manual annotation and interpretation is simpler and thus more cognitively compatible. Figure 1 shows the MultiNet annotation of a sentence from the WSJ corpus: **"Stephen Akerfeldt, currently vice president finance, will succeed Mr. McAlpine."**
In this example, there are a few relationships that illustrate the representational power of MultiNet. The main predicate *succeed* is a **ANTE** dependent of the node *now*, which indicates that the outcome of the event described by the predicate occurs at some time later than the time of the statement (i.e., the succession is taking place after the current time as captured by the future tense in the sentence). Intra-sentential coreference is indicated by the **EQU** relationship. From the previous context, we know that the *vice president* is related to a particular company, Magna International Inc. The pragmatically defined relationship between *Magna International Inc.* and *vice president finance* is captured by the **ATTCH** (conceptual attachment) relationship. This indicates that there is some relationship between these entities for which one is a member of the other (as indicated by the directed edge). *Stephen Akerfeldt* is the agent of the predicate described by this sub-network.

The semantic representation of natural language expressions by means of MultiNet is generally independent of the considered language. In contrast, the syntactic constructs used in different languages to express the same content are obviously not identical. To bridge the gap between different languages we employ the deep syntactico-semantic representation available in the Functional Generative Description framework (Sgall et al., 1986).

### 1.2 Prague Dependency Treebank

The Prague Dependency Treebank (PDT) presents a language resource containing a deep manual analysis of texts(Sgall et al., 2004). The PDT contains annotations on three layers:

**Morphological** A rich morphological annotation is provided when such information is available in the language. This includes lemmatization and detailed morphological tagging.

**Analytical** The analytical layer is a dependency analysis based purely on the syntactic interpretation.

**Tectogrammatical** The tectogrammatical annotation provides a deep-syntactic (syntactico-semantic) analysis of the text. The formalism abstracts away from word-order, function words (syn-semantic words), and morphological variation.

The units of each annotation level are linked with corresponding units on the preceding level. The morphological units are linked directly with the original tokenized text. Linking is possible as most of these interpretations are directly tied to the words in the original sentence. In MultiNet graphs, additional nodes are added and nodes are removed.

The PDT 2.0 is based on the long-standing Praguian linguistic tradition, adapted for the current

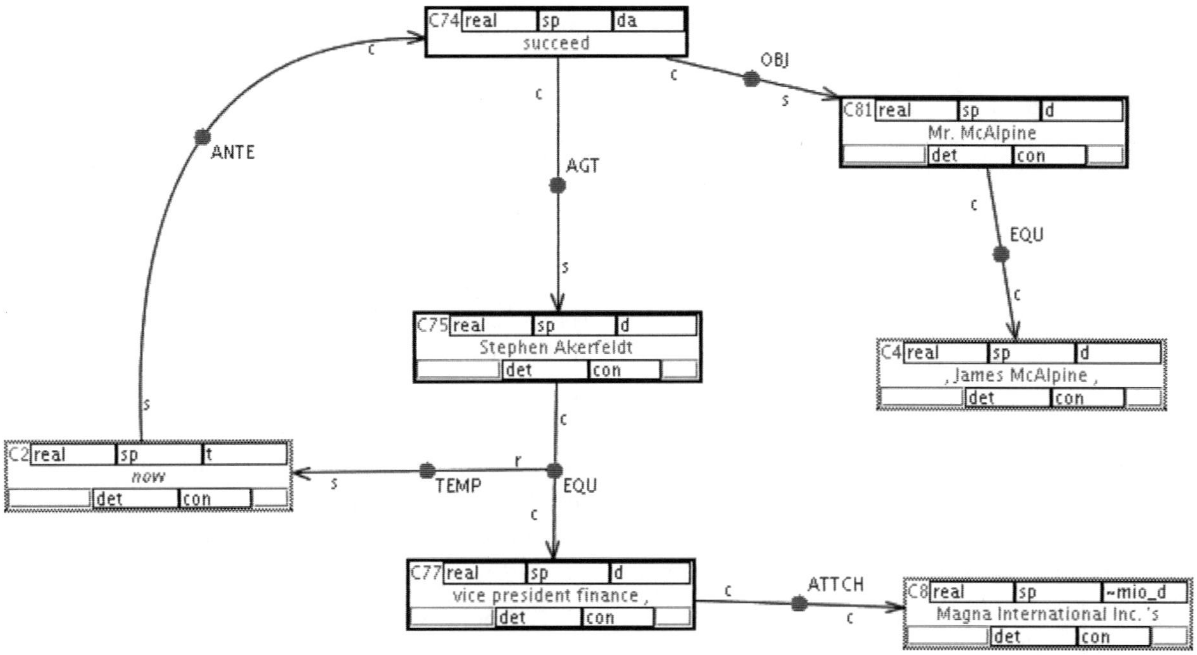


Figure 1: MultiNet annotation of sentence "Stephen Akerfeldt, currently vice president finance, will succeed Mr. McAlpine." Nodes C4 and C8 are re-used from previous sentences. Node C2 is an unexpressed (not explicitly stated in the text) annotator-created node used in previous annotations.

computational-linguistics research needs. The theoretical basis of the tectogrammatical representation lies in the Functional Generative Description of language systems (Sgall et al., 1986). Software tools for corpus search, lexicon retrieval, annotation, and language analysis are included. Extensive documentation in English is provided as well.

## 2 Integrated Annotation Process

We propose an integrated annotation procedure aimed at acquiring high-quality MultiNet semantic annotations. The procedure is based on a combination of annotation tools and annotation resources. We present these components in the this section.

### 2.1 Annotation Tool

The core annotation is facilitated by the *cedit* tool[1], which uses PML (Pajas and Štěpánek, 2005), an XML file format, as its internal representation (Novák, 2007). The annotation tool is an application with a graphical user interface implemented in Java (Sun Microsystems, Inc., 2007). The *cedit* tool is platform independent and directly connected to the annotators' wiki (see Section 2.4), where annotators can access the definitions of individual MultiNet semantic relations, functions and attributes; as well as examples, counterexamples, and discussion concerning the entity in question. If the wiki page does not contain the required information, the annotator is encouraged to edit the page with his/her questions and comments.

[1]The *cedit* annotation tool can be downloaded from http://ufal.mff.cuni.cz/~novak/files/cedit.zip.

### 2.2 Online Lexicon

The annotators in the semantic annotation project have the option to look up examples of MultiNet structures in an online version of the semantically oriented computer lexicon HaGenLex (Hartrumpf et al., 2003). The annotators can use lemmata (instead of reading IDs formed of the lemma and a numerical suffix) for the query, thus increasing the recall of related structures. English and German input is supported with outputs in English and/or German; there are approximately 3,000 and 25,000 semantic networks, respectively, in the lexicon. An example sentence for the German verb "borgen.1.1" ("to borrow") plus its automatically generated and val-

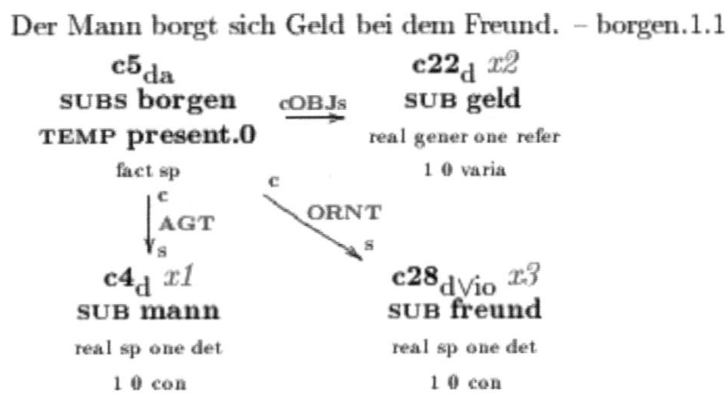


Figure 2: HaGenLex entry showing an example sentence for the German verb "borgen.1.1" ("to borrow"). The sentence is literally "The man borrows himself money from the friend."

idated semantic representation is displayed in Figure 2. The quality of example parses is assured by comparing the marked-up complements in the example to the ones in the semantic network. In the rare case that the parse is not optimal, it will not be visible to annotators.

### 2.3 Online Parser

Sometimes the annotator needs to look up a phrase or something more general than a particular noun or verb. In this case, the annotator can use the workbench for (MultiNet) knowledge bases (MWR (Gnörlich, 2000)), which provides convenient and quick access to the parser that translates German sentences or phrases into MultiNets.

### 2.4 Wiki Knowledge Base

A wiki (Leuf and Cunningham, 2001) is used collaboratively to create and maintain the knowledge base used by all the annotators. In this project we use Dokuwiki (Badger, 2007). The entries of individual annotators in the wiki are logged and a feed of changes can be observed using an RSS reader. The *cedit* annotation tool allows users to display appropriate wiki pages of individual relation types, function types and attributes directly from the tool using their preferred web browser.

## 3 Network Evaluation

We present an evaluation which has been carried out on an initial set of annotations of English articles from *The Wall Street Journal* (covering those annotated at the syntactic level in the Penn Treebank (Marcus et al., 1993)). We use the annotation from the Prague Czech-English Dependency Treebank (Cuřín et al., 2004), which contains a large portion of the WSJ Treebank annotated according to the PDT annotation scheme (including all layers of the FGD formalism).

We reserved a small set of data to be used to train our annotators and have excluded these articles from the evaluation. Three native English-speaking annotators were trained and then asked to annotate sentences from the corpus. We have a sample of 67 sentences (1793 words) annotated by two of the annotators; of those, 46 sentences (1236 words) were annotated by three annotators.[2] Agreement is measured for each individual sentences in two steps.

First, the best match between the two annotators' graphs is found and then the F-measure is computed. In order to determine the optimal graph match between two graphs, we make use of the fact that the annotators have the tectogrammatical tree from which they can select nodes as concepts in the MultiNet graph. Many of the nodes in the annotated graphs remain linked to the tectogrammatical tree, therefore we have a unique identifier for these nodes. When matching the nodes of two different annotations, we assume a node represents an identical concept if both annotators linked the node to the same tectogrammatical node. For the remaining nodes, we consider all possible one-to-one mappings and construct the optimal mapping with respect to the F-measure.

Formally, we start with a set of tectogrammatical trees containing a set of nodes $N$. The annotation is a tuple $G = (V, E, T, A)$, where $V$ are the vertices, $E \subseteq V \times V \times P$ are the directed edges and their labels (e.g., agent of an action: AGT $\in P$), $T \subseteq V \times N$ is the mapping from vertices to the tectogrammatical nodes, and finally $A$ are attributes of the nodes, which we ignore in this initial evaluation.[3] Analogously, $G' = (V', E', T', A')$ is another annotation

[2]The data associated with this experiment can be downloaded from http://ufal.mff.cuni.cz/~novak/files/data.zip. The data is in *cedit* format and can be viewed using the *cedit* editor at http://ufal.mff.cuni.cz/~novak/files/cedit.zip.

[3]We simplified the problem also by ignoring the mapping from edges to tectogrammatical nodes and the MultiNet edge attribute *knowledge type*.

of the same sentence and our goal is to measure the similarity $s(G, G') \in [0, 1]$ of $G$ and $G'$.

To measure the similarity we need a set $\Phi$ of admissible one-to-one mappings between vertices in the two annotations. A mapping is admissible if it connects vertices which are indicated by the annotators as representing the same tectogrammatical node:

$$\begin{aligned}\Phi = \Big\{ \phi \subseteq V \times V' \Big| & \forall_{\substack{n\in N\\ v\in V\\ v'\in V'}} \Big(\big((v,n)\in T \wedge (v',n)\in T'\big)\rightarrow(v,v')\in\phi\Big) \\ \wedge & \forall_{\substack{v\in V\\ v',w'\in V'}} \Big(\big((v,v')\in\phi\wedge(v,w')\in\phi\big)\rightarrow(v'=w')\Big) \\ \wedge & \forall_{\substack{v,w\in V\\ v'\in V'}} \Big(\big((v,v')\in\phi\wedge(w,v')\in\phi\big)\rightarrow(v=w)\Big)\Big\}\end{aligned} \quad (1)$$

In Equation 1, the first condition ensures that $\Phi$ is constrained by the mapping induced by the links to the tectogrammatical layer. The remaining two conditions guarantee that $\Phi$ is a one-to-one mapping.

We define the annotation agreement $s$ as:

$$s_F(G, G') = \max_{\phi\in\Phi}(F(G, G', \phi))$$

where $F$ is the F1-measure:

$$F_m(G, G', \phi) = \frac{2 \cdot m(\phi)}{|E| + |E'|}$$

where $m(\phi)$ is the number of edges that match given the mapping $\phi$.

We use four versions of $m$, which gives us four versions of $F$ and consequently four scores $s$ for every sentence:

**Directed unlabeled**: $m_{du}(\phi) =$

$$\Big|\Big\{(v,w,\rho)\in E \Big| \exists_{v',w'\in V',\rho'\in P}\Big( (v',w',\rho') \in E' \wedge (v,v') \in \phi \wedge (w,w') \in \phi\Big)\Big\}\Big|$$

**Undirected unlabeled**: $m_{uu}(\phi) =$

$$\Big|\Big\{(v,w,\rho)\in E \Big| \exists_{v',w'\in V',\rho'\in P}\Big( ((v',w',\rho') \in E' \vee (w',v',\rho') \in E') \wedge (v,v') \in \phi \wedge (w,w') \in \phi\Big)\Big\}\Big|$$

**Directed labeled**: $m_{dl}(\phi) =$

$$\Big|\Big\{(v,w,\rho)\in E \Big| \exists_{v',w'\in V'}\Big( (v',w',\rho) \in E' \wedge (v,v') \in \phi \wedge (w,w') \in \phi\Big)\Big\}\Big|$$

**Undirected labeled**: $m_{ul}(\phi) =$

$$\Big|\Big\{(v,w,\rho)\in E \Big| \exists_{v',w'\in V'}\Big( ((v',w',\rho) \in E' \vee (w',v',\rho) \in E') \wedge (v,v') \in \phi \wedge (w,w') \in \phi\Big)\Big\}\Big|$$

These four $m(\phi)$ functions give us four possible $F_m$ measures, which allows us to have four scores for every sentence: $s_{du}$, $s_{uu}$, $s_{dl}$ and $s_{ul}$.

Figure 3 shows that the inter-annotator agreement is not significantly correlated with the position of the sentence in the annotation process. This suggests that the annotations for each annotator had achieved a stable point (primarily due to the annotator training process).

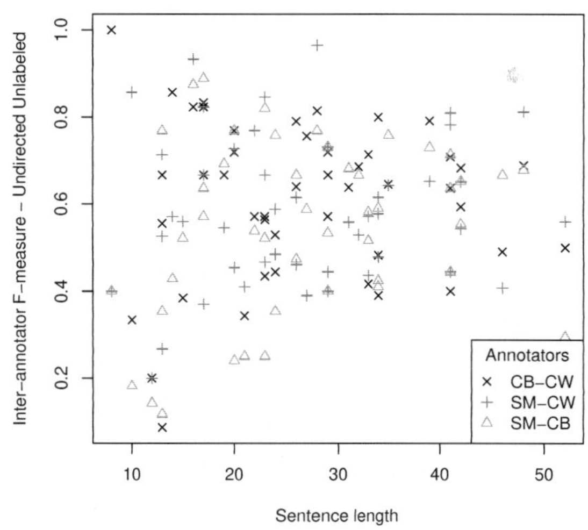


Figure 4: Inter-annotator agreement depending on the sentence length. Each point represents a sentence.

Figure 4 shows that the agreement is not correlated with the sentence length. It means that longer

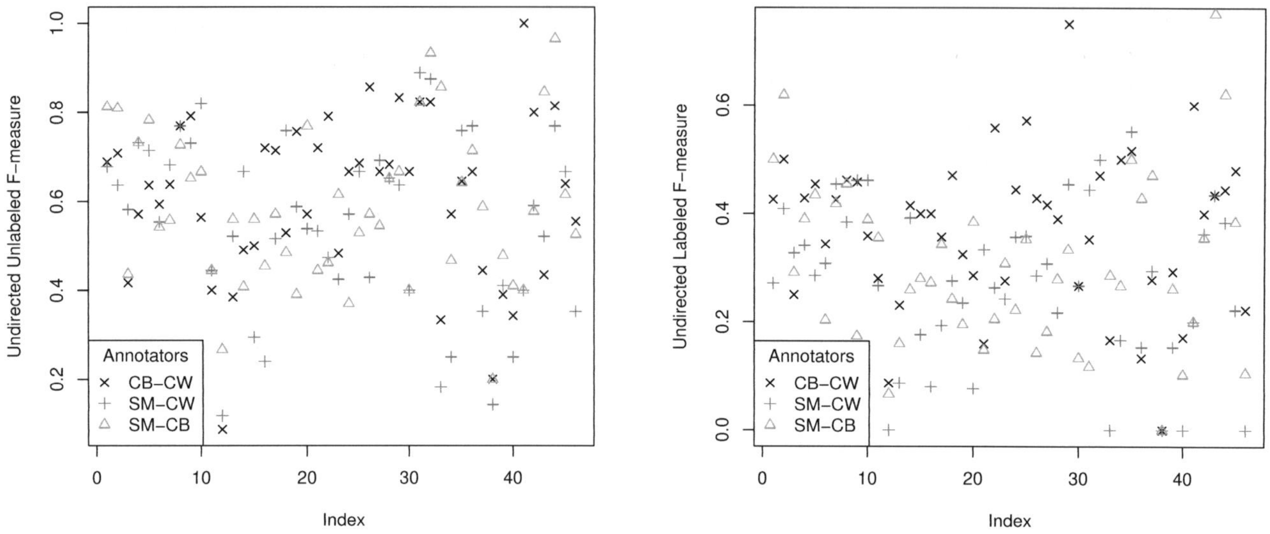


Figure 3: Inter-annotator agreement over time. Left: unlabeled, right: labeled. Each point represents a sentence; CB, CW, and SM are the annotators' IDs.

sentences are not more difficult than short sentences. The variance decreases with the sentence length as expected.

In Figure 5 we show the comparison of directed and labeled evaluations with the undirected unlabeled case. By definition the undirected unlabeled score is the upper bound for all the other scores. The directed score is well correlated and not very different from the undirected score, indicating that the annotators did not have much trouble with determining the correct direction of the edges. This might be, in part, due to support from the formalism and its tool *cedit*: each relation type is specified by a *semantic-concept type* signature; a relation that violates its signature is reported immediately to the annotator. On the other hand, labeled score is significantly lower than the unlabeled score, which suggests that the annotators have difficulties in assigning the correct relation types. The correlation coefficient between $s_{uu}$ and $s_{ul}$ (approx. $0.75$) is also much lower than than the correlation coefficient between $s_{uu}$ and $s_{du}$ (approx. $0.95$).

Figure 6 compares individual annotator pairs. The scores are similar to each other and also have a similar distribution shape.

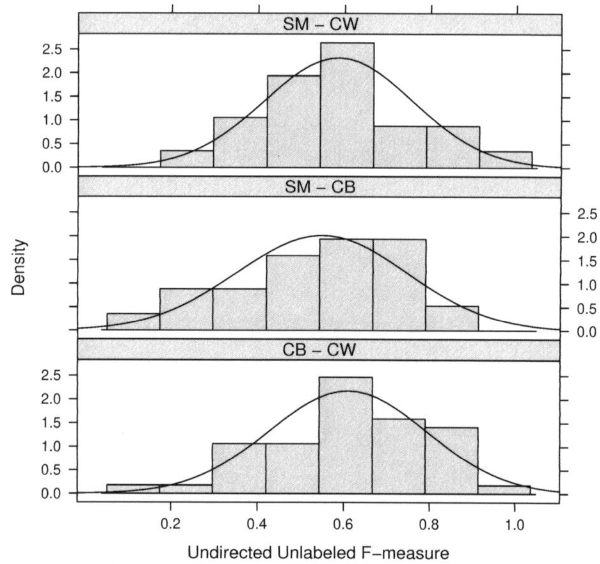


Figure 6: Comparison of individual annotator pairs.

A more detailed comparison of individual annotator pairs is depicted in Figure 7. The graph shows that there is a significant positive correlation between scores, i.e. if two annotators can agree on the

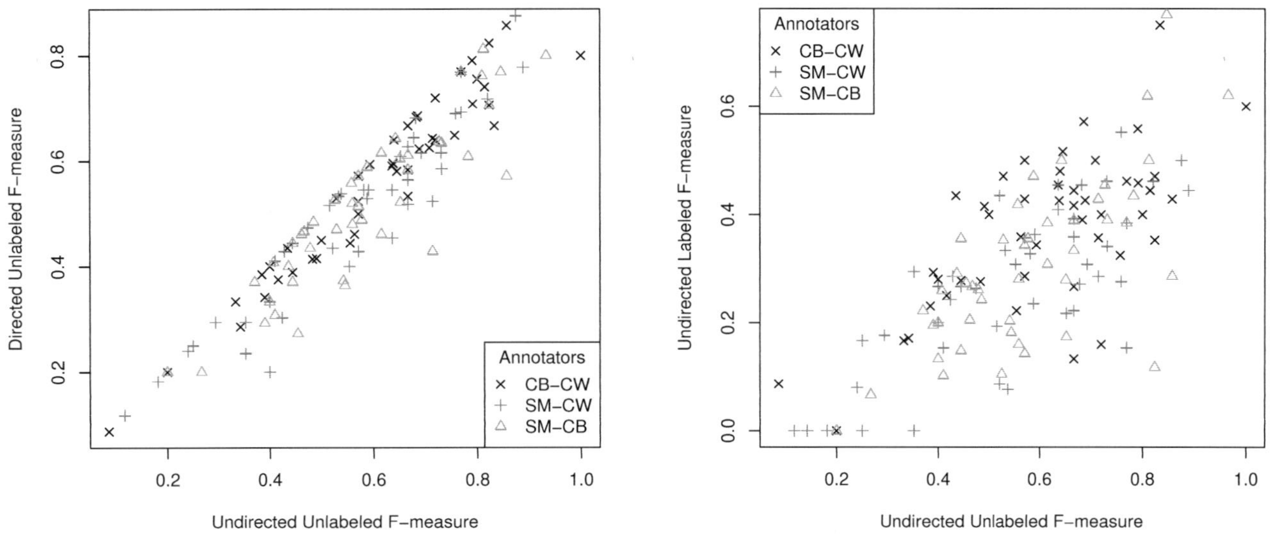


Figure 5: Left: Directed vs. undirected inter-annotator agreement. Right: Labeled vs. unlabeled inter-annotator agreement. Each point represents a sentence.

annotation, the third is likely to also agree, but this correlation is not a very strong one. The actual correlation coefficients are shown under the main diagonal of the matrix.

| Sample | Annotators | Agreement F-measure | | | |
|---|---|---|---|---|---|
| | | $s_{uu}$ | $s_{du}$ | $s_{ul}$ | $s_{dl}$ |
| Smaller | CB-CW | 61.0 | 56.3 | 37.1 | 35.0 |
| Smaller | SM-CB | 54.9 | 48.5 | 27.1 | 25.7 |
| Smaller | SM-CW | 58.5 | 50.7 | 31.3 | 30.2 |
| Smaller | average | 58.1 | 51.8 | 31.8 | 30.3 |
| Larger | CB-CW | 64.6 | 59.8 | 40.1 | 38.5 |

Table 1: Inter-annotator agreement in percents. The results come from the two samples described in the first paragraph of Section 3.

Finally, we summarize the raw result in Table 1. Note that we report simple annotator agreement here.

## 4 Conclusion and Future Work

We have presented a novel framework for the annotation of semantic network for natural language discourse. Additionally we present a technique to evaluate the agreement between the semantic networks annotated by different annotators.

Our evaluation of an initial dataset reveals that given the current tools and annotation guidelines, the annotators are able to construct the structure of the semantic network (i.e., they are good at building the directed graph). They are not, however, able to consistently label the semantic relations between the semantic nodes. In our future work, we will investigate the difficulty in labeling semantic annotations. We would like to determine whether this is a product of the annotation guidelines, the tool, or the formalism.

Our ongoing research include the annotation of inter-sentential coreference relationships between the semantic concepts within the sentence-based graphs. These relationships link the local structures, allowing for a complete semantic interpretation of the discourse. Given the current level of consistency in structural annotation, we believe the data will be useful in this analysis.

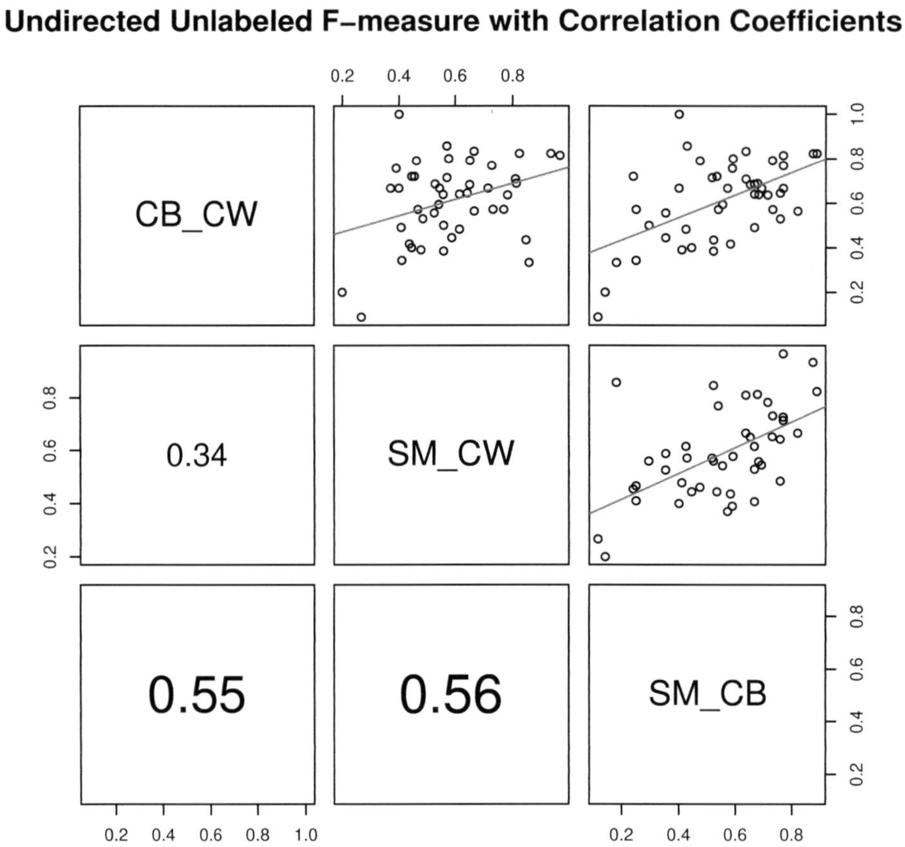


Figure 7: Undirected, unlabeled F-measure correlation of annotator pairs. Each cell represents two different pairs of annotators; cells with graphs show scatter-plots of F-scores for the annotator pairs along with the optimal linear fit; cells with values show the correlation coefficient (each point in the plot corresponds to a sentence). For example, the top row, right-most column, we are comparing the F-score agreement of annotators CB and CW with that of the F-score agreement of annotators SM and CB. This should help identify an outlier in the consistency of the annotations.

## Acknowledgment

This work was partially supported by Czech Academy of Science grants 1ET201120505 and 1ET101120503; by Czech Ministry of Education, Youth and Sports projects LC536 and MSM0021620838; and by the US National Science Foundation under grant OISE–0530118. The views expressed are not necessarily endorsed by the sponsors.

## References

Mike Badger. 2007. Dokuwiki – A Practical Open Source Knowledge Base Solution. *Enterprise Open Source Magazine*.

Johan Bos. 2008. Let's not Argue about Semantics. In European Language Resources Association (ELRA), editor, *Proceedings of the Sixth International Language Resources and Evaluation (LREC'08)*, Marrakech, Morocco, may.

Jan Cuřín, Martin Čmejrek, Jiří Havelka, and Vladislav Kuboň. 2004. Building parallel bilingual syntactically annotated corpus. In *Proceedings of The First International Joint Conference on Natural Language Processing*, pages 141–146, Hainan Island, China.

Carsten Gnörlich. 2000. MultiNet/WR: A Knowledge Engineering Toolkit for Natural Language Information. Technical Report 278, University Hagen, Hagen, Germany.

Jan Hajič, Jarmila Panevová, Eva Hajičová, Petr Sgall, Petr Pajas, Jan Štěpánek, Jiří Havelka, and Marie Mikulová. 2006. Prague Dependency Treebank 2.0.

CD-ROM, Linguistic Data Consortium, LDC Catalog No.: LDC2006T01, Philadelphia, Pennsylvania.

Sven Hartrumpf, Hermann Helbig, and Rainer Osswald. 2003. The Semantically Based Computer Lexicon HaGenLex – Structure and Technological Environment. *Traitement Automatique des Langues*, 44(2):81–105.

Hermann Helbig. 2006. *Knowledge Representation and the Semantics of Natural Language*. Springer, Berlin, Germany.

Bo Leuf and Ward Cunningham. 2001. *The Wiki Way. Quick Collaboration on the Web*. Addison-Wesley, Reading, Massachusetts.

Mitchell P. Marcus, Mary Ann Marcinkiewicz, and Beatrice Santorini. 1993. Building a large annotated corpus of English: the Penn treebank. *Computational Linguistics*, 19(2):313–330.

Václav Novák. 2007. Cedit – semantic networks manual annotation tool. In *Proceedings of Human Language Technologies: The Annual Conference of the North American Chapter of the Association for Computational Linguistics (NAACL-HLT)*, pages 11–12, Rochester, New York, April. Association for Computational Linguistics.

Petr Pajas and Jan Štěpánek. 2005. A Generic XML-Based Format for Structured Linguistic Annotation and Its Application to Prague Dependency Treebank 2.0. Technical Report 29, UFAL MFF UK, Praha, Czech Republic.

Petr Sgall, Eva Hajičová, and Jarmila Panevová. 1986. *The Meaning of the Sentence in Its Semantic and Pragmatic Aspects*. D. Reidel, Dordrecht, The Netherlands.

Petr Sgall, Jarmila Panevová, and Eva Hajičová. 2004. Deep syntactic annotation: Tectogrammatical representation and beyond. In Adam Meyers, editor, *Proceedings of the HLT-NAACL 2004 Workshop: Frontiers in Corpus Annotation*, pages 32–38, Boston, Massachusetts, May. Association for Computational Linguistics.

Sun Microsystems, Inc. 2007. *Java Platform, Standard Edition 6*. http://java.sun.com/javase/6/webnotes/README.html.

# Making Semantic Topicality Robust Through Term Abstraction*

**Paul M. Heider**
Department of Linguistics
University at Buffalo
The State University of New York
Buffalo, NY 14260, USA
pmheider@buffalo.edu

**Rohini K. Srihari**
Janya, Inc.
1408 Sweet Home Road
Suite 1
Amherst, NY 14228
rohini@cedar.buffalo.edu

## Abstract

Despite early intuitions, semantic similarity has not proven to be robust for splitting multi-party interactions into separate conversations. We discuss some initial successes with using thesaural headwords to abstract the semantics of an utterance. This simple profiling technique showed improvements over baseline conversation threading models.

## 1 Introduction

Topic segmentation is the problem of dividing a document into smaller coherent units. The segments can be hierarchical or linear; the topics can be localized or distributed; the documents can be newswire or chat logs. Of course, each of these variables is best analyzed as continuous rather than discrete. Newswire, for instance, is a more formal, monologue-style genre while a chat log tends towards the informal register with different conversations interwoven.

We present a topic segmenter which uses semantics to define coherent conversations within a larger, multi-party document. Using a word's thesaurus entry as a proxy for its underlying semantics provides a domain-neutral metric for distinguishing conversations. Also, our classifier does not rely on metalinguistic properties that may not be robust across genres.

* The first author was partially funded through a fellowship from the SUNY at Buffalo Department of Linguistics and partially through a research assistantship at Janya, Inc. (http://www.janyainc.com, Air Force Grant No.s FA8750-07-C-0077 and FA8750-07-D-0019, Task Order 0004)

## 2 Background

Most work on lexical cohesion extends from Halliday and Hasan (1976). They formalize a text as any semantic unit realized through sentences. Linguistic features found to justify binding sentences together into Halliday and Hasan's notion of a text include pronouns (Hobbs, 1979; Kehler, 2000), lexical overlap (Hearst, 1997; Kozima, 1993; Morris and Hirst, 1991), cue phrases (Manning, 1998), and discourse markers (Power et al., 2003; Reynar, 1999; Beeferman et al., 1999), among others. Of course, most of this earlier work assumes the sentences constituting any text are contiguous. Thus, a document is comprised of a series of semantic units that progress from one to the next with no returns to old topics.

Multi-party interactions[1] abide by a different set of assumptions. Namely, a multi-party interaction can include multiple floors (Aoki et al., 2006). Much like at a cocktail party, we can expect more than a single conversation at every given time. These different conversational floors are the major semantic units a topic segmentation algorithm must recognize. Spoken chat models (Aoki et al., 2006; Aoki et al., 2003) can make a simplifying assumption that speakers tend to only participate in one conversation at a time. However, in text chat models, Elsner and Charniak (2008) show that speakers seem to participate in more conversations roughly as a function of how talkative they are (cf. Camtepe et al., 2005). In both modalities, speaker tendency to stay on the same topics is a robust cue for conversational coher-

[1] See O'Neill and Martin (2003) for an analysis of differences between two- and multi-party interactions.



*Proceedings of the NAACL HLT Workshop on Semantic Evaluations: Recent Achievements and Future Directions*, pages 46–51,
Boulder, Colorado, June 2009. ©2009 Association for Computational Linguistics

ence (Elsner and Charniak, 2008; Acar et al., 2005).

Despite the initial intuitions of Halliday and Hasan (1976), semantic similarity has not proven to be a robust cue for multi-party topic segmentation. For instance, Acar et al. (2005) and Galley et al. (2003) used word repetition in their definition of coherence but found that words common to too many conversations hurt modeling performance. Elsner and Charniak (2008) used frequency binning based on the entire document to reduce the noise introduced by high-frequency words. Unfortunately, binning requires a priori knowledge of the relative frequencies of words.[2] Additionally, those authors used an on-topic/off-topic word list to bifurcate technical and non-technical utterances. Again, this technique assumes prior knowledge of the strongest on-topic cue words.

Since semantic repetition is clearly useful but simple word repetition is not a reliable measure, we investigated other measures of semantic relatedness. Elsner and Charniak (2008) conceded that context-based measures like LSA (Deerwester et al., 1990) require a clear notion of document boundary to function well. Dictionary-based models (Kozima and Furugori, 1993) are a step in the right direction because they leverage word co-occurrence within definitions to measure relatedness. The richer set of connections available in WordNet models should provide an even better measure of relatedness (Sussna, 1993; Resnik, 1995). Unfortunately, these measures have unequal distribution by part-of-speech and uneven density of lemmas by semantic domain.[3] Thesaurus-based models (Morris and Hirst, 1991) provide many of the same advantages as dictionary- and WordNet-based models.[4] In addition to the hierarchical relations encoded by the thesaurus, we can treat each thesaural category as one dimension of a topicality domain similar to the way Elsner and Charniak leveraged their list of technical terms. In sum, our model focuses on the abstraction of lemmas that is inherent to a thesaurus while limiting the domain-specific and a priori knowledge required by a classifier to divide multi-party interactions into separate conversational floors.

[2] One could use frequencies from a general corpus but that should only perform as well as a graded stop-word list.

[3] As one reviewer noted, some parts-of-speech may contribute more to a topic profile than others. Unfortunately, this empirical question must wait to be tested.

[4] Budanitsky and Hirst (2006) review the advantages.

## 3 Model

At a high level, our chat topic segmenter works like most other classifiers: each input line is tokenized[5], passed to a feature analyzer, and clustered with related lines. Unlike traditional topic segmentation models, each input represents a new utterance in the chat log. These utterances can range from single words to multiple sentences. Another aspect of our model (although not unique to it) is the on-line classification of text. We aim to model topic segmentation as if our classifier were sitting in a chat room, and not as a post-process.

While our feature analyzer focuses on semantic markers, interlocutor names are also recorded. Two intuitions were implemented with respect to individuals' names: continued affiliation with old conversations and naming interlocutors to focus attention. All else being equal, one would assume a speaker will continue in the conversations she has already participated in. Moreover, she will most likely continue with the last conversation she was part of. As the total number of conversations increases, the likelihood of sticking to the last conversation will decrease.

The second intuition derives from the observation in O'Neill and Martin (2003) that speakers accommodate for cocktail-style conversations by using direct mentions of interlocutors' names. We only model backward referencing names. That is, if a speaker uses the name of another user, we assume that the speaker is overtly affiliating with a conversation of the other user. Forward referencing is discussed under future work (see Section 6).

Following Budanitsky and Hirst (2006), we base our notion of semantic topicality on thesaural relations. Broadly speaking, two utterances are highly related if their tokenized words (hereafter, lemmas) co-occur in more of the same thesaural categories than not. We will defer further explanation of these features until we have explained our reference thesauri in Subsection 3.1. Unfortunately, many desirable and robust features are missing from our classifier. See Section 6 for a discussion of future work.

[5] We used Semantex™ (Srihari et al., 2008).

In the final stage of our processing pipeline, we use a panel of experts to generate a simple weighted classification. Each feature described above contributes a roughly equal vote towards the final sorting decision. Barring a single strong preference or a cohort of weak preferences for one conversation, the model assumes the incoming utterance introduces a new conversational floor.

### 3.1 Thesauri

We chose two machine-readable and public-domain thesauri for our model: Roget's Thesaurus (1911) and Moby Thesaurus II (2002). Both are available from Project Gutenberg (*gutenberg.org*). In the compilation notes for Roget's Thesaurus, the editor mentions a supplement of 1,000+ words to the original work. A rough count shows 1,000 headwords (the basic grouping level) and 55,000 synonyms (any word listed under a headword). The second edition of Moby Thesaurus contains some 30,000 headwords and 2.5 million synonyms. Moby Thesaurus includes many newer terms than Roget's Thesaurus. Structurally, Roget's Thesaurus has a distinct advantage over Moby Thesaurus. The former includes a six-tiered category structure with cross-indexing between headwords. The latter is only organized into headword lists.

### 3.2 Metrics

As we mentioned above, our model uses three primary metrics in classifying a new utterance: conversation affiliations of the current speaker, conversation affiliations of any explicitly mentioned interlocutors, and semantic similarity. In the end, all the conversation affiliation votes are summed with the one conversation preferred by each of the three thesaural measures.[6] The input line is then merged with the conversation that received the most votes. Details for deriving the votes follow.

Every conversation a speaker has participated in receives a vote. Moreover, his last conversation gets additional votes as a function of his total number of conversations (see Equation 1). Likewise, every conversation a named interlocutor has participated in receives a vote with extra votes given to her last conversation as a function of how gregarious she is.

[6]In the long run, a list of conversations ranked by similarity score would be better than a winner-takes-all return value.

| Headword Type | Weight Change |
|---|---|
| Direct Match | 1 |
| Co-hyponymous Headword | 0.25 |
| Cross-indexed Headword | 0.75 |

Table 1: Spreading Activation Weights.

$$Vote = \frac{3}{ln(|Conversations_{speaker}|) + 1} \quad (1)$$

Each utterance is then profiled in terms of the-saural headwords. Every lemma in an utterance matching to some headword increments the activation of that headword by one.[7] A conversation's semantic profile is a summation of the profiles of its constituent sentences. In order to simulate the drift of topic in a conversation, the conversation's semantic profile decays with every utterance. Thus, more recent headwords will be more activated than headwords activated near the beginning of a conversation. Decay is modeled by halving the activation of a headword in every cycle that it was not topical.

Moreover, a third profile was kept to simulate spreading activation within the thesaurus. For this profile, each topical headword is activated. Every cross-indexed headword listed within this category is also augmented by a fixed degree. Finally, every headword that occupies the same thesaurus section is augmented. An overview of the weight changes is listed in Table 1. The specific weights fit the authors' intuitions as good baselines. These weights can easily be trained to generate a better model.

The similarity between a new line (the test) and a conversation (the base) is computed as the sum of match bonuses and mismatch penalties in Table 2.[8] Table 3 scores an input line (TEST) against two conversations ($\text{BASE}_1$ and $\text{BASE}_2$) with respect to four headwords (A, B, C, and D). In order to control for text size, we also computed the average headword

[7]Most other models include an explicit stop-word list to reduce the effect of function words. Our model implicitly relies on the thesaurus look-up to filter out function words. One advantage to our approach is the ability to preferentially weight different headwords or lemma to headword relations.

[8]Like with Table 1, these numbers reflect the authors' intuitions and can be improved through standard machine learning methods.

| Headword Present | | | Test | | |
|---|---|---|---|---|---|
| | | | Yes | | No |
| | | Avg? | Above | Below | |
| Base | Yes | Above | +1 | +0.5 | -0.1 |
| | | Below | +0.5 | +1 | -0.05 |
| | No | | -1 | -0.5 | +0.0001 |

Table 2: Similarity Score Calculations.

| | A | B | C | D | Score |
|---|---|---|---|---|---|
| TEST | high | high | low | 0 | – |
| BASE1 | high | low | low | high | |
| | +1 | +.5 | +1 | -.1 | 2.4 |
| BASE2 | 0 | high | 0 | 0 | |
| | -1 | +1 | -.5 | +.0001 | -.4999 |

Table 3: A Example Similarity Scoring for Two Conversations. 'High' and 'low' refers to headword activation.

activation in a conversation. Intuitively, we consider it best when a headword is activated for both the base and test condition. Moreover, a headword with equally above average or equally below average activation is better than a headword with above average activation in the base but below average activation in the test. In the second best case, neither condition shows any activation in a headword. The penultimately bad condition occurs when the base contains a headword that the test does not. We do not want to penalize the test (which is usually smaller) for not containing everything that the base does. Finally, if the test condition contains a headword but the base does not, we want to penalize the conversation most.

## 4 Dataset

Our primary dataset was distributed by Elsner and Charniak (2008). They collected conversations from the IRC (Internet Relay Chat) channel ##LINUX, a very popular room on *freenode.net* with widely ranging topics. University students then annotated these chat logs into conversations. We take the collection of these annotations to be our gold standard for topic segmentation with respect to the chat logs.

### 4.1 Metrics

Elsner and Charniak (2008) use three major measures to compare annotations: a 1-to-1 comparison,

| | E&C Annotators | | | Our Model |
|---|---|---|---|---|
| | Mean | Max | Min | |
| Conversations | 81.33 | 128 | 50 | 153 |
| Avg. Length | 10.6 | 16.0 | 6.2 | 5.2 |

Table 4: General statistics for our model as compared with Elsner and Charniak's human annotators. Some numbers are taken from Table 1 (Elsner and Charniak, 2008).

| | Mean | Max | Min |
|---|---|---|---|
| Inter-annotator | 86.70 | 94.13 | 75.50 |
| Our Model | 65.17 | 74.50 | 53.38 |

Table 5: Comparative many-to-1 measures for evaluating differences in annotation granularity. Some numbers are taken from Table 1 (Elsner and Charniak, 2008).

a $loc_3$ comparison, and a many-to-1 comparison. The 1-to-1 metric tries to maximize the global conversation overlap in two annotations. The $loc_3$ scale is better at measuring local agreement. This score calculates accuracy between two annotations for each window of three utterances. Slight differences in a conversation's start and end are minimized. Finally, the many-to-1 score measures the entropy difference between annotations. In other words, simplifying a fine-grained analysis to a coarse-grained analysis will yield good results because of shared major boundaries. Disagreeing about the major conversation boundaries will yield a low score.

## 5 Analysis

Compared with the gold standard, our model has a strong preference to split conversations into smaller units. As is evident from Table 4, our model has more conversations than the maximally splitting human annotator. These results are unsurprising given that our classifier posits a new conversation in the absence of contrary evidence. Despite a low 1-to-1 score, our many-to-1 score is relatively high (see Table 5). We can interpret these results to mean that our model is splitting gold standard conversations into smaller sets rather than creating conversations across gold standard boundaries.

A similar interaction of annotation granularity shows up in Table 6. Our 1-to-1 measures are just barely above the baseline, on average. On the other

| As % of ... | Misclassified | | | All |
|---|---|---|---|---|
| Error Type | Mean | Max | Min | Mean |
| Mismatch | 25.84 | 23.78 | 28.13 | 11.93 |
| Split Error | 62.96 | 63.11 | 63.89 | 29.08 |
| Lump Error | 11.20 | 13.11 | 7.99 | 5.17 |

Table 7: Source of misclassified utterances as a percentage of misclassified utterances and all utterances.

hand, our $loc_3$ measure jumps much closer to the human annotators. In other words, the maximum annotation overlap of our model and any given human is poor[9] while the local coherence of our annotation with respect to any human annotation is high. This pattern is symptomatic of over-splitting, which is excessively penalized by the 1-to-1 metric.[10]

We also analyzed the types of errors our model made while holding the conversation history constant. We simulated a consistent conversation history by treating the gold standard's choice as an unbeatable vote and tabulating the number of times our model voted with and against the winning conversation. There were five numbers tabulated: matching new conversation votes, matching old conversation votes, mismatching old conversation votes, incorrect split vote, and incorrect lump vote. The mismatching old conversation votes occurred when our model voted for an old conversation but guessed the wrong conversation. The incorrect split vote occurred when our model wanted to create a new conversation but the gold standard voted with an old conversation. Finally, the incorrect lump vote occurred when our model matched the utterance with a old conversation when the gold standard created a new conversation.

Across all six gold standard annotations, nearly two-thirds of the errors arose from incorrect splitting votes (see Table 7). In fact, nearly one-third of all utterances fell into this category.

## 6 Future Work

The high granularity for what our model considers a conversation had a huge impact on our performance scores. The high many-to-1 scores imply that more human-like chunks will improve performance. The granularity may be very task dependent and so we will need to be careful not to overfit our model to this data set and these annotators. New features should be tested with several chat corpora to better understand the cue trading effects of genre.

At present, our model uses only a minimal set of features. Discourse cues and temporal cues are two simple measures that can be added. Our current features can also use refinement. For instance, even partially disambiguating the particular sense of the lemmas should reduce the noise in our similarity measures. Ranking the semantic similarity, in contrast with the current winner-takes-all approach, should improve our results. Accounting for forward referencing, when a speaker invokes another's name to draw them into a conversation, is also important.

Finally, understanding the different voting patterns of each feature system will help us to better understand the reliability of the different cues. Towards this end, we need to monitor and act upon the strength and type of disagreement among voters.


## Acknowledgments

Harish Srinivasan was great help in tokenizing the data. The NLP Group at Janya, Inc., Jordana Heller, Jean-Pierre Koenig, Michael Prentice, and three anonymous reviewers provided useful feedback.


## References


Evrim Acar, Seyit Ahmet Camtepe, Mukkai S. Krishnamoorthy, and Blent Yener. 2005. Modeling and multiway analysis of chatroom tensors. In Paul B. Kantor, Gheorghe Muresan, Fred Roberts, Daniel Dajun Zeng, Fei-Yue Wang, Hsinchun Chen, and Ralph C. Merkle, editors, *ISI*, volume 3495 of *Lecture Notes in Computer Science*, pages 256–268. Springer.

Paul M. Aoki, Matthew Romaine, Margaret H. Szymanski, James D. Thornton, Daniel Wilson, and Allison Woodruff. 2003. The Mad Hatter's cocktail party: A social mobile audio space supporting multiple simultaneous conversations. In *CHI 03: Proceedings of the SIGCHI Conference on Human Factors in Computing Systems*, pages 425–432, New York, NY, USA. ACM Press.

Paul M. Aoki, Margaret H. Szymanski, Luke Plurkowski, James D. Thornton, Allison Woodruff, and Weilie Yi.


[9]Elsner and Charniak (2008) found their annotators also tended to disagree on the exact point when a new conversation begins.

[10]Aoki et al. (2006) present a thorough analysis of conversational features associated with schisming, the splitting off of new conversations from old conversations.

| | Other Annotators | E&C Model | Our Model | E&C Best Baseline |
|---|---|---|---|---|
| Mean 1-to-1 | 52.98 | 40.62 | 35.77 | 34.73 |
| Max 1-to-1 | 63.50 | 51.12 | 49.88 | 56.00 |
| Min 1-to-1 | 35.63 | 33.63 | 28.25 | 28.62 |
| Mean $loc_3$ | 81.09 | 72.75 | 68.73 | 62.16 |
| Max $loc_3$ | 86.53 | 75.16 | 72.77 | 69.05 |
| Min $loc_3$ | 74.75 | 70.47 | 64.45 | 54.37 |

Table 6: Metric values for our model as compared with Elsner and Charniak's human annotators and classifier. Some numbers are taken from Table 3 (Elsner and Charniak, 2008).


2006. Where's the "party" in "multi-party"? Analyzing the structure of small-group sociable talk. In *ACM Conference on Computer Supported Cooperative Work*, pages 393–402, Banff, Alberta, Canada, November. ACM Press.

Doug Beeferman, Adam Berger, and John Lafferty. 1999. Statistical models for text segmentation. In *Machine Learning*, pages 177–210.

Alexander Budanitsky and Graeme Hirst. 2006. Evaluating WordNet-based measures of lexical semantic relatedness. *Computational Linguistics*, 32(1):13–47.

Seyit Ahmet Camtepe, Mark K. Goldberg, Malik Magdon-Ismail, and Mukkai Krishnamoorty. 2005. Detecting conversing groups of chatters: A model, algorithms, and tests. In *IADIS AC*, pages 89–96.

S. Deerwester, S. T. Dumais, G. W. Furnas, T. K. Landauer, and R. Harshman. 1990. Indexing by Latent Semantic Analysis. *Journal of the American Society of Information Science*, 41:391–407.

Micha Elsner and Eugene Charniak. 2008. You talking to me? A corpus and algorithm for conversation disentanglement. In *The Association for Computational Linguistics: Human Language Technologies (ACL-HLT 2008)*, Columbus, Ohio.

Michel Galley, Kathleen McKeown, Eric Fosler-Lussier, and Hongyan Jing. 2003. Discourse segmentation of multi-party conversation. In *Proceedings of the ACL*, pages 562–569.

Michael Halliday and Ruqaiya Hasan. 1976. *Cohesion in English*. Longman Group, New York.

Marti A. Hearst. 1997. TextTiling: Segmenting text into multi-paragraph subtopic passages. *Computational Linguistics*, 23(1):33–64.

J. R. Hobbs. 1979. Coherence and coreference. *Cognitive Science*, 3:67–90.

A. Kehler. 2000. *Coherence, Reference, and the Theory of Grammar*. CSLI Publications.

Hideki Kozima and Teiji Furugori. 1993. Similarity between words computed by spreading activation on an English dictionary. In *Proceedings of 6th Conference of the European Chapter of the Association for Computational Linguistics (EACL–93)*, pages 232–239, Utrecht.

Hideki Kozima. 1993. Text segmentation based on similarity between words. In *Proceedings of ACL'93*, pages 286–288, Ohio.

C. D. Manning. 1998. Rethinking text segmentation models: An information extraction case study. Technical Report SULTRY–98–07–01, University of Sydney.

Jane Morris and Graeme Hirst. 1991. Lexical cohesion computed by thesaural relations as an indicator of the structure of text. *Computational Linguistics*, 17(1):21–48.

Jacki O'Neill and David Martin. 2003. Text chat in action. In *GROUP '03: Proceedings of the 2003 International ACM SIGGROUP Conference on Supporting Group Work*, pages 40–49, New York, NY, USA. ACM Press.

R. Power, D. Scott, and N. Bouayad-Agha. 2003. Document structure. *Computational Linguistics*, 29(2):211–260.

Philip Resnik. 1995. Using information content to evaluate semantic similarity in a taxonomy. In *Proceedings of the 14th International Joint Conference on Artificial Intelligence*, pages 448–453.

Jeffrey C. Reynar. 1999. Statistical models for topic segmentation. In *Proceedings of the 37th Annual Meeting of the ACL*, pages 357–364, Maryland, USA, June.

Peter Mark Roget, editor. 1911. *Roget's Thesaurus*. Project Gutenberg.

R. K. Srihari, W. Li, C. Niu, and T. Cornell. 2008. Infoxtract: A customizable intermediate level information extraction engine. *Journal of Natural Language Engineering*, 14(1):33–69.

Michael Sussna. 1993. Word sense disambiguation for free-text indexing using a massive semantic network. In *Proceedings of the Second International Conference on Information and Knowledge Management (CIKMA–93)*, pages 67–74, Arlington, VA.

Grady Ward, editor. 2002. *Moby Thesaurus List*. Project Gutenberg.

# Meeting TempEval-2: Shallow Approach for Temporal Tagger

**Oleksandr Kolomiyets**
Katholieke Universiteit Leuven
Department of Computer Science
Celestijnenlaan 200A, Heverlee, Belgium
oleksandr.kolomiyets
@cs.kuleuven.be

**Marie-Francine Moens**
Katholieke Universiteit Leuven
Department of Computer Science
Celestijnenlaan 200A, Heverlee, Belgium
sien.moens@cs.kuleuven.be

## Abstract

Temporal expressions are one of the important structures in natural language. In order to understand text, temporal expressions have to be identified and normalized by providing ISO-based values. In this paper we present a shallow approach for automatic recognition of temporal expressions based on a supervised machine learning approach trained on an annotated corpus for temporal information, namely TimeBank. Our experiments demonstrate a performance level comparable to a rule-based implementation and achieve the scores of 0.872, 0.836 and 0.852 for precision, recall and F1-measure for the detection task respectively, and 0.866, 0.796, 0.828 when an exact match is required.

## 1 Introduction

The task of recognizing temporal expressions (sometimes also referred as time expressions or simply TIMEX) was first introduced in the Message Understanding Conference (MUC) in 1995. Temporal expressions were treated as a part of the Named Entity Recognition (NER) task, in which capitalized tokens in text were labeled with one of the predefined semantic labels, such as Date, Time, Person, Organization, Location, Percentage, and Money. As the types of temporal entities identified in this way were too restricted and provided little further information, the Automated Content Extraction (ACE) launched a competition campaign for Temporal Expression Recognition and Normalization (TERN 2004). The tasks were to identify temporal expressions in free text and normalize them providing an ISO-based date-time value. Later evaluations of ACE in 2005, 2006 and 2007 unfortunately did not set new challenges for temporal expression recognition and thus the participation interest in this particular task decreased.

TempEval-2 is a successor of TempEval-2007 and will take place in 2010. The new evaluation initiative sets new challenges for temporal text analysis. While TempEval-2007 was solely focused on recognition of temporal links, the TempEval-2 tasks aim at an all-around temporal processing with separate evaluations for recognition of temporal expressions and events, for the estimation of temporal relations between events and times in the same sentence, between events and document creation time, between two events in consecutive sentences and between two events, where one of them syntactically dominates the other (Pustejovsky et al., 2009). These evaluations became possible with a new freely available corpus with annotated temporal information, TimeBank (Pustejovsky et al., 2003a), and an annotation schema, called TimeML (Pustejovsky et al., 2003b).

For us all the tasks of TempEval-2 seem to be interesting. In this paper we make the first step towards a comprehensive temporal analysis and address the problem of temporal expression recognition as it is set in TempEval-2. Despite a number of previous implementations mainly done in the context of the ACE TERN competition, very few,



*Proceedings of the NAACL HLT Workshop on Semantic Evaluations: Recent Achievements and Future Directions*, pages 52–57,
Boulder, Colorado, June 2009. 

and exclusively rule-based methods were reported for temporal taggers on TimeBank developed by using the TimeML annotation scheme. As a main result of the deep analysis of relevant work (Section 2), we decided to employ a machine learning approach for constituent-based classifications with generic syntactic and lexical features.

The remainder of the paper is organized as follows: in Section 2 we provide the details of relevant work done in this field along with corpora and annotations schemes used; Section 3 describes the approach; experimental setup, results and error analysis are provided in Section 4. Finally, Section 5 gives an outlook for further improvements and research.

## 2 Related Work

For better understanding of the performance levels provided in the paper we first describe evaluation metrics defined for the temporal expression recognition task and then the methods and datasets used in previous research.

### 2.1 Evaluation metrics

With the start of the ACE TERN competition in 2004, two major evaluation conditions were proposed: Recognition+Normalization (full task) and Recognition only (TERN, 2004).

**Detection (Recognition):** Detection is a preliminary task towards the full TERN task, in which temporally relevant expressions have to be found. The scoring is very generous and implies a minimal overlap in the extent of the reference and the system output tags. As long as there is at least one overlapping character, the tags will be aligned. Any alignment of the system output tags are scored as a correct detection.

**Sloopy span:** Spans usually refer to strict match of both boundaries (the extent) of a temporal expression (see Exact Match). "Sloopy" admits recognized temporal expressions as long as their right boundary is the same as in the corresponding TimeBank's extents (Boguraev and Ando, 2005). The motivation was to assess the correctness of temporal expressions recognized in TimeBank, which was reported as inconsistent with respect to some left boundary items, such as determiners and pre-determiners.

**Exact Match (Bracketing or Extent Recognition):** Exact match measures the ability to correctly identify the extent of the TIMEX. The extent of the reference and the system output tags must match exactly the system output tag to be scored as correct.

### 2.2 Datasets

To date, there are two annotated corpora used for temporal evaluations, the ACE TERN corpus and TimeBank (Pustejovsky et al., 2003a). In this section we provide a brief description of the temporal corpora and annotation standards, which can substantially influence recognition results.

Most of the implementations referred as the state-of-the-art were developed in the scope of the ACE TERN 2004. For evaluations, a training corpus of 862 documents with about 306 thousand words was provided. Each document represents a news article formatted in XML, in which TIMEX2 tags denote temporal expressions. The total number of temporal expressions for training is 8047 TIMEX2 tags with an average of 10.5 per document. The test set comprises 192 documents with 1828 TIMEX2 tags (Ferro, 2004).

The annotation of temporal expressions in the ACE corpus was done with respect to the TIDES annotation guidelines (Ferro et al., 2003). The TIDES standard specifies so-called markable expressions, whose syntactic head must be an appropriate lexical trigger, e.g. "*minute*", "*afternoon*", "*Monday*", "*8:00*", "*future*" etc. When tagged, the full extent of the tag must correspond to one of the grammatical categories: nouns (NN, NNP), noun phrases (NP), adjectives (JJ), adjective phrases (ADJP), adverbs (RB) and adverb phrases (ADVP). According to this, all pre- and postmodifiers as well as dependent clauses are also included to the TIMEX2 extent, e.g. "*five days after he came back*", "*nearly four decades of experience*". Such a broad extent for annotations is of course necessary for correct normalization, but on the other hand, introduces difficulties for exact match. Another important characteristic of the TIDES standard are the nested temporal expressions as for example:

<TIMEX2>The<TIMEX2 VAL = "1994">1994 </TIMEX2> baseball season </TIMEX2>

The most recent annotation language for temporal expressions, TimeML (Pustejovsky et al., 2003b), with an underlying corpus TimeBank (Pustejovsky et al., 2003a), opens up new possibilities for processing temporal information in text. Besides the specification for temporal expressions, i.e. TIMEX3, which is to a large extent inherited from TIDES, TimeML provides a means to capture temporal semantics by annotations with suitably defined attributes for fine-grained specification of analytical detail (Boguraev et al., 2007). The annotation schema establishes new entity and relation marking tags along with numerous attributes for them. This advancement influenced the extent for event-based temporal expression, in which dependent clauses are no longer included into TIMEX3 tags. The TimeBank corpus includes 186 documents with 68.5 thousand words and 1423 TIMEX3 tags.

## 2.3 Approaches for temporal processing

As for any recognition problem, there are two major ways to solve it. Historically, *rule-based systems* were first implemented. Such systems are characterized by a great human effort in data analysis and rule writing. With a high precision such systems can be successfully employed for recognition of temporal expressions, whereas the recall reflects the effort put into the rule development. By contrast, *machine learning methods* require an annotated training set, and with a decent feature design and a minimal human effort can provide comparable or even better results than rule-based implementations. As the temporal expression recognition is not only about to detect them but also to provide an exact match, machine learning approaches can be divided into *token-by-token classification* following **B**(egin)-**I**(nside)-**O**(utside) encoding and *binary constituent-based classification*, in which an entire chunk-phrase is under consideration to be classified as a temporal expression or not. In this case, exact segmentation is the responsibility of the chunker or the parser used.

**Rule-based systems:** One of the first well-known implementations of temporal taggers was presented in (Many and Wilson, 2000). The approach relies on a set of hand-crafted and machine-discovered rules, which are based upon shallow lexical features. On average the system achieved a value of 83.2% for F1-measure against hand-annotated data. The dataset used comprised a set of 22 New York Times articles and 199 transcripts of Voice of America taken from the TDT2 collection (Graff et al., 1999). It should be noted that the reported performance was provided in terms of an exact match. Another example of rule-based temporal taggers is Chronos described in (Negri and Marseglia, 2004), which achieved the highest scores (F1-measure) in the TERN 2004 of 0.926 and 0.878 for recognition and exact match.

Recognition of temporal expressions using TimeBank as an annotated corpus, is reported in (Boguraev and Ando, 2005) based on a cascaded finite-state grammar (500 stages and 16000 transitions). A complex approach achieved an F1-measure value of 0.817 for exact match and 0.896 for detecting "sloopy" spans. Another known implementation for TimeBank is an adaptation of (Mani and Wilson, 2000) from TIMEX2 to TIMEX3 with no reported performance level.

**Machine learning recognition systems:** Successful machine learning TIMEX recognition systems are described in (Ahn et al., 2005; Hacioglu et al., 2005; Poveda et al., 2007). Proposed approaches made use of a token-by-token classification for temporal expressions represented by B-I-O encoding with a set of lexical and syntactic features, e.g., token itself, part-of-speech tag, label in the chunk phrase and the same features for each token in the context window. The performance levels are presented in Table 1. All the results were obtained on the ACE TERN dataset.

| Approach | *F1* (detection) | *F1* (exact match) |
|---|---|---|
| Ahn et al., 2005 | 0.914 | 0.798 |
| Hacioglu et al., 2005 | 0.935 | 0.878 |
| Poveda et al., 2007 | 0.986 | 0.757 |

Table 1. Performance of Machine Learning Approaches with B-I-O Encoding

Constituent-based classification approach for temporal expression recognition was presented in (Ahn et al., 2007). By comparing to the previous work (Ahn et al., 2005) on the same ACE TERN dataset, the method demonstrates a slight decrease in detection with F1-measure of 0.844 and a nearly equivalent F1-measure value for exact match of 0.787.

The major characteristic of machine learning approaches was a simple system design with a minimal human effort. Machine-learning based recognition systems have proven to have a comparable recognition performance level to state-of-the-art rule-based detectors.

## 3 Approach

The approach we describe in this section employs a machine-learning technique and more specifically a binary constituent based classification. In this case the entire phrase is under consideration to be labeled as a TIMEX or not. We restrict the classification for the following phrase types and grammatical categories: NN, NNP, CD, NP, JJ, ADJP, RB, ADVP and PP. In order to make it possible, for each sentence we parse the initial input line with a Maximum Entropy parser (Ratnaparkhi, 1998) and extract all phrase candidates with respect the types defined above. Each phrase candidate is examined against the manual annotations for temporal expressions found in the sentence. Those phrases, which correspond to the temporal expressions in the sentence are taken as positive examples, while the rest are considered as negative ones. Only one sub-tree from a parse is marked as positive for a distinct TIMEX at once. After that, for each candidate we produce a feature vector, which includes the following features: head phrase, head word, part-of-speech for head word, character type and character type pattern for head word as well as for the entire phrase. Character type and character type pattern[1] features are implemented following Ahn et al. (2005). The patterns are defined by using the symbols X, x and 9. X and x are used for character type as well as for character type patterns for representing capital and lower-case letters for a token. 9 is used for representing numeric tokens. Once the character types are computed, the corresponding character patterns are produced. A pattern consists of the same symbols as character types, and contains no sequential redundant occurrences of the same symbol. For example, the constituent "*January 30th*" has character type "Xxxxxxx 99xx" and pattern "X(x) (9)(x)".

On this basis, we employ a classifier that implements a Maximum Entropy model[2] and performs categorization of constituent-phrases extracted from the input.

## 4 Experiments, Results and Error Analysis

After processing the TimeBank corpus of 183 documents we had 2612 parsed sentences with 1224 temporal expressions in them. 2612 sentences resulted in 49656 phrase candidates. We separated the data in order to perform 10-fold cross validation, train the classifier and test it on an unseen dataset. The evaluations were conducted with respect to the TERN 2004 evaluation plan (TERN, 2004) and described in Section 2.1.

After running experiments the classifier demonstrated the performance in detection of TIMEX3 tags with a minimal overlap of one character with precision, recall and F1-measure at 0.872, 0.836 and 0.852 respectively. Since the candidate phrases provided by the parser do not always exactly align annotated temporal expressions, the results for the exact match experiments are constrained by an estimated upper-bound recall of 0.919. The experiments on exact match demonstrated a small decline of performance level and received scores of 0.866, 0.796 and 0.828 for precision, recall and F1-measure respectively.

Putting the received figures in context, we can say that with a very few shallow features and a standard machine learning algorithm the recognizer of temporal expressions performed at a comparable operational level to the rule-based approach of (Boguraev and Ando, 2005) and outperformed it in exact match. A comparative performance summary is presented in Table 2.

Sometimes it is very hard even for humans to identify the use of obvious temporal triggers in a specific context. As a result, many occurrences of such triggers remained unannotated for which TIMEX3 identification could not be properly carried out. Apart of obvious incorrect parses, inexact alignment between temporal expressions and candidate phrases was caused by annotations that occurred at the middle of a phrase, for example "*eight-years-long*", "*overnight*", "*yesterday's*". In total there are 99 TIMEX3 tags (or 8.1%) misaligned with the parser output, which resulted in 53 (or 4.3%) undetected TIMEX3s.

[1] In literature such patterns are also known as shorttypes.

[2] http://maxent.sourceforge.net/

| | *P* | *R* | *F1* |
|---|---|---|---|
| Detection | | | |
| Our approach | 0.872 | 0.836 | 0.852 |
| Sloopy Span | | | |
| (Boguraev and Ando, 2005) | 0.852 | 0.952 | 0.896 |
| Exact Match | | | |
| Our approach | 0.866 | 0.796 | 0.828 |
| (Boguraev and Ando, 2005) | 0.776 | 0.861 | 0.817 |

Table 2. Comparative Performance Summary

Definite and indefinite articles are unsystematically left out or included into TIMEX3 extent, which may introduce an additional bias in classification.

## 5 Conclusion and Future Work

In this paper we presented a machine learning approach for detecting temporal expression using a recent annotated corpus for temporal information, TimeBank. Employing shallow syntactic and lexical features, the performance level of the method achieved comparable results to a rule-based approach of Boguraev and Ando (2005) and for the exact match task even outperforms it. Although a direct comparison with other state-of-the-art systems is not possible, due to different evaluation corpora, annotation standards and size in particular, our experiments disclose a very important characteristic. While the recognition systems in the TERN 2004 reported a substantial drop of F1-measure between detection and exact match results (6.5 – 11.6%), our phrase-based detector demonstrates a light decrease in F1-measure (2.4%), whereas the precision declines only by 0.6%. This important finding leads us to the conclusion that most of TIMEX3s in TimeBank can be detected at a phrase-based level with a reasonably high performance.

Despite a good recognition performance level there is, of course, room for improvement. Many implementations in the TERN 2004 employ a set of apparent temporal tokens as one of the features. In our implementation, the classifier has difficulties with very simple temporal expressions such as "*now*", "*future*", "*current*", "*currently*", "*recent*", "*recently*". A direct employment of vocabularies with temporal tokens may substantially increase the F1-measure of the method, however, it yet has to be proven. As reported in (Ahn et al., 2007) a precise recognition of temporal expressions is a prerequisite for accurate normalization.

With our detector and a future normalizer we are able make the first step towards solving the TempEval-2 tasks, which introduce new challenges in temporal information processing: identification of events, identification of temporal expressions and identification of temporal relations (Pustejovsky et al., 2009). Our future work will be focused on improving current results by a new feature design, finalizing the normalization task and identification of temporal relations. All these components will result in a solid system infrastructure for all-around temporal analysis.

## Acknowledgments

This work has been partly funded by the Flemish government (through IWT) and by Space Applications Services NV as part of the ITEA2 project LINDO (ITEA2-06011).

## References

Ahn, D., Adafre, S. F., and de Rijke, M. 2005. Extracting Temporal Information from Open Domain Text: A Comparative Exploration. *Digital Information Management*, 3(1):14-20, 2005.

Ahn, D., van Rantwijk, J., and de Rijke, M. 2007. A Cascaded Machine Learning Approach to Interpreting Temporal Expressions. In *Proceedings NAACL-HLT 2007.*

Boguraev, B., and Ando, R. K. 2005. TimeBank-Driven TimeML Analysis. In *Annotating, Extracting and Reasoning about Time and Events.* Dagstuhl Seminar Proceedings. Dagstuhl, Germany

Boguraev, B., Pustejovsky, J., Ando, R., and Verhagen, M. 2007. TimeBank Evolution as a Community Resource for TimeML Parsing. *Language Resource and Evaluation*, 41(1): 91–115.

Ferro, L., Gerber, L., Mani, I., Sundheim, B., and Wilson, G. 2003. TIDES 2003 Standard for the Annotation of Temporal Expressions. Sept. 2003. timex2.mitre.org.

Ferro, L. 2004. TERN Evaluation Task Overview and Corpus, <http://fofoca.mitre.org/tern_2004/ferro1_TERN2004_task_corpus.pdf> (accessed: 5.03.2009)

Graff, D., Cieri, C., Strassel, S., and Martey, N. 1999. The TDT-2 Text and Speech Corpus. In *Proceedings of DARPA Broadcast News Workshop*, pp. 57-60.

Hacioglu, K., Chen, Y., and Douglas, B. 2005. Automatic Time Expression Labeling for English and Chinese Text. In *Proceedings of CICLing-2005*, pp. 348-359; Springer-Verlag, Lecture Notes in Computer Science, vol. 3406.

Mani, I. and Wilson, G. 2000. Robust Temporal Processing of News. In *Proceedings of the 38th Annual Meeting on Association for Computational Linguistics* (Hong Kong, October 03 - 06, 2000). Annual Meeting of the ACL. Association for Computational Linguistics, Morristown, NJ, pp. 69-76.

Negri, M. and Marseglia, L. 2004. Recognition and Normalization of Time Expressions: ITC-irst at TERN 2004. Technical Report, ITC-irst, Trento.

Poveda, J., Surdeanu, M., and Turmo, J. 2007. A Comparison of Statistical and Rule-Induction Learners for Automatic Tagging of Time Expressions in English. In *Proceedings of the International Symposium on Temporal Representation and Reasoning*, pp. 141-149.

Pustejovsky, J., Hanks, P., Saurí, R., See, A., Day, D., Ferro, L., Gaizauskas, R., Lazo, M., Setzer, A., and Sundheim, B. 2003a. The TimeBank Corpus. In *Proceedings of Corpus Linguistics 2003*, pp. 647-656.

Pustejovsky, J., Castaño, J., Ingria, R., Saurí, R., Gaizauskas, R., Setzer, A., and Katz, G. 2003b. TimeML: Robust Specification of Event and Temporal Expressions in Text. In *Proceedings of IWCS-5, Fifth International Workshop on Computational Semantics.*

Pustejovsky, J., Verhagen, M., Nianwen, X., Gaizauskas, R., Hepple, M., Schilder, F., Katz, G., Saurí, R., Saquete, E., Caselli, T., Calzolari, N., Lee, K., and Im, S. 2009. TempEval2: Evaluating Events, Time Expressions and Temporal Relations. <http://www.timeml.org/tempeval2/tempeval2-proposal.pdf> (accessed: 5.03.2009)

Ratnaparkhi, A. 1999. Learning to Parse Natural Language with Maximum Entropy Models. *Machine Learning*, 34(1): 151-175.

TERN 2004 Evaluation Plan, 2004, <http://fofoca.mitre.org/tern_2004/tern_evalplan-2004.29apr04.pdf> (accessed: 5.03.2009)

# Using Lexical Patterns in the Google Web 1T Corpus to Deduce Semantic Relations Between Nouns

**Paul Nulty**
School of Computer Science and Informatics
University College Dublin, Belfield
Dublin 4, Ireland
paul.nulty@ucd.ie

**Fintan Costello**
School of Computer Science and Informatics
University College Dublin, Belfield
Dublin 4, Ireland
fintan.costello@ucd.ie

## Abstract

This paper investigates methods for using lexical patterns in a corpus to deduce the semantic relation that holds between two nouns in a noun-noun compound phrase such as "flu virus" or "morning exercise". Much of the previous work in this area has used automated queries to commercial web search engines. In our experiments we use the Google Web 1T corpus. This corpus contains every 2,3, 4 and 5 gram occurring more than 40 times in Google's index of the web, but has the advantage of being available to researchers directly rather than through a web interface. This paper evaluates the performance of the Web 1T corpus on the task compared to similar systems in the literature, and also investigates what kind of lexical patterns are most informative when trying to identify a semantic relation between two nouns.

## 1 Introduction

Noun-noun combinations occur frequently in many languages, and the problem of semantic disambiguation of these phrases has many potential applications in natural language processing and other areas. Search engines which can identify the relations between nouns may be able to return more accurate results. Hand-built ontologies such as WordNet at present only contain a few basic semantic relations between nouns, such as hypernymy and meronymy.

If the process of discovering semantic relations from text were automated, more links could quickly be built up. Machine translation and question-answering are other potential applications. Noun compounds are very common in English, especially in technical documentation and neologisms. Latin languages tend to favour prepositional paraphrases instead of direct compound translation, and to select the correct preposition it is often necessary to know the semantic relation. One very common approach to this problem is to define a set of semantic relations which capture the interaction between the modifier and the head noun, and then attempt to assign one of these semantic relations to each noun-modifier pair. For example, the phrase *flu virus* could be assigned the semantic relation causal (the virus causes the flu); the relation for *desert wind* could be location (the storm is located in the desert).

There is no consensus as to which set of semantic relations best captures the differences in meaning of various noun phrases. Work in theoretical linguistics has suggested that noun-noun compounds may be formed by the deletion of a predicate verb or preposition (Levi 1978). However, whether the set of possible predicates numbers 5 or 50, there are likely to be some examples of noun phrases that fit into none of the categories and some that fit in multiple categories.

## 2 Related Work

The idea of searching a large corpus for specific lexicosyntactic phrases to indicate a semantic relation of interest was first described by Hearst (1992). Lauer (1995) tackled the problem of semantically disambiguating noun phrases by trying to find the preposition which best describes the relation between the modifier and head noun. His method involves searching a corpus for occurrences paraphrases of the form *"noun preposition modifier"*. Whichever preposition is most frequent in this context is chosen to represent the predicate



*Proceedings of the NAACL HLT Workshop on Semantic Evaluations: Recent Achievements and Future Directions*, pages 58–63,
Boulder, Colorado, June 2009. 

of the nominal, which poses the same problem of vagueness as Levi's approach. Lapata and Keller (2005) improved on Lauer's results on the same task by using the web as a corpus.

Turney and Littman (2005) used queries to the AltaVista search engine as the basis for their learning algorithm. Using the dataset of Nastase and Szpakowicz (2003), they experimented with a set of 64 short prepositional and conjunctive phrases they call "joining terms" to generate exact queries for AltaVista of the form *"noun joining term modifier"*, and *"modifier joining term noun"*. These hit counts were used with a nearest neighbour algorithm to assign the noun phrases semantic relations.

Nakov and Hearst (2006) present a system that discovers verbs that characterize the relation between two nouns in a compound. By writing structured queries to a web search engine and syntactically parsing the returned 'snippet', they were able to identify verbs that were suitable predicates. For example, for the compound *neck vein*, they retrieved verbs and verb-preposition such as predicates *emerge from, pass through, terminate in*, and others. However, their evaluation is qualitative; they do not attempt to use the verbs directly to categorize a compound as a particular semantic relation.

Turney (2006) examines similarity measures for semantic relations. He notes that there are at least two kinds of similarity: attributional similarity, which applies between words, and relational similarity, which holds between pairs of words.

Words that have a high attributional similarity are known as synonyms; e.g. chair and stool. When the relations in each of two pairs of words are similar, it is said that there is an analogy between the two pairs of words, e.g. stone:mason, carpenter:wood.

Turney points out that word pairs with high relational similarity do not necessarily contain words with high attributional similarity. For example, although the relations are similar in traffic:street and water:riverbed, water is not similar to traffic, nor street similar to riverbed.

Therefore, a measure of similarity of semantic relations allows a more reliable judgment of analogy than the first-order similarity of the nouns

## 3 Motivation

When looking for lexical patterns between two nouns, as is required with vector-space approaches, data sparseness is a common problem. To overcome this, many of the best-performing systems in this area rely on automated queries to web search-engines (Lapata and Keller (2005), Turney and Littman (2005), Nakov and Hearst (2006)). The most apparent advantage of using search-engine queries is simply the greater volume of data available.

Keller and Lapata (2003) demonstrated the usefulness of this extra data on a type of word-sense disambiguation test and also found that web frequencies of bigrams correlated well with frequencies in a standard corpus.

Kilgarriff (2007) argues against the use of commercial search engines for research, and outlines some of the major drawbacks. Search engine crawlers do not lemmatize or part-of-speech tag their text. This means that to obtain frequencies for may different inflectional forms, researchers must perform a separate query for each possible form and sum the results.

If part-of-speech tagging is required, the 'snippet' of text that is returned with each result may be tagged after the query has been executed, however the APIs for the major search engines have limitations on how many snippets may be retrieved for a given query (100 -1000).

Another problem is that search engine query syntax is limited, and sometimes mysterious. In the case of Google, only basic boolean operators are supported (AND, OR, NOT), and the function of the wildcard symbol (*) is limited, difficult to decipher and may have changed over time.

Kilgarriff also points out that the search API services to the major search engines have constraints on the number of searches that are allowed per user per day. Because of the multiple searches that are needed to cover inflectional variants and recover snippets for tagging, a limit of 1000 queries per day, as with the Google API, makes experimentation slow. This paper will describe the use of the Web 1T corpus, made available by Google in 2006 (Brants and Franz 2006). This corpus consists of n-grams collected from web data, and is available to researchers in its entirety, rather than through a web search interface. This means that there is no limit to the amount of searches that may be performed, and an arbitrarily complex query syntax is possible.

Despite being available since 2006, few researchers have made use of the Web 1T corpus. Hawker (2006) provides an example of using the corpus for word sense documentation, and describes a method for efficient searching. We will outline the performance of the corpus on the task of identifying the semantic relation between two nouns. Another motivation behind this paper is to examine the usefulness of different lexical patterns for the task of deducing semantic relations.

In this paper, we are interested in whether the frequency with which a joining term occurs between two nouns is related to how it indicates a semantic interaction. This is in part motivated by Zipf's theory which states that the more frequently a word occurs in a corpus the more meanings or senses it is likely to have (Zipf 1929). If this is true, we would expect that very frequent prepositions, such as "of", would have many possible meanings and therefore not reliably predict a semantic relation. However, less frequent prepositions, such as "during" would have a more limited set of senses and therefore accurately predict a semantic relation. Zipf also showed that the frequency of a term is related to its length. We will investigate whether longer lexical patterns are more useful at identifying semantic relations than shorter patterns, and whether less frequent patterns perform better than more frequent ones.

## 4 Web 1T Corpus

The Web1T corpus consists of n-grams taken from approximately one trillion words of English text taken from web pages in Google's index of web pages. The data includes all 2,3,4 and 5-grams that occur more than 40 times in these pages. The data comes in the form of approximately 110 compressed files for each of the window sizes. Each of these files consists of exactly 10 million n-grams, with their frequency counts. Below is an example of the 3-gram data:

```
ceramics collection and 43
ceramics collection at 52
ceramics collection is 68
ceramics collection | 59
ceramics collections , 66
ceramics collections . 60
```

The uncompressed 3-grams, 4-grams 5-grams together take up 80GB on disk. In order to make it possible to index and search this data, we excluded n-grams that contained any punctuation or non-alphanumeric characters. We also excluded n-grams that contained any uppercase letters, although we did allow for the first letter of the first word to be uppercase.

We indexed the data using Ferret, a Ruby port of the Java search engine package Lucene. We were able to index all of the data in under 48 hours, using 32GB of hard disk space. The resulting index was searchable by first word, last word, and intervening pattern. Only n-grams with a frequency of 40 or higher are included in the dataset, which obviously means that an average query returns fewer results than a web search. However, with the data available on local disk it is stable, reliable, and open to any kind of query syntax or lemmatization.

## 5 Lexical Patterns for Disambiguation

Modifier-noun phrases are often used interchangeably with paraphrases which contain the modifier and the noun joined by a preposition or simple verb. For example, the noun-phrase "morning exercise" may be paraphrased as "exercise in the morning" or "exercise during the morning". In a very large corpus, it is possible to find many reasonable paraphrases of noun phrases. These paraphrases contain information about the relationship between the modifier and the head noun that is not present in the bare modifier-noun phrase. By analyzing these paraphrases, we can deduce what semantic relation is most likely. For example, the paraphrases "exercise during the morning" and "exercise in the morning" are likely to occur more frequently than "exercise about the morning" or "exercise at the morning".

One method for deducing semantic relations between words in compounds involves gathering n-gram frequencies of these paraphrases, containing a noun, a modifier and a lexical pattern that links them. Some algorithm can then be used to map from lexical patterns to frequencies to semantic relations and so find the correct relation for the compound in question. This is the approach we use in our experiments.

In order to describe the semantic relation between two nouns in a compound *"noun1 noun2"* we search for ngrams that begin with *noun2* and end with *noun1*, since in English the head of the noun compound is the second word. For example, for the compound 'flu virus', we look at n-grams that begin with 'virus' and end with 'flu'. We extract the words that occur between the two nouns (a string of 1-3 words) and use these lexical patterns as features for the machine learning algorithm.

For each compound we also include n-grams which have the plural form of *noun1* or *noun2*. We assign a score to each of these lexical patterns, as the log of the frequency of the n-gram. We used the 400 most frequent lexical patterns extracted as the features for the model. Below are examples of some of the lexical patterns that were extracted:

| | |
|---|---|
| and | or |
| of the | on the |
| of | from the |
| in the | the |
| for | to |
| and the | of a |
| for the | with the |
| to the | on |
| with | that the |
| in | from |

Figure 1: The 20 most frequent patterns

The simplest way to use this vector space model to classify noun-noun combinations is to use a distance metric to compare a novel pair of nouns to ones previously annotated with semantic relations. Nulty (2007) compares these nearest neighbor models with other machine learning techniques and finds that using a support vector machine leads to improved classification.

In our experiments we used the support vector machine and k-nearest-neighbor algorithms from the WEKA machine learning toolkit. All experiments were conducted using leave-one-out cross validation: each example in the dataset is in turn tested alone, with all the other examples used for training. The first dataset used in these experiments was created by Nastase and Szpackowicz (2003) and used in experiments by Turney and Littmann (2005) and Turney (2006). The data consists of 600 noun-modifier compounds. Of the 600 examples, four contained hyphenated modifiers, for example "test-tube baby". These were excluded from our dataset, leaving 596 examples. The data is labeled with two different sets of semantic relations: one set of 30 relations with fairly specific meanings and another set of 5 relations with more abstract relations. In these experiments we use only the set of 5 relations. The reason for this is that splitting a set of 600 examples into 30 classes results in few training examples per class. This problem is compounded by the fact that the dataset is uneven, with far more examples in some classes than in others. Below are the five relations and some examples.

| Relation: | Example: |
|---|---|
| causal | flu virus, onion tear |
| temporal | summer travel, night class |
| spatial | west coast, home remedy |
| participant | mail sorter, blood donor |
| quality | rice paper, picture book |

Figure 2: Example phrases and their semantic relations

For our research we are particularly interested in noun-noun combinations. Of the 596 examples in the dataset, we found that 325 were clearly noun-noun combinations, e.g."picture book", rice paper", while in the remainder the modifier was an adjective, for example "warm air", "heavy storm". We used only the noun-noun combinations in our experiments, as this is the focus of our research. We experimented with both lemmatization of the data and excluding semantically empty stop words (determiners and conjunctions) from the lexical patterns, however neither of these methods improved performance. Below are the results obtained with the k-nearest neighbor algorithm. The optimum value of k was 3.

| Precision | Recall | f-score | class |
|---|---|---|---|
| .442 | .452 | .447 | Quality |
| .75 | .444 | .558 | Temporal |
| .243 | .167 | .198 | Causal |
| .447 | .611 | .516 | Participant |
| .571 | .138 | .222 | Spatial |

Figure 3: Results using the K-NN algorithm

The overall accuracy was 44% and the macro-averaged f-value was .39.

Below are the results obtained using the support-vector machine algorithm:

| Precision | Recall | f-score | class |
|---|---|---|---|
| .725 | .345 | .468 | Quality |
| .733 | .407 | .524 | Temporal |
| .545 | .111 | .185 | Causal |
| .472 | .885 | .615 | Participant |
| .462 | .207 | .268 | Spatial |

Figure 4: Results using the Support Vector Machine

The overall accuracy was 51.7% and the macroaveraged f-value was .42. A majority class baseline
(always predicting the largest class) would achieve an accuracy of 43.7%.

## 6 Which Lexical Patterns are Most Useful?

In addition to evaluating the Google Web 1T corpus, a motivation for this paper is to investigate what kind of lexical patterns are most useful for deducing semantic relations. In order to investigate this, we repeated the experiment one using the 3-grams, 4-grams and 5-grams separately, which gave lexical patterns of length 1, 2 and 3 respectively. Accuracy obtained using the support vector machine and k-nearest-neighbor algorithms are below:

| | 3-grams | 4grams | 5-grams | All |
|---|---|---|---|---|
| KNN | 36 | 42.5 | 42.4 | 44 |
| SVM | 44.3 | 49.2 | 43.4 | 51.7 |

Figure 5: Results for different sizes of lexical patterns

Again, in each case the support vector machine performs better than the nearest neighbor algorithm. The 4- grams (two-word lexical patterns) give the best performance. One possible explanation for this is that the single word lexical patterns don't convey a very specific relation, while the 3 word patterns are relatively rare in the corpus, leading to many missing values in the training data.

We were also interested in how the frequency of the lexical patterns related to their ability to predict the correct semantic relation. To evaluate this, we ordered the 400 lexical patterns retrieved by frequency and then split them into three groups. We took the 64 most frequent patterns, the patterns ranked 100-164 in frequency, and those ranked 300-364. We chose to include 64 patterns in each group to allow for comparison with Turney and Littman (2001), who use 64 hand-generated patterns. Examples of the most frequent patterns are shown in Fig 1. Below are examples of patterns from the other two groups.

| | |
|---|---|
| as well as | my |
| out of the | on Friday |
| of one | without |
| of fresh | which the |
| into | with my |
| for all | and their |
| was | around the |
| with your | when |
| related to the | whose |
| in the early | during |

Figure 6: Frequency Ranks 100-120

| | |
|---|---|
| to produce | one |
| but | provides |
| that cause | from your |
| of social | of edible |
| while the | levels and |
| or any other | comes from |
| such as the | chosen by the |
| are in the | producing |
| to provide | does not |
| if a | than the |
| from one | belonging to the |

Figure 7: Frequency Ranks 300-320

The accuracies obtained using patterns in the different frequency groups are shown below.

| | 1-64 | 100-164 | 300-364 |
|---|---|---|---|
| KNN | 40.9 | 43.5 | 41.9 |
| SVM | 47.6 | 45.2 | 41.5 |

Figure 8: Results for different frequency bands of patterns

Although there is no large effect to the accuracy of the KNN algorithm, the Support Vector Machine seems to perform better with the most frequent patterns. One possible explanation for this is that although the less frequent patterns seem more informative, they more often result in zero matches in the corpus, which simply leaves a missing value in the training data.

## 7 Conclusion

This paper reports several experiments on the semantic disambiguation of noun-noun phrases using the Google Web 1T corpus, and shows that the results are comparable to previous work which has relied on a web interface to search engines. Having a useful corpus based on web data that can be stored and searched locally means that results will be stable across time and can be subject to complex queries. Experiments designed to evaluate the usefulness of different lexical patterns did not yield strong results and further work is required in this area.

## References


Thorsten Brants and Alex Franz. 2006. Web 1T 5-gram Corpus Version 1.1. *Technical report, Google Research*

Tobias Hawker. 2006. Using Contexts of One Trillion Words for WSD. *Proceedings of the 10th Conference of the Pacific Association for Computational Linguistics, pages 85–93.*

Marti A. Hearst: 1992. Automatic Acquisition of Hyponyms from Large Text Corpora. *COLING: 539-545*

Keller, Frank and Mirella Lapata. 2003. Using the Web to Obtain Frequencies for Unseen Bigrams Computational Linguistics 29:3, 459-484.

Adam Kilgarriff, 2007. Googleology is Bad Science. *Comput. Linguist.* 33, 1 147-151.

Lapata, Mirella and Frank Keller. 2005. Web Based Models for Natural Language Processing. *ACM Transactions on Speech and Language Processing 2:1, 1-31.*

Mark Lauer. *Designing Statistical Language Learners: Experiments on Noun Compounds*. PhD thesis, Macquarie University NSW 2109 Australia.

Judith Levi. (1978) The Syntax and Semantics of Complex Nominals, *Academic Press, New York, NY.*

Phil Maguire *(2007) A cognitive model of conceptual combination* Unpublished PhD Thesis, UCD Dublin

Preslav Nakov and Marti Hearst. 2006. Using Verbs to Characterize Noun-Noun Relations, in the *Proceedings of AIMSA 2006*,

Preslav Nakov and Marti Hearst. 2005. Using the Web as an Implicit Training Set: Application to Structural Ambiguity Resolution, in *HLT/EMNLP'0*

Vivi Nastase and Stan Szpakowicz. 2003. Exploring Noun-Modifier Semantic Relations. *International Workshop on Computational Semantics, Tillburg, Netherlands, 2003*

Paul Nulty and Fintan Costello, 2007. Semantic Classification of Noun Phrases Using Web Counts and Learning Algorithms. *Proceedings of ACL 2007 Student Reseach Workshop.*

Barbara Rosario and Marti A. Hearst. 2001. Classifying the semantic relations in noun compounds via a domain-specific lexical hierarchy. In *Proceedings of the 2001Conference on Empirical Methods in Natural Language Processing.* ACL

Peter D. Turney. 2005. Measuring semantic similarity by latent relational analysis. In *Proceedings of the Nineteenth International Joint Conference on Artificial Intelligence (IJCAI-05)*, pages 1136-1141.

Peter D. Turney., and Michael L. Littman,. 2006. Corpus based learning of analogies and semantic relations. *Machine Learning*, 60(1–3):251–278

Ian H. Witten and Eibe Frank. 1999. *Data Mining: Practical Machine Learning Tools and Techniques with Java Implementations*, Morgan Kaufman (1999)

George K. Zipf. 1932. *Selected Studies of the Principle of Relative Frequency in Language.* Cambridge, MA

# Improvements to Monolingual English Word Sense Disambiguation*

**Weiwei Guo**
Computer Science Department
Columbia University
New York, NY, 10115, USA
wg2162@cs.columbia.edu

**Mona T. Diab**
Center for Computational Learning Systems
Columbia University
New York, NY 10115, USA
mdiab@ccls.columbia.edu

## Abstract

Word Sense Disambiguation remains one of the most complex problems facing computational linguists to date. In this paper we present modification to the graph based state of the art algorithm In-Degree. Our modifications entail augmenting the basic Lesk similarity measure with more relations based on the structure of WordNet, adding SemCor examples to the basic WordNet lexical resource and finally instead of using the LCH similarity measure for computing verb verb similarity in the In-Degree algorithm, we use JCN. We report results on three standard data sets using three different versions of WordNet. We report the highest performing monolingual unsupervised results to date on the Senseval 2 all words data set. Our system yields a performance of 62.7% using WordNet 1.7.1.

## 1 Introduction

Despite the advances in natural language processing (NLP), Word Sense Disambiguation (WSD) is still considered one of the most challenging problems in the field. Ever since the field's inception, WSD has been perceived as one of the central problems in NLP as an enabling technology that could potentially have far reaching impact on NLP applications in general. We are starting to see the beginnings of a positive effect of WSD in NLP applications such as Machine Translation (Carpuat and Wu, 2007; Chan et al., 2007). Advances in research on WSD in the current millennium can be attributed to several key factors: the availability of large scale computational lexical resources such as WordNets (Fellbaum, 1998; Miller, 1990), the availability of large scale corpora, the existence and dissemination of standardized data sets over the past 10 years through the different test beds of SENSEVAL and SEMEVAL competitions,[1] devising more robust computing algorithms to handle large scale data sets, and simply advancement in hardware machinery.

In this paper, we address the problem of WSD of all the content words in a sentence. In this framework, the task is to associate all tokens with their contextually relevant meaning definitions from some computational lexical resource. We present an enhancement on an existing graph based algorithm, In-Degree, as described in (Sinha and Mihalcea, 2007). Like the previous work, our algorithm is unsupervised. We show significant improvements over previous state of the art performance on several existing data sets, SENSEVAL2, SENSEVAL3 and SEMEVAL.

## 2 Word Sense Disambiguation

The definition of WSD has taken on several different meanings in recent years. In the latest SEMEVAL (2007) workshop, there were 18 tasks defined, several of which were on different languages, however we notably recognize the widening of the definition of the task of WSD. In addition to the traditional all words and lexical sample tasks, we note new tasks on word sense discrimination (no sense inventory is needed, the different senses are merely distinguished), lexical substitution using synonyms of words as substitutes, as well as meaning definitions obtained from different languages namely using words in translation.

Our paper is about the classical all words task of WSD. In this task, all the content bearing words in a running text are disambiguated from a static lexical

*The second author has been partially funded by DARPA GALE project. We would also like to thank the useful comments rendered by three anonymous reviewers.

[1] http://www.semeval.org



*Proceedings of the NAACL HLT Workshop on Semantic Evaluations: Recent Achievements and Future Directions*, pages 64–69,
Boulder, Colorado, June 2009. 

resource. For example a sentence such as *I walked by the bank and saw many beautiful plants there.* will have the verbs *walked, saw*, the nouns *bank, plants*, the adjectives *many, beautiful*, and the adverb *there*, be disambiguated from a standard lexical resource. Hence using WordNet,[2] *walked* will be assigned the meaning to *u*se one's feet to advance; advance by steps, *saw* will be assigned the meaning to *p*erceive by sight or have the power to perceive by sight, the noun *bank* will be assigned the meaning *s*loping land especially the slope beside a body of water and so on.

## 3 Related Works

Many systems over the years have been used for the task. A thorough review of the current state of the art is in (Navigli, 2009). Several techniques have been used to tackle the problem ranging from rule based/knowledge based approaches to unsupervised and supervised machine learning approaches. To date, the best approaches that solve the all words WSD task are supervised as illustrated in the different SenseEval and SEMEVAL All Words tasks (M. Palmer and Dang, 2001; Snyder and Palmer, 2004; Pradhan et al., 2007).

In this paper, we present an unsupervised approach to the all words WSD problem relying on WordNet similarity measures. We will review only three of the most relevant related research due to space limitations. We acknowledge the existence of many research papers that tackled the problem using unsupervised approaches.

Firstly, in work by (Pedersen and Patwardhan, 2005), the authors investigate different word similarity measures as a means of disambiguating words in context. They compare among different similarity measures. They show that using an extension on the Lesk similarity measure (Lesk, 1986) between the target words and their contexts and the contexts of those of the WordNet synset entries (Gloss Overlap), outperforms all the other similarity measures. Their approach is unsupervised. They exploit the different relations in WordNet. They also go beyond the single word overlap, they calculate the overlap in n-grams. They report results on the English Lexical sample task from Senseval 2 which comprised nouns, verbs and adjectives. The majority of the words in this set is polysemous. They achieve an F-measure of 41.2% on nouns, 21.2% on verbs, and 25.1% on adjectives.

The second related work to ours is the work by (Mihalcea, 2005). Mihalcea (2005) introduced a graph based unsupervised technique for all word sense disambiguation. Similar to the previous study, the author relied on the similarity of the WordNet entry glosses using the Lesk similarity measure. The study introduces a graph based sequence model of the problem. All the open class words in a sentence are linked via an undirected graph where all the possible senses are listed. Then dependency links are drawn between all the sense pairs. Weights on the arcs are determined based on the semantic similarity using the Lesk measure. The algorithm is basically to walk the graph and find the links with the highest possible weights deciding on the appropriate sense for the target words in question. This algorithm yields an overall F-score of 54.2% on the Senseval 2 all words data set and an F-score of 64.2% on nouns alone.

Finally, the closest study relevant to the current paper yields state of the art performance is an unsupervised approach described in (Sinha and Mihalcea, 2007). In this work, the authors combine different semantic similarity measures with different graph based algorithms as an extension to work in (Mihalcea, 2005). The authors proposed a graph-based WSD algorithm. Given a sequence of words $W = \{w_1, w_2...w_n\}$, each word $w_i$ with several senses $\{s_{i1}, s_{i2}...s_{im}\}$. A graph G = (V,E) is defined such that there exists a vertex v for each sense. Two senses of two different words may be connected by an edge $e$, depending on their distance. That two senses are connected suggests they should have influence on each other, so normally a maximum allowable distance is set. They explore 4 different graph based algorithms. The highest yielding algorithm in their work is the `In-Degree` algorithm combining different WordNet similarity measures depending on POS. They used the Jiang and Conrath (JCN) (Jiang and Conrath., 1997) similarity measure within nouns, the Leacock & Chodorow (LCH) (Leacock and Chodorow, 1998) similarity measure within verbs, and the Lesk (Lesk, 1986) similarity measure within adjectives and within adverbs and

[2] http://wordnet.princeton.edu

across different POS tags. They evaluate their work against the Senseval 2 all words task. They tune the parameters of their algorithm – specifically the normalization ratio for some of these measures — based on the Senseval 3 data set. They report a state of the art unsupervised system that yields an overall performance of 57.2%.

## 4 Our Approach

In this paper, we extend the (Sinha and Mihalcea, 2007) work (hence forth SM07) in some interesting ways. We focus on the `In-Degree` graph based algorithm as it was the best performer in the SM07 work. The *In-Degree* algorithm presents the problem as a weighted graph with senses as nodes and similarity between senses as weights on edges. The In-Degree of a vertex refers to the number of edges incident on that vertex. In the weighted graph, the In-Degree for each vertex is calculated by summing the weights on the edges that are incident on it.

After all the In-Degree values for each sense is computed, the sense with maximum value is chosen as the final sense for that word. SM07 combine different similarity measures. They show that best combination is JCN for noun pairs and LCH for verb pairs, and Lesk for within adjectives and within adverbs and also across different POS, for example comparing senses of verbs and nouns. Since different similarity measures use different similarity scales, SM07 did not directly use the value returned from the similarity metrics. Instead, the values were normalized. Lesk value is observed in a range from 0 to an arbitrary value, so values larger than 240 were set to 1, and the rest is mapped to an interval [0,1]. Similarily JCN and LCH were normalized to the interval from [0,1].[3]

In this paper, we use the basic In-Degree algorithm while applying some modifications to the basic similarity measures exploited and the WordNet lexical resource. Similar to the original In-Degree algorithm, we produce a probabilistic ranked list of senses. Our modifications are described as follows:

**JCN for Verb-Verb Similarity** In our implementation of the In-Degree algorithm, we use the JCN similarity measure for both Noun-Noun similarity calculation similar to SM07. In addition, instead of using LCH for Verb-Verb similarity, we use JCN for Verb Verb similarity based on our empirical observation on SENSEVAL 3 data, JCN yields better performance than when employing LCH among verbs.

**Expand Lesk** Following the intuition in (Pedersen and Patwardhan, 2005) – henceforth (PEA05) – we expand the basic Lesk similarity measure to take into account the glosses for all the relations for the synsets on the contextual words and compare them with the glosses of the target word senses, hence going beyond the is-a relation. The idea is based on the observation that WordNet senses are too fine-grained, therefore the neighbors share a lot of semantic meanings. To find similar senses, we use the relations: hypernym, hyponym, similar attributes, similar verb group, pertinym, holonym, and meronyms.[4] The algorithm assumes that the words in the input are POS tagged. It is worth noting the differences between our algorithm and the PEA05 algorithm, though we take our cue from it. In PEA05, the authors retrieve all the relevant neighbors to form a large bag of words for both the target sense and the surrounding sense and they specifically focus on the Lesk similarity measure. In our current work, we employ the neighbors in a disambiguation strategy using different similarity measures one pair at a time.

This algorithm takes as input a target sense and a sense pertaining to a word in the surrounding context, and returns a sense similarity score. It is worth noting that we do not apply the WN relations expansion to the target sense. It is only applied to the contextual word. We experimented with expanding both the contextual sense and the target sense and we found that the unreliability of some of the relations is detrimental to the algorithm's performance. Hence we decided empirically to expand only the contextual word.

We employ the same normalization values used in SM07 for the different similarity measures. Namely for the Lesk and Expand-Lesk we use the same cut off value of 240, accordingly, if the Lesk or Expand-Lesk similarity value returns $0 <= 240$ it is con-

[3] These values were decided on based on calibrations on the SENSEVAL 3 data set.

[4] We have run experiments varying the number of relations to employ and they all yielded relatively similar results. Hence in this paper, we report results using all the relations listed above.

verted to a real number in the interval [0,1], any similarity over 240 is by default mapped to a 1. For JCN, similar to SM07, the values are from 0.04 to 0.2, we mapped them to the interval [0,1]. It is worth noting that we did not run any calibration studies beyond the what was reported in SM07.

**SemCor Expansion of WordNet** A basic part of our approach relies on using the Lesk algorithm. Accordingly, the availability of glosses associated with the WordNet entries is extremely beneficial. Therefore, we expand the number of glosses available in WordNet by using the SemCor data set, thereby adding more examples to compare. The SemCor corpus is a corpus that is manually sense tagged (Miller, 1990). In this expansion, depending on the version of WordNet, we use the sense-index file in the WordNet Database to convert the SemCor data to the appropriate version sense annotations. We augment the sense entries for the different POS WordNet databases with example usages from SemCor. The augmentation is done as a look up table external to WordNet proper since we did not want to dabble with the WordNet offsets. We set a cap of 30 additional examples per synset. Many of the synsets had no additional examples. A total of 26875 synsets in WordNet 1.7.1 and a total of 25940 synsets are augmented with SemCor examples.[5]

## 5 Experiments and Results

### 5.1 Data

We experiment with all the standard data sets, namely, Senseval 2 (SV2) (M. Palmer and Dang, 2001), Senseval 3 (SV3) (Snyder and Palmer, 2004), and SEMEVAL (SM) (Pradhan et al., 2007) English All Words data sets. We used the true POS tag sets in the test data as rendered in the Penn Tree Bank. We exclude the data points that have a tag of "U" in the gold standard since our system does not allow for an unknown option (i.e. it has to produce a sense tag). We present our results on 3 versions of WordNet (WN), 1.7.1 for ease of comparison with previous systems, 2.1 for SEMEVAL data, and 3.0 in order to see whether the trends in performance hold across WN versions.

[5]It is worth noting that some example sentences are repeated across different synsets and POS since the SemCor data is annotated as an All-Words tagged data set.

### 5.2 Evaluation Metrics

We use the `scorer2` software to report fine-grained (P)recision and (R)ecall and (F)-measure on the different data sets.

### 5.3 Baselines

We consider here the two different baselines. 1. A random baseline (RAND) is the most appropriate baseline for an unsupervised approach. We consider the first sense baseline to be a supervised baseline since it depends crucially on SemCor in ranking the senses within WordNet.[6] It is worth pointing out that our algorithm is still an unsupervised algorithm even though we use SemCor to augment WordNet since we do not use any annotated data in our algorithm proper. 2. The SM07 baseline which we consider our true baseline.

### 5.4 Experimental Conditions

We explore 4 different experimental conditions: JCN-V which uses JCN instead of LCH for verb-verb similarity comparison, we consider this our base condition; +ExpandL is adding the Lesk Expansion to the base condition; +SemCor adds the SemCor expansion to the base condition; and finally +ExpandL_SemCor, adds the latter both conditions simultaneously.

### 5.5 Results

Table 1 illustrates the obtained results on the three data sets reporting only overall F-measure. The coverage for SV2 is 98.36% losing some of the verb and adverb target words. The coverage for SV3 is 99.7% and that of SM is 100%. These results are on the entire data set as described in Table ??. Moreover, Table 2 presents the detailed results for the Senseval 2 data set using WN 1.7.1 since it is the most studied data set and for ease of comparison with previous studies. We break the results down by POS tag (N)oun, (V)erb, (A)djective, and Adve(R)b.

[6]From an application standpoint, we do not find the first sense baseline to be of interest since it introduces a strong level of uniformity – removing semantic variability – that is not desirable. Even if the frist sense achieves higher results in these data sets, it is an artifact of the size of the data and the very limited number of documents under investigation.

| Condition | SV2-WN171 | SV2-WN30 | SV3-WN171 | SV3-WN30 | SM-WN2.1 | SM-WN30 |
|---|---|---|---|---|---|---|
| RAND | 39.9 | 41.8 | 32.9 | 33.4 | | 25.4 |
| SM07 | 59.7 | 59.8 | 54 | 53.8 | 40.4 | 40.8 |
| JCN-V | 60.2 | 60.2 | 55.9 | 55.5 | 44.1 | 45.5 |
| +ExpandL | 60.9 | 60.6 | 55.7 | 55.5 | 43.7 | 45.1 |
| +SemCor | 62.04 | 62.2 | **59.7** | **60.3** | **46.8** | **46.8** |
| +ExpandL_SemCor | **62.7** | **62.9** | 59.5 | 59.6 | 45.9 | 45.7 |

Table 1: F-measure % for all experimental conditions on all data sets

| Condition | N | V | A | R |
|---|---|---|---|---|
| RAND | 43.7 | 21 | 41.2 | 57.4 |
| SM07 | 68.7 | 33.01 | 65.2 | 63.1 |
| JCN-V | 68.7 | 35.46 | 65.2 | 63.1 |
| +ExpandL | **70** | 35.86 | 65.6 | 62.8 |
| +SemCor | 68.3 | 37.86 | **68.6** | 68.75 |
| +ExpandL_SemCor | 69.5 | **38.66** | 68.2 | **69.15** |

Table 2: F-measure results per POS tag per condition for SV2 using WN 1.7.1.

## 6 Discussion

Our overall results on all the data sets clearly outperform the baseline as well as state of the art performance using an unsupervised system (SM07) in overall accuracy across all the data sets. Our implementation of SM07 is slightly higher than those reported in (Sinha and Mihalcea, 2007), 57.12% is probably due to the fact that we do not consider the items tagged as "U" and also we resolve some of the POS tag mismatches between the gold set and the test data. We note that for the SV2 data set our coverage is not 100% due to some POS tag mismatches that could not have been resolved automatically. These POS tag problems have to do mainly with multiword expressions and the like.

In observing the performance of the overall system, we note that using JCN for verbs clearly outperforms using the LCH similarity measure across the board on all data sets as illustrated in Table 1. Using SemCor to augment WordNet examples seems to have the biggest impact on SV3 and SM compared to ExpandL. This may be attributed to the fact that the percentage of polysemous words in the latter two sets is much higher than it is for SV2. Combining SemCor with ExpandL yields the best results for the SV2 data sets. There seems to be no huge notable difference between the three versions of WN, though WN3.0 seems to yield slightly higher results maybe due to higher consistency in the overall structure when comparing WN1.7.1, WN2.1, and WN3.0. We do recognize that we can't directly compare the various WordNets except to draw conclusions on structural differences remotely. It is also worth noting that less words in WN3.0 used SemCor expansions.

Observing the results yielded per POS in Table 2, ExpandL seems to have the biggest impact on the Nouns only. This is understandable since the nouns hierachy has the most dense relations and the most consistent ones. SemCor augmentation of WN seemed to benefit all POS significantly except for nouns. In fact the performance on the nouns deteriorated from the base condition JCN-V from 68.7 to 68.3%. This maybe due to inconsistencies in the annotations of nouns in SemCor or the very fine granularity of the nouns in WN. We know that 72% of the nouns, 74% of the verbs, 68.9% of the adjectives, and 81.9% of the adverbs directly exploited the use of SemCor augmented examples. Combining SemCor and ExpandL seems to have a positive impact on the verbs and adverbs, but not on the nouns and adjectives. These trends are not held consistently across data sets. For example, we see that SemCor augmentation helps both all POS tag sets over using ExpandL alone or when combined with SemCor. In order to analyze this further, we explore the performance on the polysemous POS only in all the data sets. We note that the same trend persists, SemCor augmentation has a negative impact on the SV2 data set in both WN 1.7.1. and WN 3.0. yet it benefits all POS in the other data sets, namely SV3 WN1.7.1 and SV3 WN3.0, SM WN2.1 and SM WN3.0.

We did some basic data analysis on the items we are incapable of capturing. Several of them are cases of metonymy in examples such as "the English are known...", the sense of *English* here is clearly in reference to the people of England, however, our WSD system preferred the language sense of the word. If it had access to syntactic/semantic role we would assume it could capture that this sense of the word entails volition for example. Other types of errors resulted from the lack of a method to help identify multiwords.

## 7 Conclusions and Future Directions

In this paper, we presented improvements on state of the art monolingual all words WSD using a well established graph based algorithm coupled with enhancements on basic similarity measures. We also explored the impact of augmenting WordNet with more gloss examples from a hand annotated resource as a means of improving WSD performance. We present the best results to date for an unsupervised approach on standard data sets: Senseval 2 (62.7%) using WN1.7.1, and Senseval 3 (59.7%) using WN1.7.1. In the future, we would like to explore the incorporation of multiword chunks, document level lexical chains, and syntactic features in the modeling of the Lesk overlap measure. We would like to further explore why ExpandL conditions did not yield the expected high performance across the different POS tags. Moreover, we are still curious as to why SemCor expansion did not help the nouns performance in SV2 conditions specifically.

## References


Marine Carpuat and Dekai Wu. 2007. Improving statistical machine translation using word sense disambiguation. In *Proceedings of the 2007 Joint Conference on Empirical Methods in Natural Language Processing and Computational Natural Language Learning (EMNLP-CoNLL)*, pages 61–72, Prague, Czech Republic, June. Association for Computational Linguistics.

Yee Seng Chan, Hwee Tou Ng, and David Chiang. 2007. Word sense disambiguation improves statistical machine translation. In *Proceedings of the 45th Annual Meeting of the Association of Computational Linguistics*, pages 33–40, Prague, Czech Republic, June. Association for Computational Linguistics.

Christiane Fellbaum. 1998. "wordnet: An electronic lexical database". MIT Press.

J. Jiang and D. Conrath. 1997. Semantic similarity based on corpus statistics and lexical taxonomy. In *Proceedings of the International Conference on Research in Computational Linguistics*, Taiwan.

C. Leacock and M. Chodorow. 1998. Combining local context and wordnet sense similarity for word sense identification. In *WordNet, An Electronic Lexical Database*. The MIT Press.

M. Lesk. 1986. Automatic sense disambiguation using machine readable dictionaries: How to tell a pine cone from an ice cream cone. In *In Proceedings of the SIGDOC Conference*, Toronto, June.

S. Cotton L. Delfs M. Palmer, C. Fellbaum and H. Dang. 2001. English tasks: all-words and verb lexical sample. In *In Proceedings of ACL/SIGLEX Senseval-2*, Toulouse, France, June.

Rada Mihalcea. 2005. Unsupervised large-vocabulary word sense disambiguation with graph-based algorithms for sequence data labeling. In *Proceedings of Human Language Technology Conference and Conference on Empirical Methods in Natural Language Processing*, pages 411–418, Vancouver, British Columbia, Canada, October. Association for Computational Linguistics.

George A. Miller. 1990. Wordnet: a lexical database for english. In *Communications of the ACM*, pages 39–41.

Roberto Navigli. 2009. Word sense disambiguation: a survey. In *ACM Computing Surveys*, pages 1–69. ACM Press.

Banerjee Pedersen and Patwardhan. 2005. Maximizing semantic relatedness to perform word sense disambiguation. In *University of Minnesota Supercomputing Institute Research Report UMSI 2005/25*, Minnesotta, March.

Sameer Pradhan, Edward Loper, Dmitriy Dligach, and Martha Palmer. 2007. Semeval-2007 task-17: English lexical sample, srl and all words. In *Proceedings of the Fourth International Workshop on Semantic Evaluations (SemEval-2007)*, pages 87–92, Prague, Czech Republic, June. Association for Computational Linguistics.

Ravi Sinha and Rada Mihalcea. 2007. Unsupervised graph-based word sense disambiguation using measures of word semantic similarity. In *Proceedings of the IEEE International Conference on Semantic Computing (ICSC 2007)*, Irvine, CA.

Benjamin Snyder and Martha Palmer. 2004. The english all-words task. In Rada Mihalcea and Phil Edmonds, editors, *Senseval-3: Third International Workshop on the Evaluation of Systems for the Semantic Analysis of Text*, pages 41–43, Barcelona, Spain, July. Association for Computational Linguistics.

# SemEval-2010 Task 1: Coreference Resolution in Multiple Languages

**Marta Recasens, Toni Martí, Mariona Taulé**
Centre de Llenguatge i Computació (CLiC)
University of Barcelona
Gran Via de les Corts Catalanes 585
08007 Barcelona
{mrecasens, amarti, mtaule}
@ub.edu

**Lluís Màrquez, Emili Sapena**
TALP Research Center,
Technical University of Catalonia
Jordi Girona Salgado 1-3
08034 Barcelona
{lluism, esapena}
@lsi.upc.edu

## Abstract

This paper presents the task 'Coreference Resolution in Multiple Languages' to be run in SemEval-2010 (5th International Workshop on Semantic Evaluations). This task aims to evaluate and compare automatic coreference resolution systems for three different languages (Catalan, English, and Spanish) by means of two alternative evaluation metrics, thus providing an insight into (i) the portability of coreference resolution systems across languages, and (ii) the effect of different scoring metrics on ranking the output of the participant systems.

## 1 Introduction

Coreference information has been shown to be beneficial in many NLP applications such as Information Extraction (McCarthy and Lehnert, 1995), Text Summarization (Steinberger et al., 2007), Question Answering (Morton, 2000), and Machine Translation. In these systems, there is a need to identify the different pieces of information that refer to the same discourse entity in order to produce coherent and fluent summaries, disambiguate the references to an entity, and solve anaphoric pronouns.

Coreference is an inherently complex phenomenon. Some of the limitations of the traditional rule-based approaches (Mitkov, 1998) could be overcome by machine learning techniques, which allow automating the acquisition of knowledge from annotated corpora.

This task will promote the development of linguistic resources –annotated corpora[1]– and machine-learning techniques oriented to coreference resolution. In particular, we aim to evaluate and compare coreference resolution systems in a multilingual context, including Catalan, English, and Spanish languages, and by means of two different evaluation metrics.

By setting up a multilingual scenario, we can explore to what extent it is possible to implement a general system that is portable to the three languages, how much language-specific tuning is necessary, and the significant differences between Romance languages and English, as well as those between two closely related languages such as Spanish and Catalan. Besides, we expect to gain some useful insight into the development of multilingual NLP applications.

As far as the evaluation is concerned, by employing B-cubed (Bagga and Baldwin, 1998) and CEAF (Luo, 2005) algorithms we can consider both the advantages and drawbacks of using one or the other scoring metric. For comparison purposes, the MUC score will also be reported. Among others, we are interested in the following questions: Which evaluation metric provides a more accurate picture of the accuracy of the system performance? Is there a strong correlation between them? Can

[1] Corpora annotated with coreference are scarce, especially for languages other than English.



*Proceedings of the NAACL HLT Workshop on Semantic Evaluations: Recent Achievements and Future Directions*, pages 70–75,
Boulder, Colorado, June 2009. 

statistical systems be optimized under both metrics at the same time?

The rest of the paper is organized as follows. Section 2 describes the overall task. The corpora and the annotation scheme are presented in Section 3. Conclusions and final remarks are given in Section 4.

## 2 Task description

The SemEval-2010 task ‘Coreference Resolution in Multiple Languages’ is concerned with automatic coreference resolution for three different languages: Catalan, English, and Spanish.

### 2.1 Specific tasks

Given the complexity of the coreference phenomena, we will concentrate only in two tractable aspects, which lead to the two following subtasks for each of the languages:

i) Detection of full coreference chains, composed by named entities, pronouns, and full noun phrases (NPs).
ii) Pronominal resolution, i.e. finding the antecedents of the pronouns in the text.

> [Els beneficiaris de [pensions de [viudetat]$_3$]$_2$]$_1$ podran conservar [la paga]$_4$ encara_que [Ø]$_5$ es tornin a casar si [Ø]$_6$ compleixen [una sèrie de [condicions]$_8$]$_7$ , segons [el reial decret aprovat ahir pel [Consell_de_Ministres]$_{10}$]$_9$ .
> [La nova norma]$_{11}$ afecta [els perceptors d' [una pensió de [viudetat]$_{13}$]$_{12}$ [que]$_{14}$ contreguin [matrimoni]$_{15}$ a_partir_de [l' 1_de_gener_del_2002]$_{16}$]$_{17}$ .
> [La primera de [les condicions]$_{18}$]$_{19}$ és tenir [més de 61 anys]$_{20}$ o tenir reconeguda [una incapacitat permanent [que]$_{22}$ inhabiliti per a [tota [professió]$_{24}$ o [ofici]$_{25}$]$_{23}$]$_{21}$.
> [La segona]$_{26}$ és que [la pensió]$_{27}$ sigui [la principal o única font d' [ingressos del [pensionista]$_{30}$]$_{29}$]$_{28}$ , i sempre_que [l' import anual de [la mateixa pensió]$_{32}$]$_{31}$ representi , com_a_mínim , [el 75% del [total dels [ingressos anuals del [pensionista]$_{36}$]$_{35}$]$_{34}$]$_{33}$.

The example in Figure 1 illustrates the two subtasks.[2] Given a text in which NPs are identified and indexed (including elliptical subjects, represented as Ø), the goal of (i) is to extract all coreference chains: 1–5–6–30–36, 9–11, and 7–18; while the goal of (ii) is to identify the antecedents of pronouns 5 and 6, which are 1 and 5 (or 1), respectively. Note that (b) is a simpler subtask of (a) and that for a given pronoun there can be multiple antecedents (e.g. both 1 and 5 are correct antecedents for 6).

We restrict the task to solving ‘identity’ relations between NPs (coreference chains), and between pronouns and antecedents. Nominal predicates and appositions as well as NPs with a non-nominal antecedent (discourse deixis) will not been taken into consideration in the recognition of coreference chains (see Section 3.1 for more information about decisions concerning the annotation scheme).

Although we target at general systems addressing the full multilingual task, we will allow taking part on any subtask of any language in order to promote participation.

> [The beneficiaries of [[spouse's]$_3$ pensions]$_2$]$_1$ will be able to keep [the payment]$_4$ even if [they]$_5$ remarry provided that [they]$_6$ fulfill [a series of [conditions]$_8$]$_7$, according to [the royal decree approved yesterday by [the Council of Ministers]$_{10}$]$_9$.
> [The new rule]$_{11}$ affects [the recipients of [a [spouse's]$_{13}$ pension]$_{12}$ [that]$_{14}$ get married after [January_1_,_2002]$_{16}$]$_{17}$.
> [The first of [the conditions]$_{18}$]$_{19}$ is being older [than 61 years old]$_{20}$ or having [an officially recognized permanent disability [that]$_{22}$ makes one disabled for [any [profession]$_{24}$ or [job]$_{25}$]$_{23}$]$_{21}$.
> [The second one]$_{26}$ requires that [the pension]$_{27}$ be [the main or only source of [the [pensioner's]$_{30}$ income]$_{29}$]$_{28}$, and provided that [the annual amount of [the pension]$_{32}$]$_{31}$ represents, at least, [75% of [the total [yearly income of [the pensioner]$_{36}$]$_{35}$]$_{34}$]$_{33}$.

Figure 1. NPs in a sample from the Catalan training data (left) and the English translation (right).

[2] The example in Figure 1 is a simplified version of the annotated format. See Section 2.2 for more details.

## 2.2 Evaluation

### *2.1.1 Input information*

The input information for the task will consist of: word forms, lemmas, POS, full syntax, and semantic role labeling. Two different scenarios will be considered regarding the source of the input information:

i) In the first one, *gold standard* annotation will be provided to participants. This input annotation will correctly identify all NPs that are part of coreference chains. This scenario will be only available for Catalan and Spanish.
ii) In the second, state-of-the-art automatic linguistic analyzers for the three languages will be used to generate the input annotation of the data. The matching between the automatically generated structure and the real NPs intervening in the chains does not need to be perfect in this setting.

By defining these two experimental settings, we will be able to check the performance of coreference systems when working with perfect linguistic (syntactic/semantic) information, and the degradation in performance when moving to a more realistic scenario with noisy input annotation.

### *2.1.2 Closed/open challenges*

In parallel, we will also consider the possibility of differentiating between closed and open challenges, that is, when participants are allowed to use strictly the information contained in the training data (closed) and when they make use of some external resources/tools (open).

### *2.1.3 Scoring measures*

Regarding evaluation measures, we will have specific metrics for each of the subtasks, which will be computed by language and overall.

Several metrics have been proposed for the task of coreference resolution, and each of them presents advantages and drawbacks. For the purpose of the current task, we have selected two of them – B-cubed and CEAF – as the most appropriate ones. In what follows we justify our choice.

The MUC scoring algorithm (Vilain et al., 1995) has been the most widely used for at least two reasons. Firstly, the MUC corpora and the MUC scorer were the first available systems. Secondly, the MUC scorer is easy to understand and implement. However, this metric has two major weaknesses: (i) it does not give any credit to the correct identification of singleton entities (chains consisting of one single mention), and (ii) it intrinsically favors systems that produce fewer coreference chains, which may result in higher F-measures for worse systems.

A second well-known scoring algorithm, the ACE value (NIST, 2003), owes its popularity to the ACE evaluation campaign. Each error (a missing element, a misclassification of a coreference chain, a mention in the response not included in the key) made by the response has an associated cost, which depends on the type of entity (e.g. person, location, organization) and on the kind of mention (e.g. name, nominal, pronoun). The fact that this metric is entity-type and mention-type dependent, and that it relies on ACE-type entities makes this measure inappropriate for the current task.

The two measures that we are interested in comparing are B-cubed (Bagga and Baldwin, 1998) and CEAF (Luo, 2005). The former does not look at the links produced by a system as the MUC algorithm does, but looks at the presence/absence of mentions for each entity in the system output. Precision and recall numbers are computed for each mention, and the average gives the final precision and recall numbers.

CEAF (Luo, 2005) is a novel metric for evaluating coreference resolution that has already been used in some published papers (Ng, 2008; Denis and Baldridge, 2008). It mainly differs from B-cubed in that it finds the best one-to-one entity alignment between the gold and system responses before computing precision and recall. The best mapping is that which maximizes the similarity over pairs of chains. The CEAF measure has two variants: a mention-based, and an entity-based one. While the former scores the similarity of two chains as the absolute number of common mentions between them, the latter scores the relative number of common mentions.

Luo (2005) criticizes the fact that a response with all mentions in the same chain obtains 100% B-cubed recall, whereas a response with each mention in a different chain obtains 100% B-cubed precision. However, precision will be penalized in the first case, and recall in the second case, each captured by the corresponding F-measure. Luo's entity alignment might cause that a correctly identified link between two mentions is ignored by the scoring metric if that entity is not aligned. Finally, as far as the two CEAF metrics are concerned, the entity-based measure rewards alike a correctly identified one-mention entity and a correctly identified five-mention entity, while the mention-based measure takes into account the size of the entity.

Given this series of advantages and drawbacks, we opted for including both B-cubed and CEAF measures in the final evaluation of the systems. In this way we will be able to perform a meta-evaluation study, i.e. to evaluate and compare the performance of metrics with respect to the task objectives and system rankings. It might be interesting to break B-cubed and CEAF into partial results across different kinds of mentions in order to get a better understanding of the sources of errors made by each system. Additionally, the MUC metric will also be included for comparison purposes with previous results.

Finally, for the setting with automatically generated input information (second scenario in Section 2.1.1), it might be desirable to devise metric variants accounting for partial matches of NPs. In this case, capturing the correct NP head would give most of the credit. We plan to work in this research line in the near future.

Official scorers will be developed in advance and made available to participants when posting the trial datasets. The period in between the release of trial datasets and the start of the full evaluation will serve as a test for the evaluation metrics. Depending on the feedback obtained from the participants we might consider introducing some improvements in the evaluation setting.

## 3 AnCora-CO corpora

The corpora used in the task are AnCora-CO, which are the result of enriching the AnCora corpora (Taulé et al., 2008) with coreference information. AnCora-CO is a multilingual corpus annotated at different linguistic levels consisting of 400K words in Catalan[3], 400K words in Spanish[2], and 120K words in English. For the purpose of the task, the corpora are split into a training (85%) and test (15%) set. Each file corresponds to one newspaper text.

AnCora-CO consists mainly of newspaper and newswire articles: 200K words from the Spanish and Catalan versions of *El Periódico* newspaper, and 200K words from the EFE newswire agency in the Spanish corpus, and from the ACN newswire agency in the Catalan corpus. The source corpora for Spanish and Catalan are the AnCora corpora, which were annotated by hand with full syntax (constituents and functions) as well as with semantic information (argument structure with thematic roles, semantic verb classes, named entities, and WordNet nominal senses). The annotation of coreference constitutes an additional layer on top of the previous syntactic-semantic information.

The English part of AnCora-CO consists of a series of documents of the Reuters newswire corpus (RCV1 version).[4] The RCV1 corpus does not come with any syntactic nor semantic annotation. This is why we only count with automatic linguistic annotation produced by statistical taggers and parsers on this corpus.

Although the Catalan, English, and Spanish corpora used in the task all belong to the domain of newspaper texts, they do not form a three-way parallel corpus.

### 3.1 Coreference annotation

The annotation of a corpus with coreference information is highly complex due to (i) the lack of information in descriptive grammars about this topic, and (ii) the difficulty in generalizing the insights from one language to another. Regarding (i), a wide range of units and relations occur for which it is not straightforward to determine whether they are or not coreferent. Although there are theoretical studies for English, they cannot always be extended to Spanish or Catalan since coreference is a very language-specific phenomenon, which accounts for (ii).

In the following we present some of the linguistic issues more problematic in relation to coreference annotation, and how we decided to deal with them in AnCora-CO (Recasens, 2008). Some of them are language dependent (1); others concern

[3] Freely available for research purposes from the following URL: http://clic.ub.edu/ancora

[4] Reuters Corpus RCV1 is distributed by NIST at the following URL: http://trec.nist.gov/data/reuters/reuters.html

the internal structure of the mentions (2), or the type of coreference link (3). Finally, we present those NPs that were left out from the annotation for not being referential (4).

1. Language-specific issues
   - Since Spanish and Catalan are pro-drop languages, elliptical subjects were introduced in the syntactic annotation, and they are also annotated with coreference.
   - Expletive *it* pronouns, which are frequent in English and to a lesser extent in Spanish and Catalan are not referential, and so they do not participate in coreference links.
   - In Spanish, clitic forms for pronouns can merge into a single word with the verb; in these cases the whole verbal node is annotated for coreference.
2. Issues concerning the mention structure
   - In possessive NPs, only the reference of the thing possessed (not the possessor) is taken into account. For instance, *su libro* 'his book' is linked with a previous reference of the same book; the possessive determiner *su* 'his' does not constitute an NP on its own.
   - In the case of conjoined NPs, three (or more) links can be encoded: one between the entire NPs, and additional ones for each of the constituent NPs. AnCora-CO captures links at these different levels.
3. Issues concerning types of coreference links
   - Plural NPs can refer to two or more antecedents that appear separately in the text. In these cases an entity resulting from the addition of two or more entities is created.
   - Discourse deixis is kept under a specific link tag because not all coreference resolution systems can handle such relations.
   - Metonymy is annotated as a case of identity because both mentions pragmatically corefer.
4. Non-referential NPs
   - In order to be linguistically accurate (van Deemter and Kibble, 2000), we distinguish between referring and attributive NPs: while the first point to an entity, the latter express some of its properties. Thus, attributive NPs like apposition and predicative phrases are not treated as identity coreference in AnCora-CO (they are kept distinct under the 'predicative link' tag).
   - Bound anaphora and bridging reference go beyond coreference and so are left out from consideration.

The annotation process of the corpora is outlined in the next section.

### 3.2 Annotation process

The Ancora coreference annotation process involves: (a) marking of mentions, and (b) marking of coreference chains (entities).

(a) Referential full NPs (including proper nouns) and pronouns (including elliptical and clitic pronouns) are the potential mentions of a coreference chain.

(b) In the current task only identity relations (coreftype="ident") will be considered, which link referential NPs that point to the same discourse entity. Coreferent mentions are annotated with the attribute *entity*. Mentions that point to the same entity share the same entity number. In Figure 1, for instance, *el reial decret aprovat ahir pel Consell_de_Ministres* 'the royal decree approved yesterday by the Council of Ministers' is entity="entity9" and *la nova norma* 'the new rule' is also entity="entity9" because they corefer. Hence, mentions referring to the same discourse entity all share the same entity number.

The corpora were annotated by a total of seven annotators (qualified linguists) using the AnCoraPipe annotation tool (Bertran et al., 2008), which allows different linguistic levels to be annotated simultaneously and efficiently. AnCoraPipe supports XML in-line annotations.

An initial reliability study was performed on a small portion of the Spanish AnCora-CO corpus. In that study, eight linguists annotated the corpus material in parallel. Inter-annotator agreement was computed with Krippendorff's alpha, achieving a result above 0.8. Most of the problems detected were attributed either to a lack of training of the coders or to ambiguities that are left unresolved in the discourse itself. After carrying out this reliability study, we opted for annotating the corpora in a two-stage process: a first pass in which all mention attributes and coreference links were coded, and a second pass in which the already annotated files were revised.

## 4 Conclusions

The SemEval-2010 multilingual coreference resolution task has been presented for discussion. Firstly, we aim to promote research on coreference resolution from a learning-based perspective in a multilingual scenario in order to: (a) explore portability issues; (b) analyze language-specific tuning requirements; (c) facilitate cross-linguistic comparisons between two Romance languages and between Romance languages and English; and (d) encourage researchers to develop linguistic resources – annotated corpora – oriented to coreference resolution for other languages.

Secondly, given the complexity of the coreference phenomena we split the coreference resolution task into two (full coreference chains and pronominal resolution), and we propose two different scenarios (gold standard vs. automatically generated input information) in order to evaluate to what extent the performance of a coreference resolution system varies depending on the quality of the other levels of information.

Finally, given that the evaluation of coreference resolution systems is still an open issue, we are interested in comparing different coreference resolution metrics: B-cubed and CEAF measures. In this way we will be able to evaluate and compare the performance of these metrics with respect to the task objectives and system rankings.

## Acknowledgments

This research has been supported by the projects Lang2World (TIN2006-15265-C06), TEXT-MESS (TIN2006-15265-C04), OpenMT (TIN2006-15307-C03-02), AnCora-Nom (FFI2008-02691-E), and the FPU grant (AP2006-00994) from the Spanish Ministry of Education and Science, and the funding given by the government of the Generalitat de Catalunya.

## References

Bagga, Amit and Breck Baldwin. 1998. Algorithms for scoring coreference chains. In *Proceedings of Language Resources and Evaluation Conference*.

Bertran, Manuel, Oriol Borrega, Marta Recasens, and Bàrbara Soriano. 2008. AnCoraPipe: A tool for multilevel annotation, *Procesamiento del Lenguaje Natural*, n. 41: 291-292, SEPLN.

Denis, Pascal and Jason Baldridge. 2008. Specialized models and ranking for coreference resolution. *Proceedings of the Empirical Methods in Natural Language Processing (EMNLP 2008).*

Luo, Xiaoqiang. 2005. On coreference resolution performance metrics. *Proceedings of HLT/NAACL 2005.*

McCarthy Joseph and Wendy Lehnert. 1995. Using decision trees for coreference resolution. *Proceedings of the Fourteenth International Joint Conference on Artificial Intelligence.*

Mitkov, Ruslan. 1998. Robust pronoun resolution with limited knowledge. *Proceedings of the 36th Annual Meeting of the Association for Computational Linguistics, and 17th International Conference on Computational Linguistics (COLING-ACL98).*

Morton, Thomas. 2000. Using coreference for question answering. *Proceedings of the 8th Text REtrieval Conference (TREC-8).*

Ng, Vincent. 2008. Unsupervised models for coreference resolution. *Proceedings of the Empirical Methods in Natural Language Processing (EMNLP 2008).*

NIST. 2003. In *Proceedings of ACE 2003 workshop.* Booklet, Alexandria, VA.

Recasens, Marta. 2008. *Towards Coreference Resolution for Catalan and Spanish.* Master Thesis. University of Barcelona.

Steinberger, Josef, Massimo Poesio, Mijail Kabadjov, and Karel Jezek. 2007. Two uses of anaphora resolution in summarization. *Information Processing and Management*, 43:1663–1680.

Taulé, Mariona, Antònia Martí, and Marta Recasens. 2008. AnCora: Multilevel corpora with coreference information for Spanish and Catalan. In *Proceedings of the Language Resources and Evaluation Conference (LREC 2008).*

van Deemter, Kees and Rodger Kibble. 2000. Squibs and Discussions: On coreferring: coreference in MUC and related annotation schemes. *Computational Linguistics*, 26(4):629-637.

Vilain, Marc, John Burger, John Aberdeen, Dennis Connolly, and Lynette Hirschman. 1995. A model-theoretic coreference scoring scheme. In *Proceedings of MUC-6.*

# SemEval-2010 Task 2: Cross-Lingual Lexical Substitution

**Ravi Sinha**
University of North Texas
ravisinha@unt.edu

**Diana McCarthy**
University of Sussex
dianam@sussex.ac.uk

**Rada Mihalcea**
University of North Texas
rada@cs.unt.edu

## Abstract

In this paper we describe the SemEval-2010 Cross-Lingual Lexical Substitution task, which is based on the English Lexical Substitution task run at SemEval-2007. In the English version of the task, annotators and systems had to find an alternative substitute word or phrase for a target word in context. In this paper we propose a task where the target word and contexts will be in English, but the substitutes will be in Spanish. In this paper we provide background and motivation for the task and describe how the dataset will differ from a machine translation task and previous word sense disambiguation tasks based on parallel data. We describe the annotation process and how we anticipate scoring the system output. We finish with some ideas for participating systems.

## 1 Introduction

The Cross-Lingual Lexical Substitution task is based on the English Lexical Substitution task run at SemEval-2007. In the 2007 English Lexical Substitution Task, annotators and systems had to find an alternative substitute word or phrase for a target word in context. In this cross-lingual task the target word and contexts will be in English, but the substitutes will be in Spanish.

An automatic system for cross-lingual lexical substitution would be useful for a number of applications. For instance, such a system could be used to assist human translators in their work, by providing a number of correct translations that the human translator can choose from. Similarly, the system could be used to assist language learners, by providing them with the interpretation of the unknown words in a text written in the language they are learning. Last but not least, the output of a cross-lingual lexical substitution system could be used as input to existing systems for cross-language information retrieval or automatic machine translation.

## 2 Background: The English Lexical Substitution Task

The English Lexical substitution task (hereafter referred to as LEXSUB) was run at SemEval-2007 following earlier ideas on a method of testing WSD systems without predetermining the inventory (McCarthy, 2002). The issue of which inventory is appropriate for the task has been a long standing issue for debate, and while there is hope that coarse-grained inventories will allow for increased system performance (Ide and Wilks, 2006) we do not yet know if these will make the distinctions that will most benefit practical systems (Stokoe, 2005) or reflect cognitive processes (Kilgarriff, 2006). LEXSUB was proposed as a task which, while requiring contextual disambiguation, did not presuppose a specific sense inventory. In fact, it is quite possible to use alternative representations of meaning (Schütze, 1998; Pantel and Lin, 2002).

The motivation for a substitution task was that it would reflect capabilities that might be useful for natural language processing tasks such as paraphrasing and textual entailment, while only focusing on one aspect of the problem and therefore not requiring a complete system that might mask system capabilities at a lexical level and at the same time make



*Proceedings of the NAACL HLT Workshop on Semantic Evaluations: Recent Achievements and Future Directions*, pages 76–81,
Boulder, Colorado, June 2009. 

participation in the task difficult for small research teams.

The task required systems to produce a substitute word for a word in context. For example a substitute of *tournament* might be given for the second occurrence of *match* (shown in bold) in the following sentence:

*The ideal preparation would be a light meal about 2-2 1/2 hours pre-match, followed by a warm-up hit and perhaps a top-up with extra fluid before the* ***match****.*

In LEXSUB, the data was collected for 201 words from open class parts-of-speech (PoS) (i.e. nouns, verbs, adjectives and adverbs). Words were selected that have more than one meaning with at least one near synonym. Ten sentences for each word were extracted from the English Internet Corpus (Sharoff, 2006). There were five annotators who annotated each target word as it occurred in the context of a sentence. The annotators were each allowed to provide up to three substitutes, though they could also provide a NIL response if they could not come up with a substitute. They had to indicate if the target word was an integral part of a multiword.

A development and test dataset were provided, but no training data. Any system that relied on training data, such as sense annotated corpora, had to use resources available from other sources. The task had eight participating teams. Teams were allowed to submit up to two systems and there were a total of ten different systems. The scoring was conducted using recall and precision measures using:

- the frequency distribution of responses from the annotators and
- the mode of the annotators (the most frequent response).

The systems were scored using their **best** guess as well as an **out-of-ten** score which allowed up to 10 attempts. [1] The results are reported in McCarthy and Navigli (2007) and in more detail in McCarthy and Navigli (in press).

[1]The details are available at http://nlp.cs.swarthmore.edu/semeval/tasks/task10/task10documentation.pdf.

## 3 Motivation and Related Work

While there has been a lot of discussion on the relevant sense distinctions for monolingual WSD systems, for machine translation applications there is a consensus that the relevant sense distinctions are those that reflect different translations. One early and notable work was the SENSEVAL-2 Japanese Translation task (Kurohashi, 2001) that obtained alternative translation records of typical usages of a test word, also referred to as a *translation memory*. Systems could either select the most appropriate translation memory record for each instance and were scored against a gold-standard set of annotations, or they could provide a translation that was scored by translation experts after the results were submitted. In contrast to this work, we propose to provide actual translations for target instances in advance, rather than predetermine translations using lexicographers or rely on post-hoc evaluation, which does not permit evaluation of new systems after the competition.

Previous standalone WSD tasks based on parallel data have obtained distinct translations for senses as listed in a dictionary (Ng and Chan, 2007). In this way fine-grained senses with the same translations can be lumped together, however this does not fully allow for the fact that some senses for the same words may have some translations in common but also others that are not. An example from Resnik and Yarowsky (2000) (table 4 in that paper) is the first two senses from WordNet for the noun *interest*:

| WordNet sense | Spanish Translation |
|---|---|
| **monetary e.g. on loan** | *interés, rédito* |
| **stake/share** | *interés,participación* |

For WSD tasks, a decision can be made to lump senses with such overlap, or split them using the distinctive translation and then use the distinctive translations as a sense inventory. This sense inventory is then used to collect training from parallel data (Ng and Chan, 2007). We propose that it would be interesting to collect a dataset where the overlap in translations for an instance can remain and that this will depend on the token instance rather than mapping to a pre-defined sense inventory. Resnik and Yarowsky (2000) also conducted their experiments using words in context, rather than a predefined sense-inventory as in (Ng and Chan, 2007; Chan and Ng, 2005), however in these experiments the annotators were asked for a single preferred translation. We intend to allow annotators to supply as many translations as they feel are equally valid. This will allow us to examine more subtle relationships between usages and to allow partial credit to systems which get a close approximation to the annotators' translations. Unlike a full blown machine translation task (Carpuat and Wu, 2007), annotators and systems will not be required to translate the whole context but just the target word.

## 4 The Cross-Lingual Lexical Substitution Task

Here we discuss our proposal for a Cross-Lingual Lexical Substitution task. The task will follow LEXSUB except that the annotations will be translations rather than paraphrases.

Given a target word in context, the task is to provide several correct translations for that word in a given language. We will use English as the source language and Spanish as the target language. Multiwords are 'part and parcel' of natural language. For this reason, rather than try and filter multiwords, which is very hard to do without assuming a fixed inventory, [2] we will ask annotators to indicate where the target word is part of a multiword and what that multiword is. This way, we know what the substitute translation is replacing.

We will provide both development and test sets, but no training data. As for LEXSUB, any systems requiring data will need to obtain it from other sources. We will include nouns, verbs, adjectives and adverbs in both development and test data. Unlike LEXSUB, the annotators will be told the PoS of the current target word.

### 4.1 Annotation

We are going to use four annotators for our task, all native Spanish speakers from Mexico, with a high level of proficiency in English. The annotation interface is shown in figure 1. We will calculate intertagger agreement as pairwise agreement between sets of substitutes from annotators, as was done in LEXSUB.

### 4.2 An Example

One significant outcome of this task is that there will not necessarily be clear divisions between usages and senses because we do not use a predefined sense inventory, or restrict the annotations to distinctive translations. This will mean that there can be usages that overlap to different extents with each other but do not have identical translations. An example from our preliminary annotation trials is the target adverb *severely*. Four sentences are shown in figure 2 with the translations provided by one annotator marked in italics and {} braces. Here, all the token occurrences seem related to each other in that they share some translations, but not all. There are sentences like 1 and 2 that appear not to have anything in common. However 1, 3, and 4 seem to be partly related (they share *severamente*), and 2, 3, and 4 are also partly related (they share *seriamente*). When we look again, sentences 1 and 2, though not directly related, both have translations in common with sentences 3 and 4.

### 4.3 Scoring

We will adopt the **best** and **out-of-ten** precision and recall scores from LEXSUB. The systems can supply as many translations as they feel fit the context. The system translations will be given credit depending on the number of annotators that picked each translation. The credit will be divided by the number of annotator responses for the item and since for the **best** score the credit for the system answers for an item is also divided by the number of answers the system provides, this allows more credit to be given to instances where there is less variation. For that reason, a system is better guessing the translation that is most frequent unless it really wants to hedge its bets. Thus if $i$ is an item in the set of instances $I$, and $T_i$ is the multiset of gold standard translations from the human annotators for $i$, and a system provides a set of answers $S_i$ for $i$, then the **best** score for item $i$ will be:

$$best\ score(i) = \frac{\sum_{s \in S_i} frequency(s \in T_i)}{|S_i| \cdot |T_i|} \quad (1)$$

[2] The multiword inventories that do exist are far from complete.

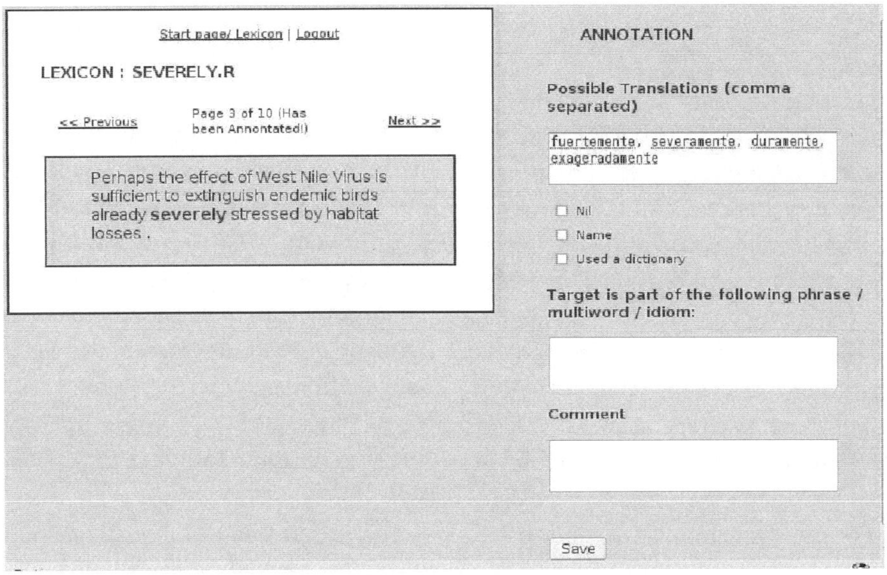


Figure 1: The Cross-Lingual Lexical Substitution Interface

1. Perhaps the effect of West Nile Virus is sufficient to extinguish endemic birds already **severely** stressed by habitat losses. {*fuertemente, severamente, duramente, exageradamente*}
2. She looked as **severely** as she could muster at Draco. {*rigurosamente, seriamente*}
3. A day before he was due to return to the United States Patton was **severely** injured in a road accident. {*seriamente, duramente, severamente*}
4. Use market tools to address environmental issues , such as eliminating subsidies for industries that **severely** harm the environment, like coal. {*peligrosamente, seriamente, severamente*}
5. This picture was **severely** damaged in the flood of 1913 and has rarely been seen until now. {*altamente, seriamente, exageradamente*}

Figure 2: Translations from one annotator for the adverb *severely*

Precision is calculated by summing the scores for each item and dividing by the number of items that the system attempted whereas recall divides the sum of scores for each item by $|I|$. Thus:

$$best\ precision = \frac{\sum_i best\ score(i)}{|i \in I : defined(S_i)|} \quad (2)$$

$$best\ recall = \frac{\sum_i best\ score(i)}{|I|} \quad (3)$$

The **out-of-ten** scorer will allow up to ten system responses and will not divide the credit attributed to each answer by the number of system responses. This allows the system to be less cautious and for the fact that there is considerable variation on the task and there may be cases where systems select a perfectly good translation that the annotators had not thought of. By allowing up to ten translations in the **out-of-ten** task the systems can hedge their bets to find the translations that the annotators supplied.

$$oot\ score(i) = \frac{\sum_{s \in S_i} frequency(s \in T_i)}{|T_i|} \quad (4)$$

$$oot\ precision = \frac{\sum_i oot\ score(i)}{|i \in I : defined(S_i)|} \quad (5)$$

$$oot\ recall = \frac{\sum_i oot\ score(i)}{|I|} \quad (6)$$

We will refine the scores before June 2009 when we will release the development data for this cross-lingual task. We note that there was an issue that the original LEXSUB **out-of-ten** scorer allowed duplicates (McCarthy and Navigli, in press). The effect of duplicates is that systems can get inflated scores because the credit for each item is not divided by the number of substitutes and because the frequency of each annotator response is used. McCarthy and Navigli (in press) describe this oversight, identify the systems that had included duplicates and explain the implications. For our task there is an option for the **out-of-ten** score. Either:

1. we remove duplicates before scoring or,

2. we allow duplicates so that systems can boost their scores with duplicates on translations with higher probability

We will probably allow duplicates but make this clear to participants.

We may calculate additional **best** and **out-of-ten** scores against the mode from the annotators responses as was done in LEXSUB, but we have not decided on this yet. We will not run a multiword task, but we will use the items identified as multiwords as an optional filter to the scoring i.e. to see how systems did without these items.

We will provide baselines and upper-bounds.

## 5 Systems

In the cross-lingual LEXSUB task, the systems will have to deal with two parts of the problem, namely:

1. candidate collection

2. candidate selection

The first sub-task, *candidate collection*, refers to consulting several resources and coming up with a list of potential translation candidates for each target word and part of speech. We do not provide any inventories, as with the original LEXSUB task, and thus leave this task of coming up with the most suitable translation list (in contrast to the synonym list required for LEXSUB) to the participants. As was observed with LEXSUB, it is our intuition that the quality of this translation list that the systems come up with will determine to a large extent how well the final performance of the system will be. Participants are free to use any ideas. However, a few possibilities might be to use parallel corpora, bilingual dictionaries, a translation engine that only translates the target word, or a machine translation system that translates the entire sentences. Several of the bilingual dictionaries or even other resources might be combined together to come up with a comprehensive translation candidate list, if that seems to improve performance.

The second phase, *candidate selection*, concerns fitting the translation candidates in context, and thus coming up with a ranking as to which translations are the most suitable for each instance. The highest ranking candidate will be the output for **best**, and the list of the top 10 ranking candidates will be the output for **out-of-ten**. Again, participants are free to use their creativity in this, while a range of possible algorithms might include using a machine translation system, using language models, word sense disambiguation models, semantic similarity-based techniques, graph-based models etc. Again, combinations of these might be used if they are feasible as far as time and space are concerned.

We anticipate a minor practical issue to come up with all participants, and that is the issue of different character encodings, especially when using bilingual dictionaries from the Web. This is directly related to the issue of dealing with characters with diacritics, and in our experience not all available software packages and programs are able to handle diacritics and different character encodings in the same way. This issue is inherent in all cross-lingual tasks, and we leave it up to the discretion of the participants to effectively deal with it.

## 6 Post Hoc Issues

In LEXSUB a post hoc evaluation was conducted using fresh annotators to ensure that the substitutes the systems came up with were not typically better than those of the original annotators. This was done as a sanity check because there was no fixed inventory for the task and there will be a lot of variation in the task and sometimes the systems might do better than the annotators. The post hoc evaluation demonstrated that the post hoc annotators typically preferred the substitutes provided by humans.

We have not yet determined whether we will run a post hoc evaluation because of the costs of doing this and the time constraints. Another option is to reannotate a portion of our data using a new set of annotators but restricting them to the translations supplied by the initial set of annotations and other translations from available resources. This would be worthwhile but it could be done at any stage when funds permit because we do not intend to supply a set of candidate translations to the annotators since we wish to evaluate candidate collection as well as candidate selection.

## 7 Conclusions

In this paper we have outlined the cross-lingual lexical substitution task to be run under the auspices of SemEval-2010. The task will require annotators and systems to find translations for a target word in context. Unlike machine translation tasks, the whole text is not translated and annotators are encouraged to supply as many translations as fit the context. Unlike previous WSD tasks based on parallel data, because we allow multiple translations and because we do not restrict translations to those that provide clear cut sense distinctions, we will be able to use the dataset collected to investigate more subtle representations of meaning.

## 8 Acknowledgements

The work of the first and third authors has been partially supported by a National Science Foundation CAREER award #0747340. The work of the second author has been supported by a Royal Society UK Dorothy Hodgkin Fellowship.

## References

Marine Carpuat and Dekai Wu. 2007. Improving statistical machine translation using word sense disambiguation. In *Proceedings of the Joint Conference on Empirical Methods in Natural Language Processing and Computational Natural Language Learning (EMNLP-CoNLL 2007)*, pages 61–72, Prague, Czech Republic, June. Association for Computational Linguistics.

Yee Seng Chan and Hwee Tou Ng. 2005. Word sense disambiguation with distribution estimation. In *Proceedings of the 19th International Joint Conference on Artificial Intelligence (IJCAI 2005)*, pages 1010–1015, Edinburgh, Scotland.

Nancy Ide and Yorick Wilks. 2006. Making sense about sense. In Eneko Agirre and Phil Edmonds, editors, *Word Sense Disambiguation, Algorithms and Applications*, pages 47–73. Springer.

Adam Kilgarriff. 2006. Word senses. In Eneko Agirre and Phil Edmonds, editors, *Word Sense Disambiguation, Algorithms and Applications*, pages 29–46. Springer.

Sadao Kurohashi. 2001. SENSEVAL-2 japanese translation task. In *Proceedings of the* SENSEVAL-2 *workshop*, pages 37–44.

Diana McCarthy and Roberto Navigli. 2007. SemEval-2007 task 10: English lexical substitution task. In *Proceedings of the 4th International Workshop on Semantic Evaluations (SemEval-2007)*, pages 48–53, Prague, Czech Republic.

Diana McCarthy and Roberto Navigli. in press. The english lexical substitution task. *Language Resources and Evaluation Special Issue on Computational Semantic Analysis of Language: SemEval-2007 and Beyond*.

Diana McCarthy. 2002. Lexical substitution as a task for wsd evaluation. In *Proceedings of the ACL Workshop on Word Sense Disambiguation: Recent Successes and Future Directions*, pages 109–115, Philadelphia, USA.

Hwee Tou Ng and Yee Seng Chan. 2007. SemEval-2007 task 11: English lexical sample task via English-Chinese parallel text. In *Proceedings of the 4th International Workshop on Semantic Evaluations (SemEval-2007)*, pages 54–58, Prague, Czech Republic.

Patrick Pantel and Dekang Lin. 2002. Discovering word senses from text. In *Proceedings of ACM SIGKDD Conference on Knowledge Discovery and Data Mining*, pages 613–619, Edmonton, Canada.

Philip Resnik and David Yarowsky. 2000. Distinguishing systems and distinguishing senses: New evaluation methods for word sense disambiguation. *Natural Language Engineering*, 5(3):113–133.

Hinrich Schütze. 1998. Automatic word sense discrimination. *Computational Linguistics*, 24(1):97–123.

Serge Sharoff. 2006. Open-source corpora: Using the net to fish for linguistic data. *International Journal of Corpus Linguistics*, 11(4):435–462.

Christopher Stokoe. 2005. Differentiating homonymy and polysemy in information retrieval. In *Proceedings of the joint conference on Human Language Technology and Empirical methods in Natural Language Processing*, pages 403–410, Vancouver, B.C., Canada.

# SemEval-2010 Task 3: Cross-lingual Word Sense Disambiguation

**Els Lefever**[1,2] **and Veronique Hoste**[1,2]

[1]LT3, Language and Translation Technology Team, University College Ghent
Groot-Brittanniëlaan 45, 9000 Gent, Belgium
[2]Department of Applied Mathematics and Computer Science, Ghent University
Krijgslaan 281 (S9), 9000 Gent, Belgium

{Els.Lefever, Veronique.Hoste}@hogent.be

## Abstract

We propose a multilingual unsupervised Word Sense Disambiguation (WSD) task for a sample of English nouns. Instead of providing manually sense-tagged examples for each sense of a polysemous noun, our sense inventory is built up on the basis of the Europarl parallel corpus. The multilingual setup involves the translations of a given English polysemous noun in five supported languages, viz. Dutch, French, German, Spanish and Italian.

The task targets the following goals: (a) the manual creation of a multilingual sense inventory for a lexical sample of English nouns and (b) the evaluation of systems on their ability to disambiguate new occurrences of the selected polysemous nouns. For the creation of the hand-tagged gold standard, all translations of a given polysemous English noun are retrieved in the five languages and clustered by meaning. Systems can participate in 5 bilingual evaluation subtasks (English - Dutch, English - German, etc.) and in a multilingual subtask covering all language pairs.

As WSD from cross-lingual evidence is gaining popularity, we believe it is important to create a multilingual gold standard and run cross-lingual WSD benchmark tests.

## 1 Introduction

The Word Sense Disambiguation (WSD) task, which consists in selecting the correct sense of a given word in a given context, has been widely studied in computational linguistics. For a recent overview of WSD algorithms, resources and applications, we refer to Agirre and Edmonds (2006) and Navigli (2009). Semantic evaluation competitions such as Senseval[1] and its successor Semeval revealed that supervised approaches to WSD usually achieve better results than unsupervised methods (Màrquez et al., 2006). The former use machine learning techniques to induce a classifier from manually sense-tagged data, where each occurrence of a polysemous word gets assigned a sense label from a predefined sense inventory such as WordNet (Fellbaum, 1998). These supervised methods, however, heavily rely on large sense-tagged corpora which are very time consuming and expensive to build. This phenomenon, well known as the *knowledge acquisition bottleneck* (Gale et al., 1992), explains the modest use and success of supervised WSD in real applications.

Although WSD has long time been studied as a stand-alone NLP task, there is a growing feeling in the WSD community that WSD should preferably be integrated in real applications such as Machine Translation or multilingual information retrieval (Agirre and Edmonds, 2006). Several studies have demonstrated that for instance Statistical Machine Translation (SMT) benefits from incorporating a dedicated WSD module (Chan et al., 2007; Carpuat and Wu, 2007). Using translations from a corpus instead of human-defined sense labels is one way of facilitating the integration of WSD in multilingual applications. It also implic-

[1]http://www.senseval.org/



*Proceedings of the NAACL HLT Workshop on Semantic Evaluations: Recent Achievements and Future Directions*, pages 82–87,
Boulder, Colorado, June 2009. 

itly deals with the granularity problem as finer sense distinctions are only relevant as far as they are lexicalized in the translations. Furthermore, this type of corpus-based approach is language-independent, which makes it a valid alternative for languages lacking sufficient sense inventories and sense-tagged corpora, although one could argue that the lack of parallel corpora for certain language pairs might be problematic as well. The methodology to deduce word senses from parallel corpora starts from the hypothesis that the different sense distinctions of a polysemous word are often lexicalized cross-linguistically. For instance, if we query the English noun *"bill"* in the English-Dutch Europarl, the following top four translations are retrieved: *"rekening" (Eng.: "invoice")* (198 occurrences), *"kosten" (Eng.: "costs")* (100 occ.), *"Bill"* (96 occ.) and *"wetsvoorstel" (Eng.: "piece of legislation")* (77 occ.). If we make the simplifying assumption for our example that (i) these are the only Dutch translations of our focus word and that (ii) all sense distinctions of *"bill"* are lexicalized in Dutch, we can infer that the English noun *"bill"* has at most four different senses. These different senses in turn can be grouped in case of synonymy. In the Dutch-French Europarl, for example, both *"rekening"* and *"kosten"*, are translated by the French *"frais"*, which might indicate that both Dutch words are synonymous.

Several WSD studies are based on the idea of cross-lingual evidence. Gale et al. (1993) use a bilingual parallel corpus for the automatic creation of a sense-tagged data set, where target words in the source language are tagged with their translation of the word in the target language. Diab and Resnik (2002) present an unsupervised approach to WSD that exploits translational correspondences in parallel corpora that were artificially created by applying commercial MT systems on a sense-tagged English corpus. Ide et al. (2002) use a multilingual parallel corpus (containing seven languages from four language families) and show that sense distinctions derived from translation equivalents are at least as reliable as those made by human annotators. Moreover, some studies present multilingual WSD systems that attain state-of-the-art performance in all-words disambiguation (Ng et al., 2003). The proposed Cross-lingual Word Sense Disambiguation task differs from earlier work (e.g. Ide et al. (2002)) through its independence from an externally defined sense set.

The remainder of this paper is organized as follows. In Section 2, we present a detailed description of the cross-lingual WSD task. It introduces the parallel corpus we used, informs on the development and test data and discusses the annotation procedure. Section 3 gives an overview of the different scoring strategies that will be applied. Section 4 concludes this paper.

## 2 Task set up

The cross-lingual Word Sense Disambiguation task involves a lexical sample of English nouns. We propose two subtasks, i.e. systems can either participate in the bilingual evaluation task (in which the answer consists of translations in one language) or in the multilingual evaluation task (in which the answer consists of translations in all five supported languages). Table 1 shows an example of the bilingual sense labels for two test occurrences of the English noun *bank* in our parallel corpus which will be further described in Section 2.1. Table 2 presents the multilingual sense labels for the same sentences.

... giving fish to people living on the [bank] of the river

| **Language** | **Sense label** |
|---|---|
| Dutch (NL) | oever/dijk |
| French (F) | rives/rivage/bord/bords |
| German (D) | Ufer |
| Italian (I) | riva |
| Spanish (ES) | orilla |

The [bank] of Scotland ...

| **Language** | **Sense label** |
|---|---|
| Dutch (NL) | bank/kredietinstelling |
| French (F) | banque/établissement de crédit |
| German (D) | Bank/Kreditinstitut |
| Italian (I) | banca |
| Spanish (ES) | banco |

Table 1: Example of bilingual sense labels for the English noun *bank*

... giving fish to people living on the [bank] of the river

| Language | Sense label |
|---|---|
| NL,F,D,I,ES | oever/dijk, rives/rivage/bord/bords, Ufer, riva, orilla |

The [bank] of Scotland ...

| Language | Sense label |
|---|---|
| NL,F,D,I,ES | bank/kredietinstelling, banque/ établissement de crédit, Bank/ Kreditinstitut, banca, banco |

Table 2: Example of multi-lingual sense labels for the English noun *bank*

### 2.1 Corpus and word selection

The document collection which serves as the basis for the gold standard construction and system evaluation is the Europarl parallel corpus[2], which is extracted from the proceedings of the European Parliament (Koehn, 2005). We selected 6 languages from the 11 European languages represented in the corpus: English (our target language), Dutch, French, German, Italian and Spanish. All sentences are aligned using a tool based on the Gale and Church (1991) algorithm. We only consider the 1-1 sentence alignments between English and the five other languages (see also Tufis et al. (2004) for a similar strategy). These 1-1 alignments will be made available to all task participants. Participants are free to use other training corpora, but additional translations which are not present in Europarl will not be included in the sense inventory that is used for evaluation.

For the competition, two data sets will be developed. The development and test sentences will be selected from the JRC-ACQUIS Multilingual Parallel Corpus[3]. The development data set contains 5 polysemous nouns, for which we provide the manually built sense inventory based on Europarl and 50 example instances, each annotated with one sense label (cluster that contains all translations that have been grouped together for that particular sense) per target language. The manual construction of the sense inventory will be discussed in Section 2.2. The test data contains 50 instances for 20 nouns from the test data as used in the Cross-Lingual Lexical Substitution Task[4]. In this task, annotators and systems are asked to provide as many correct Spanish translations as possible for an English target word. They are not bound to a predefined parallel corpus, but can freely choose the translations from any available resource. Selecting the target words from the set of nouns thats will be used for the Lexical Substitution Task should make it easier for systems to participate in both tasks.

[2]http://www.statmt.org/europarl/

[3]http://wt.jrc.it/lt/Acquis/

### 2.2 Manual annotation

The sense inventory for the 5 target nouns in the development data and the 20 nouns in the test data is manually built up in three steps.

1. In the first annotation step, the 5 translations of the English word are identified per sentence ID. In order to speed up this identification, GIZA++ (Och and Ney, 2003) is used to generate the initial word alignments for the 5 languages. All word alignments are manually verified.

   In this step, we might come across multiword translations, especially in Dutch and German which tend to glue parts of compounds together in one orthographic unit. We decided to keep these translations as such, even if they do not correspond exactly to the English target word. In following sentence, the Dutch translation *witboek* corresponds in fact to the English compound *white paper*, and not to the English target word *paper*:

   > English: the European Commission presented its white **paper**
   >
   > Dutch: de presentatie van het **witboek** door de Europese Commissie

   Although we will not remove these compound translations from our sense inventory, we will make sure that the development and test sentences do not contain target words that are part

[4]http://lit.csci.unt.edu/index.php/Semeval_2010

of a larger multiword unit, in order not to disadvantage systems that do not deal with decompounding.

2. In the second step, three annotators per language will cluster the retrieved translations per target language. On the basis of the sentence IDs, the translations in all languages will be automatically coupled. Only translations above a predefined frequency threshold are considered for inclusion in a cluster. Clustering will happen in a trilingual setting, i.e. annotators always cluster two target languages simultaneously (with English being the constant source language)[5].

   After the clustering of the translations, the annotators perform a joint evaluation per language in order to reach a consensus clustering for each target language. In case the annotators do not reach a consensus, we apply soft-clustering for that particular translation, i.e. we assign the translation to two or more different clusters.

3. In a last step, there will be a cross-lingual conflict resolution in which the resulting clusterings are checked cross-lingually by the human annotators.

The resulting sense inventory is used to annotate the sentences in the development set and the test set. This implies that a given target word is annotated with the appropriate sense cluster. This annotation is done by the same native annotators as in steps 2 and 3. The goal is to reach a consensus cluster per sentence. But again, if no consensus is reached, soft-clustering is applied and as a consequence, the correct answer for this particular test instance consists of one of the clusters that were considered for soft-clustering.

The resulting clusters are used by the three native annotators to select their top 3 translations per sentence. These potentially different translations are kept to calculate frequency information for all answer translations (discussed in section 3).

[5]The annotators will be selected from the master students at the "University College Ghent – Faculty of Translation" that trains certified translators in all six involved languages.

Table 3 shows an example of how the translation clusters for the English noun *"paper"* could look like in a trilingual setting.

## 3 System evaluation

As stated before, systems can participate in two tasks, i.e. systems can either participate in one or more bilingual evaluation tasks or they can participate in the multilingual evaluation task incorporating the five supported languages. The evaluation of the multilingual evaluation task is simply the average of the system scores on the five bilingual evaluation tasks.

### 3.1 Evaluation strategies

For the evaluation of the participating systems we will use an evaluation scheme which is inspired by the English lexical substitution task in SemEval 2007 (McCarthy and Navigli, 2007). The evaluation will be performed using precision and recall ($P$ and $R$ in the equations that follow). We perform both a *best result* evaluation and a more relaxed evaluation for the *top five results*.

Let $H$ be the set of annotators, $T$ be the set of test items and $h_i$ be the set of responses for an item $i \in T$ for annotator $h \in H$. Let $A$ be the set of items from $T$ where the system provides at least one answer and $a_i : i \in A$ be the set of guesses from the system for item $i$. For each $i$, we calculate the multiset union ($H_i$) for all $h_i$ for all $h \in H$ and for each unique type ($res$) in $H_i$ that has an associated frequency ($freq_{res}$). In the formula of (McCarthy and Navigli, 2007), the associated frequency ($freq_{res}$) is equal to the number of times an item appears in $H_i$. As we define our answer clusters by consensus, this frequency would always be "1". In order to overcome this, we ask our human annotators to indicate their top 3 translations, which enables us to also obtain meaningful associated frequencies ($freq_{res}$) ("1" in case the translation is not chosen by any annotator, "2" in case a translation is picked by 1 annotator, "3" if picked by two annotators and "4" if chosen by all three annotators).

**Best result evaluation** For the *best result* evaluation, systems can propose as many guesses as the system believes are correct, but the resulting score is divided by the number of guesses. In this way, systems that output a lot of guesses are not favoured.

$$P = \frac{\sum_{a_i:i \in A} \frac{\frac{\sum_{res \in a_i} freq_{res}}{|a_i|}}{|H_i|}}{|A|} \quad (1)$$

$$R = \frac{\sum_{a_i:i \in T} \frac{\frac{\sum_{res \in a_i} freq_{res}}{|a_i|}}{|H_i|}}{|T|} \quad (2)$$

**Relaxed evaluation** For the more relaxed evaluation, systems can propose up to five guesses. For this evaluation, the resulting score is not divided by the number of guesses.

$$P = \frac{\sum_{a_i:i \in A} \frac{\sum_{res \in a_i} freq_{res}}{|H_i|}}{|A|} \quad (3)$$

$$R = \frac{\sum_{a_i:i \in T} \frac{\sum_{res \in a_i} freq_{res}}{|H_i|}}{|T|} \quad (4)$$

### 3.2 Baseline

We will produce two, both frequency-based, baselines. The first baseline, which will be used for the *best result* evaluation, is based on the output of the GIZA++ word alignments on the Europarl corpus and just returns the most frequent translation of a given word. The second baseline outputs the five most frequent translations of a given word according to the GIZA++ word alignments. This baseline will be used for the relaxed evaluation. As a third baseline, we will consider using a baseline based on EuroWordNet[6], which is available in the five target languages.

## 4 Conclusions

We presented a multilingual unsupervised Word Sense Disambiguation task for a sample of English nouns. The lack of supervision refers to the construction of the sense inventory, that is built up on the basis of translations retrieved from the Europarl corpus in five target languages. Systems can participate in a bilingual or multilingual evaluation and are asked to provide correct translations in one or five target languages for new instances of the selected polysemous target nouns.

[6]http://www.illc.uva.nl/EuroWordNet

## References


E. Agirre and P. Edmonds, editors. 2006. *Word Sense Disambiguation*. Text, Speech and Language Technology. Springer, Dordrecht.

M. Carpuat and D. Wu. 2007. Improving statistical machine translation using word sense disambiguation. In *Proceedings of the 2007 Joint Conference on Empirical Methods in Natural Language Processing and Computational Natural Language Learning (EMNLP-CoNLL)*, pages 61–72, Prague, Czech Republic.

Y.S. Chan, H.T. Ng, and D. Chiang. 2007. Word sense disambiguation improves statistical machine translation. In *Proceedings of the 45th Annual Meeting of the Association of Computational Linguistics*, pages 33–40, Prague, Czech Republic.

M. Diab and P. Resnik. 2002. An unsupervised method for word sense tagging using parallel corpora. In *Proceedings of ACL*, pages 255–262.

C. Fellbaum. 1998. *WordNet: An Electronic Lexical Database*. MIT Press.

William A. Gale and Kenneth W. Church. 1991. A program for aligning sentences in bilingual corpora. In *Computational Linguistics*, pages 177–184.

W.A. Gale, K. Church, and D. Yarowsky. 1992. Estimating upper and lower bounds on the performance of word-sense disambiguation programs. In *Proceedings of the 30th Annual Meeting of the Association for Computational Linguistics*, pages 249–256.

W.A. Gale, K.W. Church, and D. Yarowsky. 1993. A method for disambiguating word senses in a large corpus. In *Computers and the Humanities*, volume 26, pages 415–439.

N. Ide, T. Erjavec, and D. Tufis. 2002. Sense discrimination with parallel corpora. In *Proceedings of ACL Workshop on Word Sense Disambiguation: Recent Successes and Future Directions*, pages 54–60.

P. Koehn. 2005. Europarl: A parallel corpus for statistical machine translation. In *Proceedings of the MT Summit*.

L. Màrquez, G. Escudero, D. Martìnez, and G. Rigau. 2006. Supervised corpus-based methods for WSD. In E. Agirre and P. Edmonds, editors, *Word Sense Disambiguation: Algorithms and Applications*, pages 167–216. Eds Springer, New York, NY.

D. McCarthy and R. Navigli. 2007. Semeval-2007 task 10: English lexical substitution task. In *Proceedings of the 4th International Workshop on Semantic Evaluations (SemEval-2007)*, pages 48–53.

R. Navigli. 2009. Word sense disambiguation: a survey. In *ACM Computing Surveys*, volume 41, pages 1–69.

H.T. Ng, B. Wang, and Y.S. Chan. 2003. Exploiting parallel texts for word sense disambiguation: An empirical study. In *Proceedings of the 41st Annual Meeting of the Association for Computational Linguistics*, pages 455–462, Santa Cruz.

F.J. Och and H. Ney. 2003. A systematic comparison of various statistical alignment models. *Computational Linguistics*, 29(1):19–51.

Dan Tufiş, Radu Ion, and Nancy Ide. 2004. Fine-Grained Word Sense Disambiguation Based on Parallel Corpora, Word Alignment, Word Clustering and Aligned Wordnets. In *Proceedings of the 20th International Conference on Computational Linguistics (COLING 2004)*, pages 1312–1318, Geneva, Switzerland, August. Association for Computational Linguistics.

| English "paper" | Dutch | French | Italian |
|---|---|---|---|
| Cluster 1<br>*green paper* | boek, verslag, wetsvoorstel<br>kaderbesluit | livre, document,<br>paquet | libro |
| Cluster 2<br>*present a paper* | document, voorstel, paper<br>nota, stuk, notitie | document, rapport, travail<br>publication, note<br>proposition, avis | documento, rapporto<br>testo, nota |
| Cluster 3<br>*read a paper* | krant, dagblad<br>weekblad | journal, quotidien<br>hebdomadaire | giornale, quotidiano,<br>settimanale, rivista |
| Cluster 4<br>*reams of paper* | papier | papier | carta, cartina |
| Cluster 5<br>*of paper, paper industry, paper basket* | papieren, papier<br>prullenmand | papeterie, papetière<br>papier | cartastraccia, cartaceo<br>cartiera |
| Cluster 6<br>*voting paper, ballot paper* | stembiljet,<br>stembriefje | bulletin, vote | scheda, scheda di voto |
| Cluster 7<br>*piece of paper* | papiertje | papier volant | foglio, foglietto |
| Cluster 8<br>*excess of paper, generate paper* | papier, administratie<br>administratief | paperasse, paperasserie<br>papier, administratif<br>bureaucratie | carta, amministrativo<br>burocratico, cartaceo |
| Cluster 9<br>*on paper* | in theorie, op papier,<br>papieren, bij woorden | en théorie,<br>conceptuellement | in teoria,<br>di parole |
| Cluster 10<br>*on paper* | op papier | écrit, dans les textes,<br>de nature typographique, par voie<br>épistolaire, sur (le) papier | nero su bianco, (di natura)<br>tipografica, per iscritto,<br>cartaceo, di parole |
| Cluster 11<br>*order paper* | agenda, zittingstuk,<br>stuk | ordre du jour,<br>ordre des votes | ordine del giorno |

Table 3: translation clusters for the English noun "paper"

# SemEval-2010 Task 7: Argument Selection and Coercion

**James Pustejovsky**
Computer Science Department
Brandeis University
Waltham, Massachusetts, USA
jamesp@cs.brandeis.edu

**Anna Rumshisky**
Computer Science Department
Brandeis University
Waltham, Massachusetts, USA
arum@cs.brandeis.edu

## Abstract

In this paper, we describe the *Argument Selection and Coercion* task, currently in development for the SemEval-2 evaluation exercise scheduled for 2010. This task involves characterizing the type of compositional operation that exists between a predicate and the arguments it selects. Specifically, the goal is to identify whether the type that a verb selects is satisfied directly by the argument, or whether the argument must change type to satisfy the verb typing. We discuss the problem in detail and describe the data preparation for the task.

## 1 Introduction

In recent years, a number of annotation schemes that encode semantic information have been developed and used to produce data sets for training machine learning algorithms. Semantic markup schemes that have focused on annotating entity types and, more generally, word senses, have been extended to include semantic relationships between sentence elements, such as the semantic role (or label) assigned to the argument by the predicate (Palmer et al., 2005; Ruppenhofer et al., 2006; Kipper, 2005; Burchardt et al., 2006; Ohara, 2008; Subirats, 2004).

In this task, we take this one step further, in that this task attempts to capture the "compositional history" of the argument selection relative to the predicate. In particular, this task attempts to identify the operations of type adjustment induced by a predicate over its arguments when they do not match its selectional properties. The task is defined as follows: for each argument of a predicate, identify whether the entity in that argument position satisfies the type expected by the predicate. If not, then one needs to identify how the entity in that position satisfies the typing expected by the predicate; that is, to identify the source and target types in a type-shifting (or coercion) operation.

Consider the example below, where the verb *report* normally selects for a human in subject position as in (1). Notice, however, that through a metonymic interpretation, this constraint can be violated as demonstrated in (1).

(1) a. John reported in late from Washington.
b. Washington reported in late.

Neither the surface annotation of entity extents and types, nor assigning semantic roles associated with the predicate would reflect in this case a crucial point: namely, that in order for the typing requirements of the predicate to be satisfied, what has been referred to a *type coercion* or a *metonymy* (Hobbs et al., 1993; Pustejovsky, 1991; Nunberg, 1979; Egg, 2005) has taken place.

The SemEval Metonymy task (Markert and Nissim, 2007) was a good attempt to annotate such metonymic relations over a larger data set. This task involved two types with their metonymic variants:

(2) i. **Categories for Locations**: literal, place-for-people, place-for-event, place-for-product;
ii. **Categories for Organizations**: literal, organization-for-members, organization-for-event, organization-for-product, organization-for-facility.

One of the limitations of this approach, however, is that, while appropriate for these specialized metonymy relations, the annotation specification and resulting corpus are not an informative



*Proceedings of the NAACL HLT Workshop on Semantic Evaluations: Recent Achievements and Future Directions*, pages 88–93,
Boulder, Colorado, June 2009. 

guide for extending the annotation of argument selection more broadly.

In fact, the metonymy example in (1) is an instance of a much more pervasive phenomenon of type shifting and coercion in argument selection. For example, in (3) below, the sense annotation for the verb *enjoy* should arguably assign similar values to both (3a) and (3b).

(3) a. Mary enjoyed drinking her beer .
b. Mary enjoyed her beer.

The consequence of this, however, is that, under current sense and role annotation strategies, the mapping to a syntactic realization for a given sense is made more complex, and is in fact, perplexing for a clustering or learning algorithm operating over subcategorization types for the verb.

## 2 Methodology of Annotation

Before introducing the specifics of the argument selection and coercion task, let us review briefly our assumptions regarding the role of annotation within the development and deployment of computational linguistic systems.

We assume that the features we use for encoding a specific linguistic phenomenon are rich enough to capture the desired behavior. These linguistic descriptions are typically distilled from extensive theoretical modeling of the phenomenon. The descriptions in turn form the basis for the annotation values of the specification language, which are themselves the features used in a development cycle for training and testing an identification or labeling algorithm over text. Finally, based on an analysis and evaluation of the performance of a system, the model of the phenomenon may be revised, for retraining and testing.

We call this particular cycle of development the MATTER methodology:

(4) a. **Model**: Structural descriptions provide theoretically-informed attributes derived from empirical observations over the data;

b. **Annotate**: Annotation scheme assumes a feature set that encodes specific structural descriptions and properties of the input data;

c. **Train**: Algorithm is trained over a corpus annotated with the target feature set;

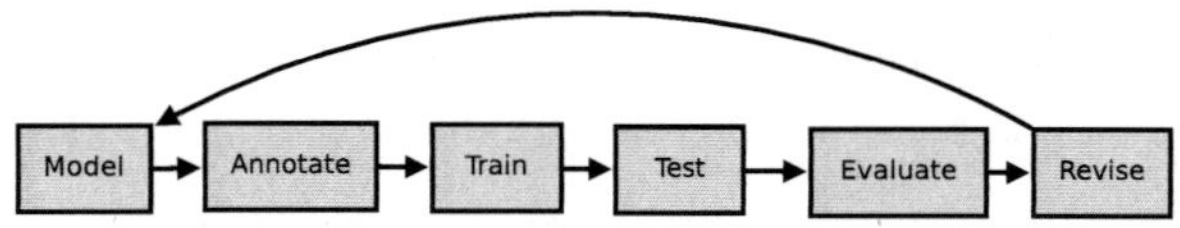


Figure 1: The MATTER Methodology

d. **Test**: Algorithm is tested against held-out data;

e. **Evaluate**: Standardized evaluation of results;

f. **Revise**: Revisit the model, annotation specification, or algorithm, in order to make the annotation more robust and reliable.

Some of the current and completed annotation efforts that have undergone such a development cycle include:

- PropBank (Palmer et al., 2005)
- NomBank (Meyers et al., 2004)
- TimeBank (Pustejovsky et al., 2005)
- Opinion Corpus (Wiebe et al., 2005)
- Penn Discourse TreeBank (Miltsakaki et al., 2004)

## 3 Task Description

This task involves identifying the selectional mechanism used by the predicate over a particular argument.[1] For the purposes of this task, the possible relations between the predicate and a given argument are restricted to *selection* and *coercion*. In *selection*, the argument NP satisfies the typing requirements of the predicate, as in (5).

(5) a. The spokesman denied the statement (PROPOSITION).
b. The child threw the stone (PHYSICAL OBJECT).
c. The audience didn't believe the rumor (PROPOSITION).

*Coercion* encompasses all cases when a type-shifting operation must be performed on the complement NP in order to satisfy selectional requirements of the predicate, as in (6). Note that coercion operations may apply to any argument position in a sentence, including the subject, as seen in (6b). Coercion can also be seen as an object of a proposition as in (6c).

(6) a. The president denied the attack (EVENT → PROPOSITION).
b. The White House (LOCATION → HUMAN) denied this statement.
c. The Boston office called with an update (EVENT → INFO).

[1] This task is part of a larger effort to annotate text with compositional operations (Pustejovsky et al., 2009).

The definition of *coercion* will be extended to include instances of type-shifting due to what we term the *qua*-relation.

(7) a. You can crush the pill (PHYSICAL OBJECT) between two spoons. (*Selection*)
b. It is always possible to crush imagination (ABSTRACT ENTITY *qua* PHYSICAL OBJECT) under the weight of numbers. (*Coercion/qua-relation*)

In order to determine whether type-shifting has taken place, the classification task must then involve the following (1) identifying the verb sense and the associated syntactic frame, (2) identifying selectional requirements imposed by that verb sense on the target argument, and (3) identifying semantic type of the target argument. Sense inventories for the verbs and the type templates associated with different syntactic frames will be provided to the participants.

### 3.1 Semantic Types

In the present task, we use a subset of semantic types from the Brandeis Shallow Ontology (BSO), which is a shallow hierarchy of types developed as a part of the CPA effort (Hanks, 2009; Pustejovsky et al., 2004; Rumshisky et al., 2006). The BSO types were selected for their prevalence in manually identified selection context patterns developed for several hundreds English verbs. That is, they capture common semantic distinctions associated with the selectional properties of many verbs.

The following list of types is currently being used for annotation:

(8) HUMAN, ANIMATE, PHYSICAL OBJECT, ARTIFACT, ORGANIZATION, EVENT, PROPOSITION, INFORMATION, SENSATION, LOCATION, TIME PERIOD, ABSTRACT ENTITY, ATTITUDE, EMOTION, PROPERTY, PRIVILEGE, OBLIGATION, RULE

The subset of types chosen for annotation is purposefully shallow, and is not structured in a hierarchy. For example, we include both HUMAN and ANIMATE in the type system along with PHYSICAL OBJECT. While HUMAN is a subtype of both ANIMATE and PHYSICAL OBJECT, the system should simply choose the most relevant type (i.e. HUMAN) and not be concerned with type inheritance. The present set of types may be revised if necessary as the annotation proceeds.

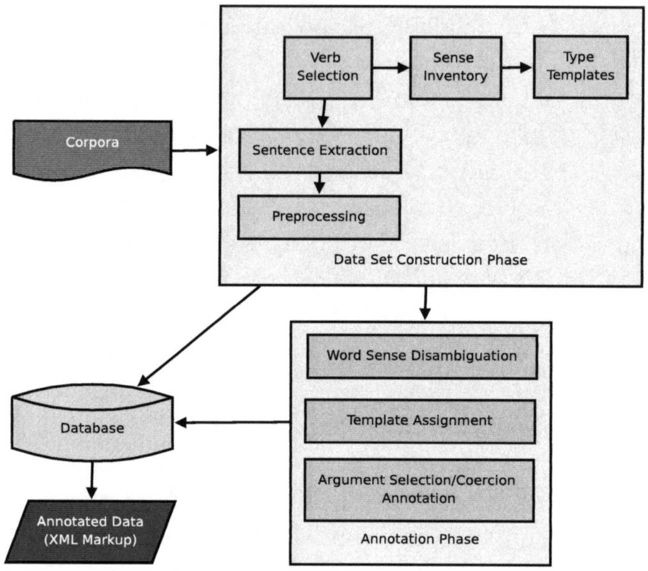


Figure 2: Corpus Development Architecture

## 4 Resources and Corpus Development

Preparing the data for this task will be done in two phases: *the data set construction phase* and *the annotation phase*. The first phase consists of (1) selecting the target verbs to be annotated and compiling a sense inventory for each target, and (2) data extraction and preprocessing. The prepared data is then loaded into the annotation interface. During the annotation phase, the annotation judgments are entered into the database, and the adjudicator resolves disagreements. The resulting database representation is used by the exporting module to generate the corresponding XML markup or stand-off annotation. The corpus development architecture is shown in Fig. 2.

### 4.1 Data Set Construction Phase

In the set of target verbs selected for the task, preference will be given to the verbs that are strongly coercive in at least one of their senses, i.e. tend to impose semantic typing on one of their arguments. The verbs will be selected by examining the data from several sources, using the Sketch Engine (Kilgarriff et al., 2004) as described in (Rumshisky and Batiukova, 2008).

An inventory of senses will be compiled for each verb. Whenever possible, the senses will be mapped to OntoNotes (Pradhan et al., 2007) and to the CPA patterns (Hanks, 2009). For each sense, a set of type templates will be compiled, associating each sense with one or more syntactic patterns which will include type specification for all arguments. For example, one of the senses of the verb *deny* is *refuse to grant*. This sense is associated with the following type templates:

(9) HUMAN deny ENTITY to HUMAN
HUMAN deny HUMAN ENTITY

The set of type templates for each verb will be built using a modification of the CPA technique (Hanks and Pustejovsky, 2005; Pustejovsky et al., 2004)).

A set of sentences will be randomly extracted for each target verb from the BNC (BNC, 2000) and the American National Corpus (Ide and Suderman, 2004). This choice of corpora should ensure a more balanced representation of language than is available in commonly annotated WSJ and other newswire text. Each extracted sentence will be automatically parsed, and the sentences organized according to the grammatical relation involving the target verb. Sentences will be excluded from the set if the target argument is expressed as anaphor, or is not present in the sentence. Semantic head for the target grammatical relation will be identified in each case.

### 4.2 Annotation Phase

Word sense disambiguation will need to be performed as a preliminary stage for the annotation of compositional operations. The annotation task is thus divided into two subtasks, presented successively to the annotator:

(1) Word sense disambiguation of the target predicate

(2) Identification of the compositional relationship between target predicate and its arguments

In the first subtask, the annotator is presented with a set of sentences containing the target verb and the chosen grammatical relation. The annotator is asked to select the most fitting sense of the target verb, or to throw out the example (pick the "N/A" option) if no sense can be chosen either due to insufficient context, because the appropriate sense does not appear in the inventory, or simply no disambiguation can be made in good faith. The interface is shown in Fig. 3. After this step is complete, the appropriate sense is saved into the database, along with the associated type template.

In the second subtask, the annotator is presented with a list of sentences in which the target verb is used in the same sense. The data is annotated one grammatical relation at a time. The annotator is asked to determine whether the argument in the specified grammatical relation to the target belongs to the type associated with that sense in the corresponding template. The illustration of this can be seen in Fig. 4. We will perform double annotation and subsequent adjudication at each of the above annotation stages.

## 5 Data Format

The test and training data will be provided in XML format. The relation between the predicate (viewed as function) and its argument will be represented by a composition link (`CompLink`) as shown below. In case of *coercion*, there is a mismatch between the source and the target types, and both types need to be identified:

*The State Department repeatedly denied the attack.*

```
The State Department repeatedly
<SELECTOR sid="s1">denied</SELECTOR>
the
<NOUN nid="n1">attack</NOUN> .
<CompLink cid="cid1" sID="s1"
relatedToNoun="n1" gramRel="dobj"
compType="COERCION"
sourceType="EVENT"
targetType="PROPOSITION"/>
```

When the compositional operation is *selection*, the source and the target types must match:

*The State Department repeatedly denied this statement.*

```
The State Department repeatedly
<SELECTOR sid="s1">denied</SELECTOR>
this
<NOUN nid="n1">statement</NOUN> .
<CompLink cid="cid1" sID="s1"
relatedToNoun="n1" gramRel="dobj"
compType="selection"
sourceType="PROPOSITION"
targetType="PROPOSITION"/>
```

## 6 Evaluation Methodology

Precision and recall will be used as evaluation metrics. A scoring program will be supplied for participants. Two subtasks will be evaluated separately:

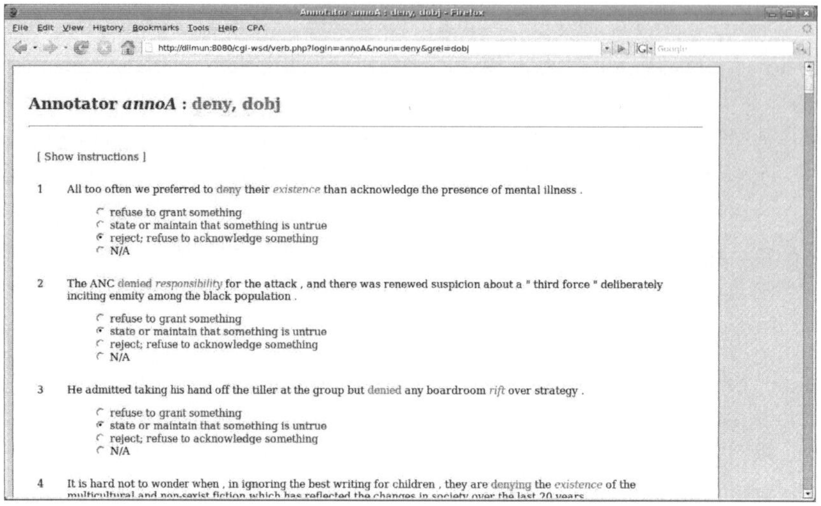


Figure 3: Predicate Sense Disambiguation for *deny*.

(1) identifying the compositional operation (i.e. selection vs. coercion) and (2) identifying the source and target argument type, for each relevant argument. Both subtasks require sense disambiguation which will not be evaluated separately.

Since type-shifting is by its nature a relatively rare event, the distribution between different types of compositional operations in the data set will be necessarily skewed. One of the standard sampling methods for handling class imbalance is downsizing (Japkowicz, 2000; Monard and Batista, 2002), where the number of instances of the major class in the training set is artificially reduced. Another possible alternative is to assign higher error costs to misclassification of minor class instances (Chawla et al., 2004; Domingos, 1999).

## 7 Conclusion

In this paper, we have described the Argument Selection and Coercion task for SemEval-2, to be held in 2010. This task involves the identifying the relation between a predicate and its argument as one that encodes the compositional history of the selection process. This allows us to distinguish surface forms that directly satisfy the selectional (type) requirements of a predicate from those that are coerced in context. We described some details of a specification language for selection and the annotation task using this specification to identify argument selection behavior. Finally, we discussed data preparation for the task and evaluation techniques for analyzing the results.

## References


BNC. 2000. *The British National Corpus*. The BNC Consortium, University of Oxford, *http://www.natcorp.ox.ac.uk/*.

Aljoscha Burchardt, Katrin Erk, Anette Frank, Andrea Kowalski, Sebastian Pado, and Manfred Pinkal. 2006. The salsa corpus: a german corpus resource for lexical semantics. In *Proceedings of LREC*, Genoa, Italy.

N. Chawla, N. Japkowicz, and A. Kotcz. 2004. Editorial: special issue on learning from imbalanced data sets. *ACM SIGKDD Explorations Newsletter*, 6(1):1–6.

P. Domingos. 1999. Metacost: A general method for making classifiers cost-sensitive. In *Proceedings of the fifth ACM SIGKDD international conference on Knowledge discovery and data mining*, pages 155–164. ACM New York, NY, USA.

Marcus Egg. 2005. *Flexible semantics for reinterpretation phenomena*. CSLI, Stanford.

P. Hanks and J. Pustejovsky. 2005. A pattern dictionary for natural language processing. *Revue Française de Linguistique Appliquée*.

P. Hanks. 2009. Corpus pattern analysis. CPA Project Page. Retrieved April 11, 2009, from http://nlp.fi.muni.cz/projekty/cpa/.

J. R. Hobbs, M. Stickel, and P. Martin. 1993. Interpretation as abduction. *Artificial Intelligence*, 63:69–142.

N. Ide and K. Suderman. 2004. The American National Corpus first release. In *Proceedings of LREC 2004*, pages 1681–1684.

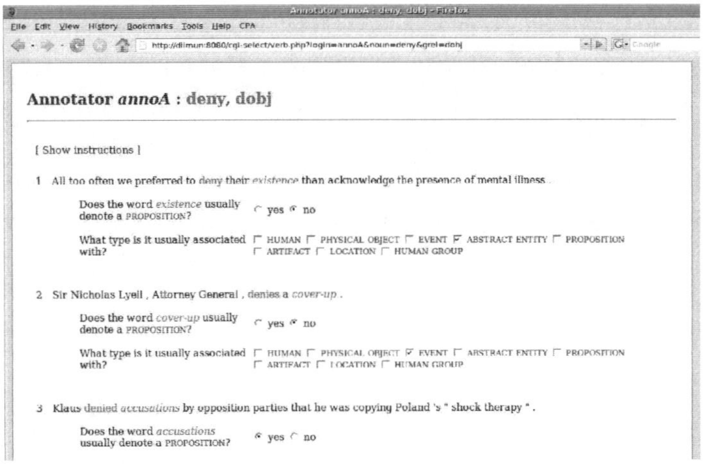


Figure 4: Identifying Compositional Relationship for *deny*.


N. Japkowicz. 2000. Learning from imbalanced data sets: a comparison of various strategies. In *AAAI workshop on learning from imbalanced data sets*, pages 00–05.

A. Kilgarriff, P. Rychly, P. Smrz, and D. Tugwell. 2004. The Sketch Engine. *Proceedings of Euralex, Lorient, France*, pages 105–116.

Karin Kipper. 2005. *VerbNet: A broad-coverage, comprehensive verb lexicon*. Phd dissertation, University of Pennsylvania, PA.

K. Markert and M. Nissim. 2007. Metonymy resolution at SemEval I: Guidelines for participants. In *Proceedings of the ACL 2007 Conference*.

A. Meyers, R. Reeves, C. Macleod, R. Szekely, V. Zielinska, B. Young, and R. Grishman. 2004. The NomBank project: An interim report. In *HLT-NAACL 2004 Workshop: Frontiers in Corpus Annotation*, pages 24–31.

E. Miltsakaki, R. Prasad, A. Joshi, and B. Webber. 2004. The Penn Discourse Treebank. In *Proceedings of the 4th International Conference on Language Resources and Evaluation*.

M.C. Monard and G.E. Batista. 2002. Learning with skewed class distributions. *Advances in logic, artificial intelligence and robotics (LAPTEC'02)*.

Geoffrey Nunberg. 1979. The non-uniqueness of semantic solutions: Polysemy. *Linguistics and Philosophy*, 3:143–184.

Kyoko Hirose Ohara. 2008. Lexicon, grammar, and multilinguality in the japanese framenet. In *Proceedings of LREC*, Marrakech, Marocco.

M. Palmer, D. Gildea, and P. Kingsbury. 2005. The proposition bank: An annotated corpus of semantic roles. *Computational Linguistics*, 31(1):71–106.

S. Pradhan, E. Loper, D. Dligach, and M. Palmer. 2007. Semeval-2007 task-17: English lexical sample, srl and all words. In *Proceedings of the Fourth International Workshop on Semantic Evaluations (SemEval-2007)*, pages 87–92, Prague, Czech Republic, June. Association for Computational Linguistics.

J. Pustejovsky, P. Hanks, and A. Rumshisky. 2004. Automated Induction of Sense in Context. In *COLING 2004, Geneva, Switzerland*, pages 924–931.

J. Pustejovsky, R. Knippen, J. Littman, and R. Sauri. 2005. Temporal and event information in natural language text. *Language Resources and Evaluation*, 39(2):123–164.

J. Pustejovsky, A. Rumshisky, J. Moszkowicz, and O. Batiukova. 2009. GLML: Annotating argument selection and coercion. *IWCS-8: Eighth International Conference on Computational Semantics*.

J. Pustejovsky. 1991. The generative lexicon. *Computational Linguistics*, 17(4).

A. Rumshisky and O. Batiukova. 2008. Polysemy in verbs: systematic relations between senses and their effect on annotation. In *COLING Workshop on Human Judgement in Computational Linguistics (HJCL-2008)*, Manchester, England.

A. Rumshisky, P. Hanks, C. Havasi, and J. Pustejovsky. 2006. Constructing a corpus-based ontology using model bias. In *The 19th International FLAIRS Conference, FLAIRS 2006*, Melbourne Beach, Florida, USA.

J. Ruppenhofer, M. Ellsworth, M. Petruck, C. Johnson, and J. Scheffczyk. 2006. *FrameNet II: Extended Theory and Practice*.

Carlos Subirats. 2004. FrameNet Español. Una red semántica de marcos conceptuales. In *VI International Congress of Hispanic Linguistics*, Leipzig.

J. Wiebe, T. Wilson, and C. Cardie. 2005. Annotating expressions of opinions and emotions in language. *Language Resources and Evaluation*, 39(2):165–210.

# SemEval-2010 Task 8: Multi-Way Classification of Semantic Relations Between Pairs of Nominals

**Iris Hendrickx[*], Su Nam Kim[†], Zornitsa Kozareva[‡], Preslav Nakov[§], Diarmuid Ó Séaghdha[¶], Sebastian Padó[‖], Marco Pennacchiotti[**], Lorenza Romano[††], Stan Szpakowicz[‡‡]**

## Abstract

We present a brief overview of the main challenges in the extraction of semantic relations from English text, and discuss the shortcomings of previous data sets and shared tasks. This leads us to introduce a new task, which will be part of SemEval-2010: multi-way classification of mutually exclusive semantic relations between pairs of common nominals. The task is designed to compare different approaches to the problem and to provide a standard testbed for future research, which can benefit many applications in Natural Language Processing.

## 1 Introduction

The computational linguistics community has a considerable interest in robust knowledge extraction, both as an end in itself and as an intermediate step in a variety of Natural Language Processing (NLP) applications. *Semantic relations between pairs of words* are an interesting case of such semantic knowledge. It can guide the recovery of useful facts about the world, the interpretation of a sentence, or even discourse processing. For example, *pears* and *bowl* are connected in a CONTENT-CONTAINER relation in the sentence "*The bowl contained apples, pears, and oranges.*", while *ginseng* and *taste* are in an ENTITY-ORIGIN relation in "*The taste is not from alcohol, but from the ginseng.*".

The automatic recognition of semantic relations can have many applications, such as information extraction (IE), document summarization, machine translation, or construction of thesauri and semantic networks. It can also facilitate auxiliary tasks such as word sense disambiguation, language modeling, paraphrasing or recognizing textual entailment. For example, semantic network construction can benefit from detecting a FUNCTION relation between *airplane* and *transportation* in "*the airplane is used for transportation*" or a PART-WHOLE relation in "*the car has an engine*". Similarly, all domains that require deep understanding of text relations can benefit from knowing the relations that describe events like ACQUISITION between named entities in "*Yahoo has made a definitive agreement to acquire Flickr*".

In this paper, we focus on the recognition of *semantic relations between pairs of common nominals*. We present a task which will be part of the SemEval-2010 evaluation exercise and for which we are developing a new benchmark data set. This data set and the associated task address three significant problems encountered in previous work: (1) the definition of a suitable set of relations; (2) the incorporation of context; (3) the desire for a realistic experimental design. We outline these issues in Section 2. Section 3 describes the inventory of relations we adopted for the task. The annotation process, the design of the task itself and the evaluation methodology are presented in Sections 4-6.

[*] University of Antwerp, iris.hendrickx@ua.ac.be
[†] University of Melbourne, snkim@csse.unimelb.edu.au
[‡] University of Alicante, zkozareva@dlsi.ua.es
[§] National University of Singapore, nakov@comp.nus.edu.sg
[¶] University of Cambridge, do242@cl.cam.ac.uk
[‖] University of Stuttgart, pado@stanford.edu
[**] Yahoo! Inc., pennacc@yahoo-inc.com
[††] Fondazione Bruno Kessler, romano@fbk.eu
[‡‡] University of Ottawa *and* Polish Academy of Sciences, szpak@site.uottawa.ca



*Proceedings of the NAACL HLT Workshop on Semantic Evaluations: Recent Achievements and Future Directions*, pages 94–99, Boulder, Colorado, June 2009. 

## 2 Semantic Relation Classification: Issues

### 2.1 Defining the Relation Inventory

A wide variety of relation classification schemes exist in the literature, reflecting the needs and granularities of various applications. Some researchers only investigate relations between named entities or internal to noun-noun compounds, while others have a more general focus. Some schemes are specific to a domain such as biomedical text.

Rosario and Hearst (2001) classify noun compounds from the domain of medicine into 13 classes that describe the semantic relation between the head noun and the modifier. Rosario et al. (2002) classify noun compounds using the MeSH hierarchy and a multi-level hierarchy of semantic relations, with 15 classes at the top level. Stephens et al. (2001) propose 17 very specific classes targeting relations between genes. Nastase and Szpakowicz (2003) address the problem of classifying noun-modifier relations in general text. They propose a two-level hierarchy, with 5 classes at the first level and 30 classes at the second one; other researchers (Kim and Baldwin, 2005; Nakov and Hearst, 2008; Nastase et al., 2006; Turney, 2005; Turney and Littman, 2005) have used their class scheme and data set. Moldovan et al. (2004) propose a 35-class scheme to classify relations in various phrases; the same scheme has been applied to noun compounds and other noun phrases (Girju et al., 2005). Lapata (2002) presents a binary classification of relations in nominalizations. Pantel and Pennacchiotti (2006) concentrate on five relations in an IE-style setting. In short, there is little agreement on relation inventories.

### 2.2 The Role of Context

A fundamental question in relation classification is whether the relations between nominals should be considered *out of context* or *in context*. When one looks at real data, it becomes clear that context does indeed play a role. Consider, for example, the noun compound *wood shed*: it may refer either to a shed *made of* wood, or to a shed of any material *used to store* wood. This ambiguity is likely to be resolved in particular contexts. In fact, most NLP applications will want to determine not all possible relations between two words, but rather the relation between two instances in a particular context. While the integration of context is common in the field of IE (cf. work in the context of ACE[1]), much of the existing literature on relation extraction considers word pairs out of context (thus, types rather than tokens). A notable exception is SemEval-2007 Task 4 *Classification of Semantic Relations between Nominals* (Girju et al., 2007; Girju et al., 2008), the first to offer a standard benchmark data set for seven semantic relations between common nouns in context.

### 2.3 Style of Classification

The design of SemEval-2007 Task 4 had an important limitation. The data set avoided the challenge of defining a single unified standard classification scheme by creating seven separate training and test sets, one for each semantic relation. That made the relation recognition task on each data set a simple *binary* (positive / negative) classification task.[2] Clearly, this does not easily transfer to practical NLP settings, where *any* relation can hold between a pair of nominals which occur in a sentence or a discourse.

### 2.4 Summary

While there is a substantial amount of work on relation extraction, the lack of standardization makes it difficult to compare different approaches. It is known from other fields that the availability of standard benchmark data sets can provide a boost to the advancement of a field. As a first step, SemEval-2007 Task 4 offered many useful insights into the performance of different approaches to semantic relation classification; it has also motivated follow-up research (Davidov and Rappoport, 2008; Katrenko and Adriaans, 2008; Nakov and Hearst, 2008; Ó Séaghdha and Copestake, 2008).

Our objective is to build on the achievements of SemEval-2007 Task 4 while addressing its shortcomings. In particular, we consider a larger set of semantic relations (9 instead of 7), we assume a proper multi-class classification setting, we emulate the effect of an "open" relation inventory by means of a tenth class OTHER, and we will release to the research community a data set with a considerably

[1] `http://www.itl.nist.gov/iad/mig/tests/ace/`

[2] Although it was not designed for a multi-class set-up, some subsequent publications tried to use the data sets in that manner.

larger number of examples than SemEval-2007 Task 4 or other comparable data sets. The last point is crucial for ensuring the robustness of the performance estimates for competing systems.

## 3 Designing an Inventory of Semantic Relations Between Nominals

We begin by considering the first of the problems listed above: defining of an inventory of semantic relations. Ideally, it should be exhaustive (should allow the description of relations between any pair of nominals) and mutually exclusive (each pair of nominals in context should map onto only one relation). The literature, however, suggests no such inventory that could satisfy all needs. In practice, one always must decide on a trade-off between these two properties. For example, the gene-gene relation inventory of Stephens et al. (2001), with relations like *X phosphorylates Y*, arguably allows no overlaps, but is too specific for applications to general text.

On the other hand, schemes aimed at exhaustiveness tend to run into overlap issues, due to such fundamental linguistic phenomena as metaphor (Lakoff, 1987). For example, in the sentence *Dark clouds gather over Nepal.*, the relation between *dark clouds* and *Nepal* is literally a type of ENTITY-DESTINATION, but in fact it refers to the ethnic unrest in Nepal.

We seek a pragmatic compromise between the two extremes. We have selected nine relations with sufficiently broad coverage to be of general and practical interest. We aim at avoiding "real" overlap to the extent that this is possible, but we include two sets of similar relations (ENTITY-ORIGIN/ENTITY-DESTINATION and CONTENT-CONTAINER/COMPONENT-WHOLE/MEMBER-COLLECTION), which can help assess the models' ability to make such fine-grained distinctions.[3]

As in Semeval-2007 Task 4, we give ordered two-word names to the relations, where each word describes the role of the corresponding argument. The full list of our nine relations follows[4] (the definitions we show here are intended to be indicative rather than complete):

**Cause-Effect.** An event or object leads to an effect. Example: *Smoking causes cancer.*

**Instrument-Agency.** An agent uses an instrument. Example: *laser printer*

**Product-Producer.** A producer causes a product to exist. Example: *The farmer grows apples.*

**Content-Container.** An object is physically stored in a delineated area of space, the container. Example: *Earth is located in the Milky Way.*

**Entity-Origin.** An entity is coming or is derived from an origin (e.g., position or material). Example: *letters from foreign countries*

**Entity-Destination.** An entity is moving towards a destination. Example: *The boy went to bed.*

**Component-Whole.** An object is a component of a larger whole. Example: *My apartment has a large kitchen.*

**Member-Collection.** A member forms a nonfunctional part of a collection. Example: *There are many trees in the forest.*

**Communication-Topic.** An act of communication, whether written or spoken, is about a topic. Example: *The lecture was about semantics.*

We add a tenth element to this set, the pseudo-relation OTHER. It stands for any relation which is not one of the nine explicitly annotated relations. This is motivated by modelling considerations. Presumably, the data for OTHER will be very nonhomogeneous. By including it, we force any model of the complete data set to correctly identify the decision boundaries between the individual relations and "everything else". This encourages good generalization behaviour to larger, noisier data sets commonly seen in real-world applications.

### 3.1 Semantic Relations versus Semantic Roles

There are three main differences between our task (classification of semantic relations between nominals) and the related task of automatic labeling of semantic roles (Gildea and Jurafsky, 2002).

The first difference is to do with the linguistic phenomena described. Lexical resources for theories of semantic roles such as FrameNet (Fillmore et

[3]COMPONENT-WHOLE and MEMBER-COLLECTION are proper subsets of PART-WHOLE, one of the relations in SemEval-2007 Task 4.

[4]We have taken the first five from SemEval-2007 Task 4.

al., 2003) and PropBank (Palmer et al., 2005) have been developed to describe the linguistic realization patterns of events and states. Thus, they target primarily verbs (or event nominalizations) and their dependents, which are typically nouns. In contrast, semantic relations may occur between all parts of speech, although we limit our attention to nominals *in this task*. Also, semantic role descriptions typically relate an event to a set of multiple participants and props, while semantic relations are in practice (although not necessarily) binary.

The second major difference is the syntactic context. Theories of semantic roles usually developed out of syntactic descriptions of verb valencies, and thus they focus on describing the linking patterns of verbs and their direct dependents, phenomena like raising and noninstantiations notwithstanding (Fillmore, 2002). Semantic relations are not tied to predicate-argument structures. They can also be established within noun phrases, noun compounds, or sentences more generally (cf. the examples above).

The third difference is that of the level of generalization. FrameNet currently contains more than 825 different frames (event classes). Since the semantic roles are designed to be interpreted at the frame level, there is *a priori* a very large number of unrelated semantic roles. There is a rudimentary frame hierarchy that defines mappings between roles of individual frames,[5] but it is far from complete. The situation is similar in PropBank. PropBank does use a small number of semantic roles, but these are again to be interpreted at the level of individual predicates, with little cross-predicate generalization. In contrast, all of the semantic relation inventories discussed in Section 1 contain fewer than 50 types of semantic relations. More generally, semantic relation inventories attempt to generalize relations across wide groups of verbs (Chklovski and Pantel, 2004) and include relations that are not verb-centered (Nastase and Szpakowicz, 2003; Moldovan et al., 2004). Using the same labels for similar semantic relations facilitates supervised learning. For example, a model trained with examples of *sell* relations should be able to transfer what it has learned to *give* relations. This has the potential of adding crucial robustness and coverage to analysis tools in NLP applications based on semantic relations.

[5]For example, it relates the BUYER role of the COMMERCE_SELL frame (verb *sell*) to the RECIPIENT role of the GIVING frame (verb *give*).

1. People in Hawaii might be feeling <e1>aftershocks</e1> from that powerful <e2>earthquake</e2> for weeks.

2. My new <e1>apartment</e1> has a <e2>large kitchen</e2>.

Figure 1: Two example sentences with annotation

## 4 Annotation

The next step in our study will be the actual annotation of relations between nominals. For the purpose of annotation, we define a *nominal* as a noun or a base noun phrase. A base noun phrase is a noun and its pre-modifiers (e.g., nouns, adjectives, determiners). We do not include complex noun phrases (e.g., noun phrases with attached prepositional phrases or relative clauses). For example, *lawn* is a noun, *lawn mower* is a base noun phrase, and *the engine of the lawn mower* is a complex noun phrase.

We focus on heads that are common nouns. This emphasis distinguishes our task from much work in IE, which focuses on named entities and on considerably more fine-grained relations than we do. For example, Patwardhan and Riloff (2007) identify categories like *Terrorist organization* as participants in terror-related semantic relations, which consists predominantly of named entities. We feel that named entities are a specific category of nominal expressions best dealt with using techniques which do not apply to common nouns; for example, they do not lend themselves well to semantic generalization.

Figure 1 shows two examples of annotated sentences. The XML tags <e1> and <e2> mark the target nominals. Since all nine proper semantic relations in this task are asymmetric, the ordering of the two nominals must be taken into account. In example 1, CAUSE-EFFECT(e1, e2) does not hold, although CAUSE-EFFECT(e2, e1) would. In example 2, COMPONENT-WHOLE(e2, e1) holds.

We are currently developing annotation guidelines for each of the relations. They will give a precise definition for each relation and some prototypical examples, similarly to SemEval-2007 Task 4.

The annotation will take place in two rounds. In the first round, we will do a coarse-grained search for positive examples for each relation. We will collect data from the Web using a semi-automatic, pattern-based search procedure. In order to ensure a wide variety of example sentences, we will use several dozen patterns per relation. We will also ensure that patterns retrieve both positive and negative example sentences; the latter will help populate the OTHER relation with realistic *near-miss* negative examples of the other relations. The patterns will be manually constructed following the approach of Hearst (1992) and Nakov and Hearst (2008).[6]

The example collection for each relation $R$ will be passed to two independent annotators. In order to maintain exclusivity of relations, only examples that are negative for all relations but $R$ will be included as positive and only examples that are negative for all nine relations will be included as OTHER. Next, the annotators will compare their decisions and assess inter-annotator agreement. Consensus will be sought; if the annotators cannot agree on an example it will not be included in the data set, but it will be recorded for future analysis.

Finally, two other task organizers will look for overlap across all relations. They will discard any example marked as positive in two or more relations, as well as examples in OTHER marked as positive in any of the other classes. The OTHER relation will, then, consist of examples that are negatives for all other relations and near-misses for any relation.

**Data sets.** The annotated data will be divided into a training set, a development set and a test set. There will be 1000 annotated examples for each of the ten relations: 700 for training, 100 for development and 200 for testing. All data will be released under the *Creative Commons Attribution 3.0 Unported License*[7]. The annotation guidelines will be included in the distribution.

## 5 The Classification Task

The actual task that we will run at SemEval-2010 will be a multi-way classification task. Not all pairs of nominals in each sentence will be labeled, so the gold-standard boundaries of the nominals to be classified will be provided as part of the test data.

In contrast with Semeval 2007 Task 4, in which the ordering of the entities was provided with each example, we aim at a more realistic scenario in which the ordering of the labels is not given. Participants in the task will be asked to discover both the relation and the order of the arguments. Thus, the more challenging task is to identify the *most informative ordering and relation* between a pair of nominals. The stipulation "most informative" is necessary since with our current set of asymmetrical relations that includes OTHER, each pair of nominals that instantiates a relation in one direction (e.g., REL(e1, e2)), instantiates OTHER in the inverse direction (OTHER (e2, e1)). Thus, the correct answers for the two examples in Figure 1 are CAUSE-EFFECT (earthquake, aftershocks) and COMPONENT-WHOLE (large kitchen, apartment).

Note that unlike in SemEval-2007 Task 4, we will not provide manually annotated WordNet senses, thus making the task more realistic. WordNet senses did, however, serve for disambiguation purposes in SemEval-2007 Task 4. We will therefore have to assess the effect of this change on inter-annotator agreement.

## 6 Evaluation Methodology

The official ranking of the participating systems will be based on their macro-averaged *F-scores* for the nine proper relations. We will also compute and report their *accuracy* over all ten relations, including OTHER. We will further analyze the results quantitatively and qualitatively to gauge which relations are most difficult to classify.

Similarly to SemEval-2007 Task 4, in order to assess the effect of varying quantities of training data, we will ask the teams to submit several sets of guesses for the labels for the test data, using varying fractions of the training data. We may, for example, request test results when training on the first 50, 100, 200, 400 and all 700 examples from each relation.

We will provide a Perl-based automatic evaluation tool that the participants can use when training/tuning/testing their systems. We will use the same tool for the official evaluation.

## 7 Conclusion

We have introduced a new task, which will be part of SemEval-2010: multi-way classification of semantic

[6] Note that, unlike in Semeval 2007 Task 4, we will not release the patterns to the participants.

[7] `http://creativecommons.org/licenses/by/3.0/`

relations between pairs of common nominals. The task will compare different approaches to the problem and provide a standard testbed for future research, which can benefit many NLP applications.

The description we have presented here should be considered preliminary. We invite the interested reader to visit the official task website `http://semeval2.fbk.eu/semeval2.php?location=tasks\#T11`, where up-to-date information will be published; there is also a discussion group and a mailing list.

## References


Timothy Chklovski and Patrick Pantel. 2004. VerbOcean: Mining the web for fine-grained semantic verb relations. In *Proc. EMNLP 2004*, pages 33–40.

Dmitry Davidov and Ari Rappoport. 2008. Classification of semantic relationships between nominals using pattern clusters. In *Proc. ACL-08: HLT*, pages 227–235.

Charles J. Fillmore, Christopher R. Johnson, and Miriam R.L. Petruck. 2003. Background to FrameNet. *International Journal of Lexicography*, 16:235–250.

Charles J. Fillmore. 2002. FrameNet and the linking between semantic and syntactic relations. In *Proc. COLING 2002*, pages 28–36.

Daniel Gildea and Daniel Jurafsky. 2002. Automatic labeling of semantic roles. *Computational Linguistics*, 28(3):245–288.

Roxana Girju, Dan Moldovan, Marta Tatu, , and Dan Antohe. 2005. On the semantics of noun compounds. *Computer Speech and Language*, 19:479–496.

Roxana Girju, Preslav Nakov, Vivi Nastase, Stan Szpakowicz, Peter Turney, and Deniz Yuret. 2007. SemEval-2007 task 04: Classification of semantic relations between nominals. In *Proc. 4th Semantic Evaluation Workshop (SemEval-2007)*.

Roxana Girju, Preslav Nakov, Vivi Nastase, Stan Szpakowicz, Peter Turney, and Deniz Yuret. 2008. Classification of semantic relations between nominals. *Language Resources and Evaluation*. In print.

Marti A. Hearst. 1992. Automatic acquisition of hyponyms from large text corpora. In *Proc. COLING 92*, pages 539–545.

Sophia Katrenko and Pieter Adriaans. 2008. Semantic types of some generic relation arguments: Detection and evaluation. In *Proc. ACL-08: HLT, Short Papers*, pages 185–188.

Su Nam Kim and Timothy Baldwin. 2005. Automatic interpretation of noun compounds using WordNet similarity. In *Proc. IJCAI*, pages 945–956.

George Lakoff. 1987. *Women, fire, and dangerous things*. University of Chicago Press, Chicago, IL.

Maria Lapata. 2002. The disambiguation of nominalisations. *Computational Linguistics*, 28:357–388.

Dan Moldovan, Adriana Badulescu, Marta Tatu, Daniel Antohe, and Roxana Girju. 2004. Models for the semantic classification of noun phrases. In *HLT-NAACL 2004: Workshop on Computational Lexical Semantics*, pages 60–67.

Preslav Nakov and Marti A. Hearst. 2008. Solving relational similarity problems using the web as a corpus. In *Proc. ACL-08: HLT*, pages 452–460.

Vivi Nastase and Stan Szpakowicz. 2003. Exploring noun-modifier semantic relations. In *Fifth International Workshop on Computational Semantics (IWCS-5)*, pages 285–301.

Vivi Nastase, Jelber Sayyad-Shirabad, Marina Sokolova, and Stan Szpakowicz. 2006. Learning noun-modifier semantic relations with corpus-based and WordNet-based features. In *Proc. AAAI*, pages 781–787.

Diarmuid Ó Séaghdha and Ann Copestake. 2008. Semantic classification with distributional kernels. In *Proc. COLING 2008*, pages 649–656.

Martha Palmer, Dan Gildea, and Paul Kingsbury. 2005. The Proposition Bank: An annotated corpus of semantic roles. *Computational Linguistics*, 31(1):71–106.

Patrick Pantel and Marco Pennacchiotti. 2006. Espresso: Leveraging generic patterns for automatically harvesting semantic relations. In *Proc. COLING/ACL*, pages 113–120.

Siddharth Patwardhan and Ellen Riloff. 2007. Effective information extraction with semantic affinity patterns and relevant regions. In *Proc. EMNLP-CoNLL)*, pages 717–727.

Barbara Rosario and Marti Hearst. 2001. Classifying the semantic relations in noun compounds via a domain-specific lexical hierarchy. In *Proc. EMNLP 2001*, pages 82–90.

Barbara Rosario, Marti Hearst, and Charles Fillmore. 2002. The descent of hierarchy, and selection in relational semantics. In *Proc. ACL-02*, pages 247–254.

Matthew Stephens, Mathew Palakal, Snehasis Mukhopadhyay, Rajeev Raje, and Javed Mostafa. 2001. Detecting gene relations from Medline abstracts. In *Pacific Symposium on Biocomputing*, pages 483–495.

Peter D. Turney and Michael L. Littman. 2005. Corpus-based learning of analogies and semantic relations. *Machine Learning*, 60(1-3):251–278.

Peter D. Turney. 2005. Measuring semantic similarity by latent relational analysis. In *Proc. IJCAI*, pages 1136–1141.

# SemEval-2010 Task 9: The Interpretation of Noun Compounds Using Paraphrasing Verbs and Prepositions

**Cristina Butnariu**
University College Dublin
ioana.butnariu@ucd.ie

**Su Nam Kim**
University of Melbourne
nkim@csse.unimelb.edu.au

**Preslav Nakov**
National University of Singapore
nakov@comp.nus.edu.sg

**Diarmuid Ó Séaghdha**
University of Cambridge
do242@cam.ac.uk

**Stan Szpakowicz**
University of Ottawa
Polish Academy of Sciences
szpak@site.uottawa.ca

**Tony Veale**
University College Dublin
tony.veale@ucd.ie

## Abstract

We present a brief overview of the main challenges in understanding the semantics of noun compounds and consider some known methods. We introduce a new task to be part of SemEval-2010: the interpretation of noun compounds using paraphrasing verbs and prepositions. The task is meant to provide a standard testbed for future research on noun compound semantics. It should also promote paraphrase-based approaches to the problem, which can benefit many NLP applications.

## 1 Introduction

Noun compounds (NCs) – sequences of two or more nouns acting as a single noun,[1] e.g., *colon cancer tumor suppressor protein* – are abundant in English and pose a major challenge to the automatic analysis of written text. Baldwin and Tanaka (2004) calculated that 3.9% and 2.6% of the tokens in the *Reuters corpus* and the *British National Corpus (BNC)*, respectively, are part of a noun compound. Compounding is also an extremely productive process in English. The frequency spectrum of compound types follows a Zipfian or power-law distribution (Ó Séaghdha, 2008), so in practice many compound tokens encountered belong to a "long tail" of low-frequency types. For example, over half of the two-noun NC types in the BNC occur just once (Lapata and Lascarides, 2003). Even for relatively frequent NCs that occur ten or more times in the BNC, static English dictionaries give only 27% coverage (Tanaka and Baldwin, 2003). Taken together, the factors of high frequency and high productivity mean that achieving robust NC interpretation is an important goal for broad-coverage semantic processing. NCs provide a concise means of evoking a relationship between two or more nouns, and natural language processing (NLP) systems that do not try to recover these implicit relations from NCs are effectively discarding valuable semantic information. Broad coverage should therefore be achieved by post-hoc interpretation rather than pre-hoc enumeration, since it is impossible to build a lexicon of all NCs likely to be encountered.

The challenges presented by NCs and their semantics have generated significant ongoing interest in NC interpretation in the NLP community. Representative publications include (Butnariu and Veale, 2008; Girju, 2007; Kim and Baldwin, 2006; Nakov, 2008b; Nastase and Szpakowicz, 2003; Ó Séaghdha and Copestake, 2007). Applications that have been suggested include Question Answering, Machine Translation, Information Retrieval and Information Extraction. For example, a question-answering system may need to determine whether *headaches induced by caffeine withdrawal* is a good paraphrase for *caffeine headaches* when answering questions about the causes of headaches, while an information extraction system may need to decide whether *caffeine withdrawal headache* and *caffeine headache* refer to the same concept when used in the same document. Similarly, a machine translation system facing the unknown NC *WTO Geneva headquarters* might benefit from the ability to paraphrase it as *Geneva headquarters of the WTO* or as *WTO headquarters located in Geneva*. Given a query like *can-*

[1] We follow the definition in (Downing, 1977).



*Proceedings of the NAACL HLT Workshop on Semantic Evaluations: Recent Achievements and Future Directions*, pages 100–105,
Boulder, Colorado, June 2009. 

*cer treatment*, an information retrieval system could use suitable paraphrasing verbs like *relieve* and *prevent* for page ranking and query refinement.

In this paper, we introduce a new task, which will be part of the SemEval-2010 competition: NC interpretation using paraphrasing verbs and prepositions. The task is intended to provide a standard testbed for future research on noun compound semantics. We also hope that it will promote paraphrase-based approaches to the problem, which can benefit many NLP applications.

The remainder of the paper is organized as follows: Section 2 presents a brief overview of the existing approaches to NC semantic interpretation and introduces the one we will adopt for SemEval-2010 Task 9; Section 3 provides a general description of the task, the data collection, and the evaluation methodology; Section 4 offers a conclusion.

## 2 Models of Relational Semantics in NCs

### 2.1 Inventory-Based Semantics

The prevalent view in theoretical and computational linguistics holds that the semantic relations that implicitly link the nouns of an NC can be adequately enumerated via a small inventory of abstract relational categories. In this view, *mountain hut*, *field mouse* and *village feast* all express 'location in space', while the relation implicit in *history book* and *nativity play* can be characterized as 'topicality' or 'aboutness'. A sample of some of the most influential relation inventories appears in Table 1.

Levi (1978) proposes that complex nominals – a general concept grouping together nominal compounds (e.g., *peanut butter*), nominalizations (e.g., *dream analysis*) and non-predicative noun phrases (e.g., *electric shock*) – are derived through the complementary processes of *recoverable predicate deletion* and *nominalization*; each process is associated with its own inventory of semantic categories. Table 1 lists the categories for the former.

Warren (1978) posits a hierarchical classification scheme derived from a large-scale corpus study of NCs. The top-level relations in her hierarchy are listed in Table 1, while the next level subdivides CONSTITUTE into SOURCE-RESULT, RESULT-SOURCE and COPULA; COPULA is then further subdivided at two additional levels.

In computational linguistics, popular inventories of semantic relations have been proposed by Nastase and Szpakowicz (2003) and Girju et al. (2005), among others. The former groups 30 fine-grained relations into five coarse-grained super-categories, while the latter is a flat list of 21 relations. Both schemes are intended to be suitable for broad-coverage analysis of text. For specialized applications, however, it is often useful to use domain-specific relations. For example, Rosario and Hearst (2001) propose 18 abstract relations for interpreting NCs in biomedical text, e.g., DEFECT, MATERIAL, PERSON AFFILIATED, ATTRIBUTE OF CLINICAL STUDY.

Inventory-based analyses offer significant advantages. Abstract relations such as 'location' and 'possession' capture valuable generalizations about NC semantics in a parsimonious framework. Unlike paraphrase-based analyses (Section 2.2), they are not tied to specific lexical items, which may themselves be semantically ambiguous. They also lend themselves particularly well to automatic interpretation methods based on multi-class classification.

On the other hand, relation inventories have been criticized on a number of fronts, most influentially by Downing (1977). She argues that the great variety of NC relations makes listing them all impossible; creative NCs like *plate length* ('what your hair is when it drags in your food') are intuitively compositional, but cannot be assigned to any standard inventory category. A second criticism is that restricted inventories are too impoverished a representation scheme for NC semantics, e.g., *headache pills* and *sleeping pills* would both be analyzed as FOR in Levi's classification, but express very different (indeed, contrary) relationships. Downing writes (p. 826): *"These interpretations are at best reducible to underlying relationships. . . , but only with the loss of much of the semantic material considered by subjects to be relevant or essential to the definitions."* A further drawback associated with sets of abstract relations is that it is difficult to identify the "correct" inventory or to decide whether one proposed classification scheme should be favored over another.

### 2.2 Interpretation Using Verbal Paraphrases

An alternative approach to NC interpretation associates each compound with an explanatory para-

| Author(s) | Relation Inventory |
|---|---|
| Levi (1978) | CAUSE, HAVE, MAKE, USE, BE, IN, FOR, FROM, ABOUT |
| Warren (1978) | POSSESSION, LOCATION, PURPOSE, ACTIVITY-ACTOR, RESEMBLANCE, CONSTITUTE |
| Nastase and Szpakowicz (2003) | CAUSALITY (cause, effect, detraction, purpose), PARTICIPANT (agent, beneficiary, instrument, object_property, object, part, possessor, property, product, source, whole, stative), QUALITY (container, content, equative, material, measure, topic, type), SPATIAL (direction, location_at, location_from, location), TEMPORALITY (frequency, time_at, time_through) |
| Girju et al. (2005) | POSSESSION, ATTRIBUTE-HOLDER, AGENT, TEMPORAL, PART-WHOLE, IS-A, CAUSE, MAKE/PRODUCE, INSTRUMENT, LOCATION/SPACE, PURPOSE, SOURCE, TOPIC, MANNER, MEANS, THEME, ACCOMPANIMENT, EXPERIENCER, RECIPIENT, MEASURE, RESULT |
| Lauer (1995) | OF, FOR, IN, AT, ON, FROM, WITH, ABOUT |

Table 1: Previously proposed inventories of semantic relations for noun compound interpretation. The first two come from linguistic theories; the rest have been proposed in computational linguistics.

phrase. Thus, *cheese knife* and *kitchen knife* can be expanded as a *knife for cutting cheese* and a *knife used in a kitchen*, respectively. In the paraphrase-based paradigm, semantic relations need not come from a small set; it is possible to have many subtle distinctions afforded by the vocabulary of the paraphrasing language (in our case, English). This paradigm avoids the problems of coverage and representational poverty, which Downing (1977) observed in inventory-based approaches. It also reflects cognitive-linguistic theories of NC semantics, in which compounds are held to express underlying *event frames* and whose constituents are held to denote event participants (Ryder, 1994).

Lauer (1995) associates NC semantics with prepositional paraphrases. As Lauer only considers a handful of prepositions (about, at, for, from, in, of, on, with), his model is essentially inventory-based. On the other hand, noun-preposition co-occurrences can easily be identified in a corpus, so an automatic interpretation can be implemented through simple unsupervised methods. The disadvantage of this approach is the absence of a one-to-one mapping from prepositions to meanings; prepositions can be ambiguous (of indicates many different relations) or synonymous (at, in and on all express 'location'). This concern arises with all paraphrasing models, but it is exacerbated by the restricted nature of prepositions. Furthermore, many NCs cannot be paraphrased adequately with prepositions, e.g., *woman driver*, *honey bee*.

A richer, more flexible paraphrasing model is afforded by the use of verbs. In such a model, a *honey bee* is a *bee that produces honey*, a *sleeping pill* is a *pill that induces sleeping* and a *headache pill* is a *pill that relieves headaches*. In some previous computational work on NC interpretation, manually constructed dictionaries provided typical activities or functions associated with nouns (Finin, 1980; Isabelle, 1984; Johnston and Busa, 1996). It is, however, impractical to build large structured lexicons for broad-coverage systems; these methods can only be applied to specialized domains. On the other hand, we expect that the ready availability of large text corpora should facilitate the automatic mining of rich paraphrase information.

The SemEval-2010 task we present here builds on the work of Nakov (Nakov and Hearst, 2006; Nakov, 2007; Nakov, 2008b), where NCs are paraphrased by combinations of verbs and prepositions. Given the problem of synonymy, we do not provide a single correct paraphrase for a given NC but a probability distribution over a range of candidates. For example, highly probable paraphrases for *chocolate bar* are *bar made of chocolate* and *bar that tastes like chocolate*, while *bar that eats chocolate* is very unlikely. As described in Section 3.3, a set of gold-standard paraphrase distributions can be constructed by collating responses from a large number of human subjects.

In this framework, the task of interpretation becomes one of identifying the most likely paraphrases for an NC. Nakov (2008b) and Butnariu and Veale (2008) have demonstrated that paraphrasing information can be collected from corpora in an unsupervised fashion; we expect that participants in

SemEval-2010 Task 9 will further develop suitable techniques for this problem. Paraphrases of this kind have been shown to be useful in applications such as machine translation (Nakov, 2008a) and as an intermediate step in inventory-based classification of abstract relations (Kim and Baldwin, 2006; Nakov and Hearst, 2008). Progress in paraphrasing is therefore likely to have follow-on benefits in many areas.

## 3 Task Description

The description of the task we present below is preliminary. We invite the interested reader to visit the official Website of SemEval-2010 Task 9, where up-to-date information will be published; there is also a discussion group and a mailing list.[2]

### 3.1 Preliminary Study

In a preliminary study, we asked 25-30 human subjects to paraphrase 250 noun-noun compounds using suitable paraphrasing verbs. This is the *Levi-250* dataset (Levi, 1978); see (Nakov, 2008b) for details.[3] The most popular paraphrases tend to be quite apt, while some less frequent choices are questionable. For example, for *chocolate bar* we obtained the following paraphrases (the number of subjects who proposed each one is shown in parentheses):

> contain (17); be made of (16); be made from (10); taste like (7); be composed of (7); consist of (5); be (3); have (2); smell of (2); be manufactured from (2); be formed from (2); melt into (2); serve (1); sell (1); incorporate (1); be made with (1); be comprised of (1); be constituted by (1); be solidified from (1); be flavored with (1); store (1); be flavored with (1); be created from (1); taste of (1)

### 3.2 Objective

We propose a task in which participating systems must estimate the quality of paraphrases for a test set of NCs. A list of verb/preposition paraphrases will be provided for each NC, and for each list a participating system will be asked to provide aptness scores that correlate well (in terms of frequency distribution) with the human judgments collated from our test subjects.

### 3.3 Datasets

**Trial/Development Data.** As trial/development data, we will release the previously collected paraphrase sets for the *Levi-250* dataset (after further review and cleaning). This dataset consists of 250 noun-noun compounds, each paraphrased by 25-30 human subjects (Nakov, 2008b).

**Test Data.** The test data will consist of approximately 300 NCs, each accompanied by a set of paraphrasing verbs and prepositions. Following the methodology of Nakov (2008b), we will use the *Amazon Mechanical Turk* Web service[4] to recruit human subjects. This service offers an inexpensive way to recruit subjects for tasks that require human intelligence, and provides an API which allows a computer program to easily run tasks and collate the responses from human subjects. The Mechanical Turk is becoming a popular means to elicit and collect linguistic intuitions for NLP research; see Snow et al. (2008) for an overview and a discussion of issues that arise.

We intend to recruit 100 annotators for each NC, and we will require each annotator to paraphrase at least five NCs. Annotators will be given clear instructions and will be asked to produce one or more paraphrases for a given NC. To help us filter out subjects with an insufficient grasp of English or an insufficient interest in the task, annotators will be asked to complete a short and simple multiple-choice pretest on NC comprehension before proceeding to the paraphrasing step.

**Post-processing.** We will manually check the trial/development data and the test data. Depending on the quality of the paraphrases, we may decide to drop the least frequent verbs.

**License.** All data will be released under the *Creative Commons Attribution 3.0 Unported license*[5].

### 3.4 Evaluation

**Single-NC Scores.** For each NC, we will compare human scores (our gold standard) with those proposed by each participating system. We have con-

[2] Please follow the Task #9 link at the SemEval-2010 homepage http://semeval2.fbk.eu

[3] This dataset is available from http://sourceforge.net/projects/multiword/

[4] http://www.mturk.com

[5] http://creativecommons.org/licenses/by/3.0/

sidered three scores: (1) Pearson's correlation, (2) cosine similarity, and (3) Spearman's rank correlation.

*Pearson's correlation coefficient* is a standard measure of the correlation strength between two distributions; it can be calculated as follows:

$$\rho = \frac{E(XY) - E(X)E(Y)}{\sqrt{E(X^2) - [E(X)]^2}\sqrt{E(Y^2) - [E(Y)]^2} \quad (1)$$

where $X = (x_1, \ldots, x_n)$ and $Y = (y_1, \ldots, y_n)$ are vectors of numerical scores for each paraphrase provided by the humans and the competing systems, respectively, $n$ is the number of paraphrases to score, and $E(X)$ is the expectation of $X$.

*Cosine correlation coefficient* is another popular alternative and was used by Nakov and Hearst (2008); it can be seen as an uncentered version of Pearson's correlation coefficient:

$$\rho = \frac{X.Y}{\|X\|\|Y\|} \quad (2)$$

*Spearman's rank correlation coefficient* is suitable for comparing rankings of sets of items; it is a special case of Pearson's correlation, derived by considering rank indices (1,2,...) as item scores . It is defined as follows:

$$\rho = \frac{n\sum x_i y_i - (\sum x_i)(\sum y_i)}{\sqrt{n\sum x_i^2 - (\sum x_i)^2}\sqrt{n\sum y_i^2 - (\sum y_i)^2}} \quad (3)$$

One problem with using Spearman's rank coefficient for the current task is the assumption that swapping any two ranks has the same effect. The often-skewed nature of paraphrase frequency distributions means that swapping some ranks is intuitively less "wrong" than swapping others. Consider, for example, the following list of human-proposed paraphrasing verbs for *child actor*, which is given in Nakov (2007):

> be (22); look like (4); portray (3); start as (1); include (1); play (1); have (1); involve (1); act like (1); star as (1); work as (1); mimic (1); pass as (1); resemble (1); be classified as (1); substitute for (1); qualify as (1); act as (1)

Clearly, a system that swaps the positions for *be (22)* and *look like (4)* for *child actor* will have made a significant error, while swapping *contain (17)* and *be made of (16)* for *chocolate bar* (see Section 3.1) would be less inappropriate. However, Spearman's coefficient treats both alterations identically since it only looks at ranks; thus, we do not plan to use it for official evaluation, though it may be useful for post-hoc analysis.

**Final Score.** A participating system's final score will be the average of the scores it achieves over all test examples.

**Scoring Tool.** We will provide an automatic evaluation tool that participants can use when training/tuning/testing their systems. We will use the same tool for the official evaluation.

## 4 Conclusion

We have presented a noun compound paraphrasing task that will run as part of SemEval-2010. The goal of the task is to promote and explore the feasibility of paraphrase-based methods for compound interpretation. We believe paraphrasing holds some key advantages over more traditional inventory-based approaches, such as the ability of paraphrases to represent fine-grained and overlapping meanings, and the utility of the resulting paraphrases for other applications such as Question Answering, Information Extraction/Retrieval and Machine Translation.

The proposed paraphrasing task is predicated on two important assumptions: first, that paraphrasing via a combination of verbs and prepositions provides a powerful framework for representing and interpreting the meaning of compositional nonlexicalized noun compounds; and second, that humans can agree amongst themselves about what constitutes a good paraphrase for any given NC. As researchers in this area and as proponents of this task, we believe that both assumptions are valid, but if the analysis of the task were to raise doubts about either assumption (e.g., by showing poor agreement amongst human annotators), then this in itself would be a meaningful and successful output of the task. As such, we anticipate that the task and its associated dataset will inspire further research, both on the theory and development of paraphrase-based compound interpretation and on its practical applications.

## References


Timothy Baldwin and Takaaki Tanaka. 2004. Translation by machine of compound nominals: Getting it right. In *Proceedings of the ACL 2004 Workshop on Multiword Expressions: Integrating Processing*, pages 24–31.

Cristina Butnariu and Tony Veale. 2008. A concept-centered approach to noun-compound interpretation. In *Proceedings of the 22nd International Conference on Computational Linguistics (COLING 2008)*, pages 81–88.

Pamela Downing. 1977. On the creation and use of English compound nouns. *Language*, 53(4):810–842.

Timothy Finin. 1980. *The Semantic Interpretation of Compound Nominals*. Ph.D. Dissertation, University of Illinois, Urbana, Illinois.

Roxana Girju, Dan Moldovan, Marta Tatu, and Daniel Antohe. 2005. On the semantics of noun compounds. *Journal of Computer Speech and Language - Special Issue on Multiword Expressions*, 4(19):479–496.

Roxana Girju. 2007. Improving the interpretation of noun phrases with cross-linguistic information. In *Proceedings of the 45th Annual Meeting of the Association of Computational Linguistics (ACL 2007)*, pages 568–575.

Pierre Isabelle. 1984. Another look at nominal compounds. In *Proceedings of the 10th International Conference on Computational Linguistics*, pages 509–516.

Michael Johnston and Frederica Busa. 1996. Qualia structure and the compositional interpretation of compounds. In *Proceedings of the ACL 1996 Workshop on Breadth and Depth of Semantic Lexicons*, pages 77–88.

Su Nam Kim and Timothy Baldwin. 2006. Interpreting semantic relations in noun compounds via verb semantics. In *Proceedings of the 45th Annual Meeting of the Association of Computational Linguistics (COLING/ACL 2006) Main Conference Poster Sessions*, pages 491–498.

Mirella Lapata and Alex Lascarides. 2003. Detecting novel compounds: the role of distributional evidence. In *Proceedings of the 10th conference of the European chapter of the Association for Computational Linguistics (EACL 2003)*, pages 235–242.

Mark Lauer. 1995. *Designing Statistical Language Learners: Experiments on Noun Compounds*. Ph.D. thesis, Dept. of Computing, Macquarie University, Australia.

Judith Levi. 1978. *The Syntax and Semantics of Complex Nominals*. Academic Press, New York.

Preslav Nakov and Marti A. Hearst. 2006. Using verbs to characterize noun-noun relations. In *LNCS vol. 4183: Proceedings of the 12th international conference on Artificial Intelligence: Methodology, Systems and Applications (AIMSA 2006)*, pages 233–244. Springer.

Preslav Nakov and Marti A. Hearst. 2008. Solving relational similarity problems using the web as a corpus. In *Proceedings of the 46th Annual Meeting of the Association of Computational Linguistics (ACL 2008)*, pages 452–460.

Preslav Nakov. 2007. *Using the Web as an Implicit Training Set: Application to Noun Compound Syntax and Semantics*. Ph.D. thesis, EECS Department, University of California, Berkeley, UCB/EECS-2007-173.

Preslav Nakov. 2008a. Improved statistical machine translation using monolingual paraphrases. In *Proceedings of the 18th European Conference on Artificial Intelligence (ECAI'2008)*, pages 338–342.

Preslav Nakov. 2008b. Noun compound interpretation using paraphrasing verbs: Feasibility study. In *LNAI vol. 5253: Proceedings of the 13th international conference on Artificial Intelligence: Methodology, Systems and Applications (AIMSA 2008)*, pages 103–117. Springer.

Vivi Nastase and Stan Szpakowicz. 2003. Exploring noun-modifier semantic relations. In *Proceedings of the 5th International Workshop on Computational Semantics*, pages 285–301.

Diarmuid Ó Séaghdha and Ann Copestake. 2007. Co-occurrence contexts for noun compound interpretation. In *Proceedings of the Workshop on A Broader Perspective on Multiword Expressions*, pages 57–64.

Diarmuid Ó Séaghdha. 2008. *Learning Compound Noun Semantics*. Ph.D. thesis, University of Cambridge.

Barbara Rosario and Marti Hearst. 2001. Classifying the semantic relations in noun compounds via a domain-specific lexical hierarchy. In *Proceedings of the 2001 Conference on Empirical Methods in Natural Language Processing (EMNLP 2005)*, pages 82–90.

Mary Ellen Ryder. 1994. *Ordered Chaos: The Interpretation of English Noun-Noun Compounds*. University of California Press, Berkeley, CA.

Rion Snow, Brendan O'Connor, Daniel Jurafsky, and Andrew Ng. 2008. Cheap and fast – but is it good? evaluating non-expert annotations for natural language tasks. In *Proceedings of the 2008 Conference on Empirical Methods in Natural Language Processing (EMNLP 2008)*, pages 254–263.

Takaaki Tanaka and Timothy Baldwin. 2003. Noun-noun compound machine translation: a feasibility study on shallow processing. In *Proceedings of the ACL 2003 workshop on Multiword expressions*, pages 17–24.

Beatrice Warren. 1978. Semantic patterns of noun-noun compounds. In *Gothenburg Studies in English 41, Goteburg, Acta Universtatis Gothoburgensis*.

# SemEval-2010 Task 10: Linking Events and Their Participants in Discourse

**Josef Ruppenhofer** and **Caroline Sporleder**
Computational Linguistics
Saarland University
{josefr,csporled}@coli.uni-sb.de

**Roser Morante**
CNTS
University of Antwerp
Roser.Morante@ua.ac.be

**Collin Baker**
ICSI
Berkeley, CA 94704
collin@icsi.berkeley.edu

**Martha Palmer**
Department of Linguistics
University of Colorado at Boulder
martha.palmer@colorado.edu

## Abstract

In this paper, we describe the SemEval-2010 shared task on "Linking Events and Their Participants in Discourse". This task is a variant of the classical semantic role labelling task. The novel aspect is that we focus on linking local semantic argument structures across sentence boundaries. Specifically, the task aims at linking locally uninstantiated roles to their co-referents in the wider discourse context (if such co-referents exist). This task is potentially beneficial for a number of NLP applications and we hope that it will not only attract researchers from the semantic role labelling community but also from co-reference resolution and information extraction.

## 1 Introduction

Semantic role labelling (SRL) has been defined as a sentence-level natural-language processing task in which semantic roles are assigned to the syntactic arguments of a predicate (Gildea and Jurafsky, 2002). Semantic roles describe the function of the participants in an event. Identifying the semantic roles of the predicates in a text allows knowing who did what to whom when where how, etc.

SRL has attracted much attention in recent years, as witnessed by several shared tasks in Senseval/SemEval (Màrquez et al., 2007; Litkowski, 2004; Baker et al., 2007; Diab et al., 2007), and CoNLL (Carreras and Màrquez, 2004; Carreras and Màrquez, 2005; Surdeanu et al., 2008). The state-of-the-art in semantic role labelling has now advanced so much that a number of studies have shown that automatically inferred semantic argument structures can lead to tangible performance gains in NLP applications such as information extraction (Surdeanu et al., 2003), question answering (Shen and Lapata, 2007) or recognising textual entailment (Burchardt and Frank, 2006).

However, semantic role labelling as it is currently defined also misses a lot of information that would be beneficial for NLP applications that deal with text understanding (in the broadest sense), such as information extraction, summarisation, or question answering. The reason for this is that SRL has traditionally been viewed as a sentence-internal task. Hence, relations between different local semantic argument structures are disregarded and this leads to a loss of important semantic information.

This view of SRL as a sentence-internal task is partly due to the fact that large-scale manual annotation projects such as FrameNet[1] and PropBank[2] typically present their annotations lexicographically by lemma rather than by source text. Furthermore, in the case of FrameNet, the annotation effort did not start out with the goal of exhaustive corpus annotation but instead focused on isolated instances of the target words sampled from a very large corpus, which did not allow for a view of the data as 'full-text annotation'.

It is clear that there is an interplay between local argument structure and the surrounding discourse (Fillmore, 1977). In early work, Palmer et al. (1986) discussed filling null complements from context by using knowledge about individual predicates and ten-

[1] http://framenet.icsi.berkeley.edu/
[2] http://verbs.colorado.edu/~mpalmer/projects/ace.html



*Proceedings of the NAACL HLT Workshop on Semantic Evaluations: Recent Achievements and Future Directions*, pages 106–111,
Boulder, Colorado, June 2009. 

dencies of referential chaining across sentences. But so far there have been few attempts to find links between argument structures across clause and sentence boundaries explicitly on the basis of semantic relations between the predicates involved. Two notable exceptions are Fillmore and Baker (2001) and Burchardt et al. (2005). Fillmore and Baker (2001) analyse a short newspaper article and discuss how frame semantics could benefit discourse processing but without making concrete suggestions of how to model this. Burchardt et al. (2005) provide a detailed analysis of the links between the local semantic argument structures in a short text; however their system is not fully implemented either.

In the shared task, we intend to make a first step towards taking SRL beyond the domain of individual sentences by linking local semantic argument structures to the wider discourse context. In particular, we address the problem of finding fillers for roles which are neither instantiated as direct dependents of our target predicates nor displaced through long-distance dependency or coinstantatiation constructions. Often a referent for an uninstantiated role can be found in the wider context, i.e. in preceding or following sentences. An example is given in (1), where the CHARGES role (ARG2 in PropBank) of *cleared* is left empty but can be linked to *murder* in the previous sentence.

(1) In a lengthy court case the defendant was tried for murder. In the end, he was cleared.

Another very rich example is provided by (2), where, for instance, the experiencer and the object of jealousy are not overtly expressed as syntactic dependents of the noun *jealousy* but can be inferred to be Watson and the speaker, Holmes, respectively.

(2) Watson won't allow that I know anything of art but that is mere jealousy because our views upon the subject differ.

NIs are also very frequent in clinical reports. For example, in (3) the EXPERIENCER role of "cough", "tachypnea", and "breathing" can be linked to "twenty-two month old". Text mining systems in the biomedical domain focus on extracting relations between biomedical entities and information about patients. It is important that these systems extract information as accurately as possible. Thus, finding co-referents for NIs is also very relevant for improving results on mining relations in biomedical texts.

(3) Twenty-two month old with history of recurrent right middle lobe infiltrate. Increased cough, tachypnea, and work of breathing.

In the following sections we describe the task in more detail. We start by providing some background on null instantiations (Section 2). Section 3 gives an overview of the task, followed by a description of how we intend to create the data (Section 4). Section 5 provides a short description of how null instantiations could be resolved automatically given the provided data. Finally, Section 6 discusses the evaluation measures and we wrap up in Section 7.

## 2 Background on Null Instantiation

The theory of null complementation used here is the one adopted by FrameNet, which derives from the work of Fillmore (1986).[3] Briefly, omissions of core arguments of predicates are categorised along two dimensions, the licensor and the interpretation they receive. The idea of a licensor refers to the fact that either a particular lexical item or a particular grammatical construction must be present for the omission of a frame element (FE) to occur. For instance, the omission of the agent in (4) is licensed by the passive construction.

(4) No doubt, mistakes were made $0^{Protagonist}$.

The omission is a constructional omission because it can apply to any predicate with an appropriate semantics that allows it to combine with the passive construction. On the other hand, the omission in (5) is lexically specific: the verb *arrive* allows the Goal to be unspecified but the verb *reach*, also a member of the Arriving frame, does not.

(5) We arrived $0^{Goal}$ at 8pm.

The above two examples also illustrate the second major dimension of variation. Whereas, in (4) the protagonist making the mistake is only existentially bound within the discourse (instance of indefinite null

[3]Palmer et al.'s (1986) treatment of uninstantiated 'essential roles' is very similar (see also Palmer (1990)).

instantiation, INI), the Goal location in (5) is an entity that must be accessible to speaker and hearer from the discourse or its context (definite null instantiation, DNI). Finally note that the licensing construction or lexical item fully and reliably determines the interpretation. Missing by-phrases always have an indefinite interpretation and whenever *arrive* omits the Goal lexically, the Goal has to be interpreted as definite, as it is in (5).

The import of this classification to the task here is that we will concentrate on cases of DNI whether they are licensed lexically or constructionally.

## 3 Task Description

We plan to run the task in the following two modes:

**Full Task** For the full task we supply a test set in which the target words are marked and labelled with the correct sense (i.e. frame).[4] The participants then have to:

1. find the overt semantic arguments of the target (role recognition)
2. label them with the correct role (role labelling)
3. recognize definite null instantiations and find links to antecedents in the wider context (NI linking)

**NIs only** In the second mode, participants will be supplied with a test set which is annotated with gold standard local semantic argument structure.[5] The task is then restricted to recognizing that a core role is missing, ascertaining that it must have a definite interpretation and finding a filler for it (i.e., sub-task 3 from the full task).

The full task and the null instantiation linking task will be evaluated separately. By setting up a SRL task, we expect to attract participants from the established SRL community. Furthermore, by allowing participants to only address the second task, we hope to also attract researchers from areas such as coreference resolution or information extraction who do not want to implement a complete SRL system. We also plan to provide the data with both FrameNet and PropBank style annotations to encourage researchers from both areas to take part.

## 4 Data

The data will come from one of Arthur Conan Doyle's fiction works. We chose fiction rather than news because we believe that fiction texts with a linear narrative generally contain more context-resolvable null instantiations. They also tend to be longer and have a simpler structure than news texts which typically revisit the same facts repeatedly at different levels of detail (in the so-called 'inverted pyramid' structure) and which mix event reports with commentary and evaluation, thus sequencing material that is understood as running in parallel. Fiction texts should lend themselves more readily to a first attempt at integrating discourse structure into semantic role labeling. We chose Conan Doyle's work because most of his books are not subject to copyright restrictions anymore, which allows us to freely release the annotated data.

We plan to make the data sets available with both FrameNet and PropBank semantic argument annotation, so that participants can choose which framework they want to work in. The annotations will originally be made using FrameNet-style and will later be mapped semi-automatically to PropBank annotations. The data set for the FrameNet version of the task will be built at Saarland University, in close co-operation with the FrameNet team in Berkeley. We aim for the same density of annotation as is exhibited by FrameNet's existing full-text annotation[6] and are currently investigating whether the semantic argument annotation can be done semi-automatically, e.g., by starting the annotation with a run of the Shalmaneser role labeller (Erk and Padó, 2006), whose output is then corrected and expanded manually. To ensure a high annotation quality, at least part of the data will be annotated by two annotators and then manually adjudicated. We also provide detailed annotation guidelines (largely following the FrameNet

[4] We supply the correct sense to ensure that all systems use the same role inventory for each target (i.e., the role inventory associated with the gold standard sense). This makes it easier to evaluate the systems consistently with respect to role assignments and null instantiation linking, which is our main focus.

[5] The training set is identical for both set-ups and will contain the full annotation, i.e., frames, semantic roles and their fillers, and referents of null instantiations in the wider context (see Section 4 for details).

[6] `http://framenet.icsi.berkeley.edu/index.php?option=com_wrapper&Itemid=84`

guidelines) and any open questions are discussed in a weekly annotation meeting.

For the annotation of null instantiations and their links to the surrounding discourse we have to create new guidelines as this is a novel annotation task. We will adopt ideas from the annotation of co-reference information, linking locally unrealised roles to all mentions of the referents in the surrounding discourse, where available. We will mark only identity relations but not part-whole or bridging relations between referents. The set of unrealised roles under consideration includes only the core arguments but not adjuncts (peripheral or extra-thematic roles in FrameNet's terminology). Possible antecedents are not restricted to noun phrases but include all constituents that can be (local) role fillers for some predicate plus complete sentences (which can sometimes fill roles such as MESSAGE).

The data-set for PropBank will be created by mapping the FrameNet annotations onto PropBank and NomBank labels. For verbal targets, we use the Semlink[7] mappings. For nominal targets, there is no existing hand-checked mapping between FrameNet and NomBank but we will explore a way of building a FrameNet - NomBank mapping at least for eventive nouns indirectly with the help of Semlink. This would take advantage of the fact that PropBank verbs and eventive NomBank nouns both have a mapping to VerbNet classes, which are referenced also by Semlink. Time permitting, non-eventive nouns could be mapped manually. For FrameNet targets of other parts of speech, in particular adjectives and prepositions, no equivalent PropBank-style counterparts will be available. The result of the automatic mappings will be partly hand-checked. The annotations resolving null instantiations need no adjustment.

We intend to annotate at least two data sets of around 4,000 words. One set for testing and one for training. Because we realise that the training set will not be large enough to train a semantic role labelling system on it, we permit the participants to boost the training data for the SRL task by making use of the existing FrameNet and PropBank corpora.[8]

[7] `http://verbs.colorado.edu/semlink/`

[8] This may require some genre adaption but we believe this is feasible.

## 5 Resolving Null Instantiations

We conceive of null instantiation resolution as a three step problem. First, one needs to determine whether a core role is missing. This involves looking up which core roles are overtly expressed and which are not.

In the second step, one needs to determine what licenses an omission and what its interpretation is. To do this, one can use rules and heuristics based on various syntactic and lexical facts of English. As an example of a relevant syntactic fact, consider that subjects in English can only be omitted when licensed by a construction. One such construction is the imperative (e.g. *Please, sit down*). Since this construction also specifies that the missing referent must be the addressee of the speaker of the imperative, it is clear what referent one has to try to find.

As for using lexical knowledge, consider omissions of the Goods FE of the verb *steal* in the Theft frame. FrameNet annotation shows that whenever the Goods FE of *steal* is missing it is interpreted indefinitely, suggesting that a new instance of the FE being missing should have the same interpretation.

More evidence to the same effect can be derived using Ruppenhofer's (2004) observation that the interpretation of a lexically licensed omission is definite if the overt instances of the FE have mostly definite form (i.e. have definite determiners such as *that*, *the* , *this*), and indefinite if they are mostly indefinite (i.e. have bare or indefinite determiners such as *a(n)* or *some*). The morphology of overt instances of an FE could be inspected in the FrameNet data, or if the predicate has only one sense or a very dominant one, then the frequencies could even be estimated from unannotated corpora.

The third step is linking definite omissions to referents in the context. This linking problem could be modelled as a co-reference resolution task. While the work of Palmer et al. (1986) relied on special lexicons, one might instead want to learn information about the semantic content of different role fillers and then assess for each of the potential referents in the discourse context whether their semantic content is close enough to the expected content of the null instantiated role.

Information about the likely fillers of a role can be obtained from annotated data sets (e.g., FrameNet or PropBank). For instance, typical fillers of the

CHARGES role of *clear* might be *murder*, *accusations*, *allegations*, *fraud* etc. The semantic content of the role could then be represented in a vector space model, using additional unannotated data to build meaning vectors for the attested role fillers. Meaning vectors for potential role fillers in the context of the null instantiation could be built in a similar fashion. The likelihood of a potential filler filling the target role can then be modelled as the distance between the meaning vector of the filler and the role in the vector space model (see Padó et al. (2008) for a similar approach for semi-automatic SRL).

We envisage that the manually annotated null instantiated data can be used to learn additionally heuristics for the filler resolution task, such as information about the average distance between a null instantiation and its most recent co-referent.

## 6 Evaluation

As mentioned above we allow participants to address either the full role recognition and labelling task plus the linking of null instantiations or to make use of the gold standard semantic argument structure and look only at the null instantiations. We also permit systems to perform either FrameNet or PropBank style SRL. Hence, systems can be entered for four subtasks which will be evaluated separately:

- full task, FrameNet
- null instantiations, FrameNet
- full task, PropBank
- null instantiations, PropBank

The focus for the proposed task is on the null instantiation linking, however, for completeness, we also evaluate the standard SRL task. For role recognition and labelling we use a standard evaluation set-up, i.e., for role recognition we will evaluate the accuracy with respect to the manually created gold standard, for role labelling we will evaluate precision, recall, and F-Score.

The null instantiation linkings are evaluated slightly differently. In the gold standard, we will identify referents for null instantiations in the discourse context. In some cases, more than one referent might be appropriate, e.g., because the omitted argument refers to an entity that is mentioned multiple times in the context. In this case, a system should be given credit if the null instantiation is linked to any of these expressions. To achieve this we create equivalence sets for the referents of null instantiations. If the null instantiation is linked to any item in the equivalence set, the link is counted as a true positive. We can then define **NI linking precision** as the number of all true positive links divided by the number of links made by a system, and **NI linking recall** as the number of true positive links divided by the number of links between a null instantiation and its equivalence set in the gold standard. **NI linking F-Score** is then the harmonic mean between NI linking precision and recall.

Since it may sometimes be difficult to determine the correct extend of the filler of an NI, we score an automatic annotation as correct if it includes the head of the gold standard filler in the predicted filler. However, in order to not favour systems which link NIs to excessively large spans of text to maximise the likelihood of linking to a correct referent, we introduce a second evaluation measure, which computes the overlap (Dice coefficient) between the words in the predicted filler (P) of a null instantiation and the words in the gold standard one (G):

$$\textbf{NI linking overlap} = \frac{2|P \cap G|}{|P| + |G|} \quad (6)$$

Example (7) illustrates this point. The verb *won* in the second sentence evokes the Finish_competition frame whose COMPETITION role is null instantiated. From the context it is clear that the competition role is semantically filled by *their first TV debate* (head: *debate*) and *last night's debate* (head: *debate*) in the previous sentences. These two expressions make up the equivalence set for the COMPETITION role in the last sentence. Any system that would predict a linkage to a filler that covers the head of either of these two expressions would score a true positive for this NI. However, a system that linked to *last night's debate* would have an NI linking overlap of 1 (i.e., 2*3/(3+3)) while a system linking the whole second sentence *Last night's debate was eagerly anticipated* to the NI would have an NI linking overlap of 0.67 (i.e., 2*3/(6+3))

(7) US presidential rivals Republican John McCain and Democrat Barack Obama have yesterday evening attacked each other over

foreign policy and the economy, in [their first TV debate]$_{Competition}$. [Last night's debate]$_{Competition}$ was eagerly anticipated. Two national flash polls suggest that [Obama]$_{Competitor}$ <u>won</u>$_{Finish\_competition}$ $0^{Competition}$.

## 7 Conclusion

In this paper, we described the SemEval-2010 shared task on "Linking Events and Their Participants in Discourse". With this task, we intend to take a first step towards viewing semantic role labelling not as a sentence internal problem but as a task which should really take the discourse context into account. Specifically, we focus on finding referents for roles which are null instantiated in the local context. This is potentially useful for various NLP applications. We believe that the task is timely and interesting for a number of researchers not only from the semantic role labelling community but also from fields such as co-reference resolution or information extraction.

While our task focuses specifically on finding links between null instantiated roles and the discourse context, we hope that in setting it up, we can stimulate research on the interaction between discourse structure and semantic argument structure in general. Possible future editions of the task could then focus on additional connections between local semantic argument structures (e.g., linking argument structures that refer to the same event).

## 8 Acknowledgements

Josef Ruppenhofer and Caroline Sporleder are supported by the German Research Foundation DFG (under grant PI 154/9-3 and the Cluster of Excellence Multimodal Computing and Interaction (MMCI), respectively). Roser Morante's research is funded by the GOA project BIOGRAPH of the University of Antwerp.

## References

C. Baker, M. Ellsworth, and K. Erk. 2007. SemEval-2007 Task 19: Frame semantic structure extraction. In *Proceedings of SemEval-07.*

A. Burchardt and A. Frank. 2006. Approximating textual entailment with LFG and framenet frames. In *Proceedings of the Second Recognising Textual Entailment Workshop.*

A. Burchardt, A. Frank, and M. Pinkal. 2005. Building text meaning representations from contextually related frames – A case study. In *Proceedings of IWCS-6.*

X. Carreras and Ll. Màrquez. 2004. Introduction to the CoNLL-2004 shared task: Semantic role labeling. In *Proceedings of CoNLL-04*, pages 89–97.

X. Carreras and Ll. Màrquez. 2005. Introduction to the CoNLL-2005 shared task: Semantic role labeling. In *Proceedings of CoNLL-05*, pages 152–164.

M. Diab, M. Alkhalifa, S. ElKateb, C. Fellbaum, A. Mansouri, and M. Palmer. 2007. SemEval-2007 Task 18: Arabic semantic labeling. In *Proc. of SemEval-07.*

K. Erk and S. Padó. 2006. Shalmaneser - a flexible toolbox for semantic role assignment. In *Proceedings of LREC-06.*

C.J. Fillmore and C.F. Baker. 2001. Frame semantics for text understanding. In *Proc. of the NAACL-01 Workshop on WordNet and Other Lexical Resources.*

C.J. Fillmore. 1977. Scenes-and-frames semantics, linguistic structures processing. In Antonio Zampolli, editor, *Fundamental Studies in Computer Science, No. 59*, pages 55–88. North Holland Publishing.

C.J. Fillmore. 1986. Pragmatically controlled zero anaphora. In *Proceedings of the Twelfth Annual Meeting of the Berkeley Liguistics Society.*

D. Gildea and D. Jurafsky. 2002. Automatic labeling of semantic roles. *Computational Linguistics*, 28(3):245–288.

K. Litkowski. 2004. SENSEVAL-3 Task: Automatic labeling of semantic roles. In *Proc. of SENSEVAL-3.*

L. Màrquez, L. Villarejo, M. A. Martì, and M. Taulè. 2007. SemEval-2007 Task 09: Multilevel semantic annotation of Catalan and Spanish. In *Proceedings of SemEval-07.*

S. Padó, M. Pennacchiotti, and C. Sporleder. 2008. Semantic role assignment for event nominalisations by leveraging verbal data. In *Proceedings of Coling-2008.*

M. Palmer, D. Dahl, R. Passonneau, L. Hirschman, M. Linebarger, and J. Dowding. 1986. Recovering implicit information. In *Proceedings of ACL-1986.*

M. Palmer. 1990. *Semantic Processing for Finite Domains.* CUP, Cambridge, England.

J. Ruppenhofer. 2004. *The interaction of valence and information structure.* Ph.d., University of California, Berkeley, CA.

D. Shen and M. Lapata. 2007. Using semantic roles to improve question answering. In *Proc. of EMNLP-07.*

M. Surdeanu, S. Harabagiu, J. Williams, and P. Aarseth. 2003. Using predicate arguments structures for information extraction. In *Proceedings of ACL-2003.*

M. Surdeanu, R. Johansson, A. Meyers, Ll. Màrquez, and J. Nivre. 2008. The CoNLL-2008 shared task on joint parsing of syntactic and semantic dependencies. In *Proceedings of CoNLL-2008*, pages 159–177.

# SemEval-2010 Task 13: Evaluating Events, Time Expressions, and Temporal Relations (TempEval-2)

**James Pustejovsky**
Computer Science Department
Brandeis University
Waltham, Massachusetts, USA
jamesp@cs.brandeis.edu

**Marc Verhagen**
Computer Science Department
Brandeis University
Waltham, Massachusetts, USA
marc@cs.brandeis.edu

### Abstract

We describe the TempEval-2 task which is currently in preparation for the SemEval-2010 evaluation exercise. This task involves identifying the temporal relations between events and temporal expressions in text. Six distinct subtasks are defined, ranging from identifying temporal and event expressions, to anchoring events to temporal expressions, and ordering events relative to each other.

## 1 Introduction

Newspaper texts, narratives and other such texts describe events which occur in time and specify the temporal location and order of these events. Text comprehension, even at the most general level, involves the capability to identify the events described in a text and locate these in time. This capability is crucial to a wide range of NLP applications, from document summarization and question answering to machine translation. As in many areas of NLP, an open evaluation challenge in the area of temporal annotation will serve to drive research forward.

The automatic identification of all temporal referring expressions, events, and temporal relations within a text is the ultimate aim of research in this area. However, addressing this aim in a first evaluation challenge was deemed too difficult and a staged approach was suggested. The 2007 SemEval task, TempEval (henceforth TempEval-1), was an initial evaluation exercise based on three limited tasks that were considered realistic both from the perspective of assembling resources for development and testing and from the perspective of developing systems capable of addressing the tasks.

We are now preparing TempEval-2, a temporal evaluation task based on TempEval-1. TempEval-2 is more elaborate in two respects: (i) it is a multilingual task, and (ii) it consists of six subtasks rather than three.

## 2 TempEval-1

TempEval-1 consisted of three tasks:

A. determine the relation between an event and a timex in the same sentence;

B. determine the relation between an event and the document creation time;

C. determine the relation between the main events of two consecutive sentences.

The data sets were based on TimeBank (Pustejovsky et al., 2003; Boguraev et al., 2007), a hand-built gold standard of annotated texts using the TimeML markup scheme.[1] The data sets included sentence boundaries, TIMEX3 tags (including the special document creation time tag), and EVENT tags. For tasks A and B, a restricted set of events was used, namely those events that occur more than 5 times in TimeBank. For all three tasks, the relation labels used were BEFORE, AFTER, OVERLAP, BEFORE-OR-OVERLAP, OVERLAP-OR-AFTER and VAGUE.[2] For a more elaborate description of TempEval-1, see (Verhagen et al., 2007; Verhagen et al., 2009).

[1] See www.timeml.org for details on TimeML, TimeBank is distributed free of charge by the Linguistic Data Consortium (www.ldc.upenn.edu), catalog number LDC2006T08.

[2] Which is different from the set of 13 labels from TimeML. The set of labels for TempEval-1 was simplified to aid data preparation and to reduce the complexity of the task.



*Proceedings of the NAACL HLT Workshop on Semantic Evaluations: Recent Achievements and Future Directions*, pages 112–116, Boulder, Colorado, June 2009. 

There were six systems competing in TempEval-1: University of Colorado at Boulder (CU-TMP); Language Computer Corporation (LCC-TE); Nara Institute of Science and Technology (NAIST); University of Sheffield (USFD); Universities of Wolverhampton and Allicante (WVALI); and XEROX Research Centre Europe (XRCE-T).

The difference between these systems was not large, and details of system performance, along with comparisons and evaluation, are presented in (Verhagen et al., 2009). The scores for WVALI's hybrid approach were noticeably higher than those of the other systems in task B and, using relaxed scoring, in task C as well. But for task A, the highest scoring systems are barely ahead of the rest of the field. Similarly, for task C using strict scoring, there is no system that clearly separates itself from the field. Interestingly, the baseline is close to the average system performance on task A, but for other tasks the system scores noticeably exceed the baseline. Note that the XRCE-T system is somewhat conservative in assigning TLINKS for tasks A and B, producing lower recall scores than other systems, which in turn yield lower f-measure scores. For task A, this is mostly due to a decision only to assign a temporal relation between elements that can also be linked by the syntactic analyzer.

## 3 TempEval-2

The set of tasks chosen for TempEval-1 was by no means complete, but was a first step towards a fuller set of tasks for temporal parsing of texts. While the main goal of the division in subtasks was to aid evaluation, the larger goal of temporal annotation in order to create a complete temporal characterization of a document was not accomplished. Results from the first competition indicate that task A was defined too generally. As originally defined, it asks to temporally link all events in a sentence to all time expressions in the same sentence. A clearer task would have been to solicit local anchorings and to separate these from the less well-defined temporal relations between arbitrary events and times in the same sentence. We expect both inter-annotator agreement and system performance to be higher with a more precise subtask. Thus, the set of tasks used in TempEval-1 is far from complete and the tasks could have been made more restrictive. As a result, inter-annotator agreement scores lag, making precise evaluation more challenging.

The overall goal of temporal tagging of a text is to provide a temporal characterization of a set of events that is as complete as possible. If the annotation graph of a document is not completely connected then it is impossible to determine temporal relations between two arbitrary events because these events could be in separate subgraphs. Hence, for the current competition, TempEval-2, we have enriched the task description to bring us closer to creating such a temporal characterization for a text. We have enriched the TempEval-2 task definition to include six distinct subtasks:

A. Determine the extent of the time expressions in a text as defined by the TimeML TIMEX3 tag. In addition, determine value of the features TYPE and VAL. The possible values of TYPE are TIME, DATE, DURATION, and SET; the value of VAL is a normalized value as defined by the TIMEX2 and TIMEX3 standards.

B. Determine the extent of the events in a text as defined by the TimeML EVENT tag. In addition, determine the value of the features TENSE, ASPECT, POLARITY, and MODALITY.

C. Determine the temporal relation between an event and a time expression in the same sentence. For TempEval-2, this task is further restricted by requiring that either the event syntactically dominates the time expression or the event and time expression occur in the same noun phrase.

D. Determine the temporal relation between an event and the document creation time.

E. Determine the temporal relation between two main events in consecutive sentences.

F. Determine the temporal relation between two events where one event syntactically dominates the other event. This refers to examples like "she *heard* an *explosion*" and "he *said* they *postponed* the meeting".

The complete TimeML specification assumes the temporal interval relations as defined by Allen (Allen, 1983) in Figure 1.

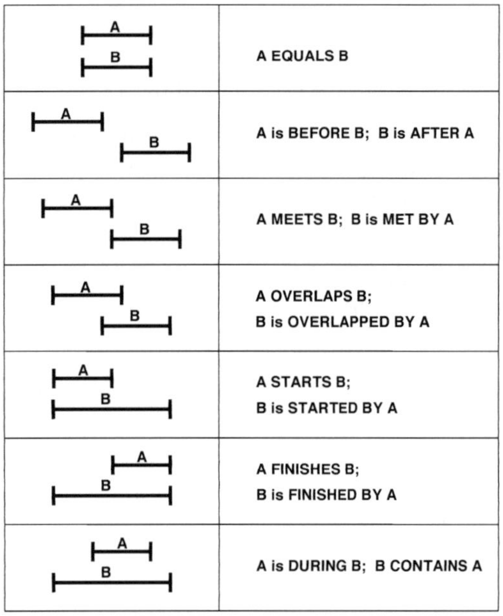


Figure 1: Allen Relations

For this task, however, we assume a reduced subset, as introduced in TempEval-1: BEFORE, AFTER, OVERLAP, BEFORE-OR-OVERLAP, OVERLAP-OR-AFTER and VAGUE. However, we are investigating whether for some tasks the more precise set of TimeML relations could be used.

Task participants may choose to either do all tasks, focus on the time expression task, focus on the event task, or focus on the four temporal relation tasks. In addition, participants may choose one or more of the five languages for which we provide data: English, Italian, Chinese, Spanish, and Korean.

### 3.1 Extent of Time Expression

This task involves identification of the EXTENT, TYPE, and VAL of temporal expressions in the text. Times can be expressed syntactically by adverbial or prepositional phrases, as shown in the following:

(1) a. on Thursday
 b. November 15, 2004
 c. Thursday evening
 d. in the late 80's
 e. Later this afternoon
 f. yesterday

The TYPE of the temporal extent must be identified. There are four temporal types that will be distinguished for this task;

(2) a. Time: *at 2:45 p.m.*
 b. Date: *January 27, 1920, yesterday*
 c. Duration *two weeks*
 d. Set: *every Monday morning*

The VAL attribute will assume values according to an extension of the ISO 8601 standard, as enhanced by TIMEX2.

(3) *November 22, 2004*

```
<TIMEX3 tid="t1" type="DATE"
value="2004-11-22"/>
```

### 3.2 Extent of Event Expression

The `EVENT` tag is used to annotate those elements in a text that describe what is conventionally referred to as an *eventuality*. Syntactically, events are typically expressed as inflected verbs, although event nominals, such as "crash" in *killed by the crash*, should also be annotated as `EVENTs`.

In this task, event extents must be identified and tagged with EVENT, along with values for the features TENSE, ASPECT, POLARITY, and MODALITY. Examples of these features are shown below:

(4) should have *bought*

```
<EVENT id="e1" pred="BUY" pos="VERB"
tense="PAST" aspect="PERFECTIVE"
modality="SHOULD" polarity="POS"/>
```

(5) did not *teach*

```
<EVENT id="e2" pred="TEACH" pos="VERB"
tense="PAST" aspect="NONE"
modality="NONE" polarity="NEG"/>
```

The specifics on the definition of event extent will follow the published TimeML guideline (cf. timeml.org).

### 3.3 Within-sentence Event-Time Anchoring

This task involves determining the temporal relation between an event and a time expression in the same sentence. This was present in TempEval-1, but here, in TempEval-2, this problem is further restricted by requiring that the event either syntactically dominates the time expression or the event and time expression occur in the same noun phrase. For example, the following constructions will be targeted for temporal labeling:

(6) Mary *taught*$_{e1}$ on *Tuesday morning*$_{t1}$
OVERLAP(e1,t1)

(7) They cancelled the *evening*$_{t2}$ *class*$_{e2}$
OVERLAP(e2,t2)

### 3.4 Neighboring Sentence Event-Event Ordering

In this task, the goal is to identify the temporal relation between two main events in consecutive sentences. This task was covered in the previous competition, and includes pairs such as that shown below:

(8) The President *spoke*$_{e1}$ to the nation on Tuesday on the financial crisis. He had *conferred*$_{e2}$ with his cabinet regarding policy the day before.
AFTER(e1,e2)

### 3.5 Sentence Event-DCT Ordering

This task was also included in TempEval-1 and requires the identification of the temporal order between the matrix event of the sentence and the Document Creation Time (DCT) of the article or text. For example, the text fragment below specifies a fixed DCT, relative to which matrix events from the two sentences are ordered:

(9) DCT: MARCH 5, 2009
a. Most troops will *leave*$_{e1}$ Iraq by August of 2010. AFTER(e1,dct)
b. The country *defaulted*$_{e2}$ on debts for that entire year. BEFORE(e2,dct)

### 3.6 Within-sentence Event-Event Ordering

The final task involves identifying the temporal relation between two events, where one event syntactically dominates the other event. This includes examples such as those illustrated below.

(10) The students *heard*$_{e1}$ a *fire alarm*$_{e2}$.
OVERLAP(e1,e2)

(11) He *said*$_{e1}$ they had *postponed*$_{e2}$ the meeting.
AFTER(e1,e2)

## 4 Resources and Evaluation

### 4.1 Data

The development corpus will contain the following data:

1. Sentence boundaries;
2. The document creation time (DCT) for each document;
3. All temporal expressions in accordance with the TimeML TIMEX3 tag;
4. All events in accordance with the TimeML EVENT tag;
5. Main event markers for each sentence;
6. All temporal relations defined by tasks C through F.

The data for the five languages are being prepared independently of each other. We do not provide a parallel corpus. However, annotation specifications and guidelines for the five languages will be developed in conjunction with one other. For some languages, we may not use all four temporal linking tasks. Data preparation is currently underway for English and will start soon for the other languages. Obviously, data preparation is a large task. For English and Chinese, the data are being developed at Brandeis University under three existing grants.

For evaluation data, we will provide two data sets, each consisting of different documents. DataSet1 is for tasks A and B and will contain data item 1 and 2 from the list above. DataSet2 is for tasks C though F and will contain data items 1 through 5.

### 4.2 Data Preparation

For all languages, annotation guidelines are defined for all tasks, based on version 1.2.1 of the TimeML annotation guidelines for English[3]. The most notable changes relative to the previous TimeML guidelines are the following:

- The guidelines are not all presented in one document, but are split up according to the seven TempEval-2 tasks. Full temporal annotation has proven to be a very complex task, splitting it into subtasks with separate guidelines for

[3]See `http://www.timeml.org`.

each task has proven to make temporal annotation more manageable.

- It is not required that all tasks for temporal linking (tasks C through F) use the same relation set. One of the goals during the data preparation phase is to determine what kind of relation set makes sense for each individual task.
- The guidelines can be different depending on the language. This is obviously required because time expressions, events, and relations are expressed differently across languages.

Annotation proceeds in two phases: a dual annotation phase where two annotators annotate each document and an adjudication phase where a judge resolves disagreements between the annotators. We are expanding the annotation tool used for TempEval-1, making sure that we can quickly annotate data for all tasks while making it easy for a language to define an annotation task in a slightly different way from another language. The Brandeis Annotation Tool (BAT) is a generic web-based annotation tool that is centered around the notion of annotation tasks. With the task decomposition allowed by BAT, it is possible to flexibly structure the complex task of temporal annotation by splitting it up in as many sub tasks as seems useful. As such, BAT is well-suited for TempEval-2 annotation. Comparison of annotation speed with tools that do not allow task decomposition showed that annotation with BAT is up to ten times faster. Annotation has started for Italian and English.

For all tasks, precision and recall are used as evaluation metrics. A scoring program will be supplied for participants.

## 5 Conclusion

In this paper, we described the TempEval-2 task within the SemEval 2010 competition. This task involves identifying the temporal relations between events and temporal expressions in text. Using a subset of TimeML temporal relations, we show how temporal relations and anchorings can be annotated and identified in five different languages. The markup language adopted presents a descriptive framework with which to examine the temporal aspects of natural language information, demonstrating in particular, how tense and temporal information is encoded in specific sentences, and how temporal relations are encoded between events and temporal expressions. This work paves the way towards establishing a broad and open standard metadata markup language for natural language texts, examining events, temporal expressions, and their orderings.

## References


James Allen. 1983. Maintaining knowledge about temporal intervals. *Communications of the ACM*, 26(11):832–843.

Bran Boguraev, James Pustejovsky, Rie Ando, and Marc Verhagen. 2007. Timebank evolution as a community resource for timeml parsing. *Language Resource and Evaluation*, 41(1):91–115.

James Pustejovsky, David Day, Lisa Ferro, Robert Gaizauskas, Patrick Hanks, Marcia Lazo, Roser Saurí, Andrew See, Andrea Setzer, and Beth Sundheim. 2003. The TimeBank Corpus. *Corpus Linguistics*, March.

Marc Verhagen, Robert Gaizauskas, Frank Schilder, Mark Hepple, Graham Katz, and James Pustejovsky. 2007. Semeval-2007 task 15: Tempeval temporal relation identification. In *Proc. of the Fourth Int. Workshop on Semantic Evaluations (SemEval-2007)*, pages 75–80, Prague, Czech Republic, June. Association for Computational Linguistics.

Marc Verhagen, Robert Gaizauskas, Frank Schilder, Mark Hepple, Jessica Moszkowicz, and James Pustejovsky. 2009. The tempeval challenge: identifying temporal relations in text. *Language Resources and Evaluation*.

# SemEval-2010 Task 14: Evaluation Setting for Word Sense Induction & Disambiguation Systems

**Suresh Manandhar**
Department of Computer Science
University of York
York, UK, YO10 5DD
*suresh@cs.york.ac.uk*

**Ioannis P. Klapaftis**
Department of Computer Science
University of York
York, UK, YO10 5DD
*giannis@cs.york.ac.uk*

## Abstract

This paper presents the evaluation setting for the SemEval-2010 Word Sense Induction (WSI) task. The setting of the SemEval-2007 WSI task consists of two evaluation schemes, i.e. *unsupervised evaluation* and *supervised evaluation*. The first one evaluates WSI methods in a similar fashion to Information Retrieval exercises using F-Score. However, F-Score suffers from the *matching problem* which does not allow: (1) the assessment of the entire membership of clusters, and (2) the evaluation of all clusters in a given solution. In this paper, we present the use of V-measure as a measure of objectively assessing WSI methods in an unsupervised setting, and we also suggest a small modification on the supervised evaluation.

## 1 Introduction

WSI is the task of identifying the different senses (uses) of a target word in a given text. WSI is a field of significant value, because it aims to overcome the limitations originated by representing word senses as a fixed-list of dictionary definitions. These limitations of hand-crafted lexicons include the use of general sense definitions, the lack of explicit semantic and topical relations between concepts (Agirre et al., 2001), and the inability to reflect the exact content of the context in which a target word appears (Véronis, 2004).

Given the significance of WSI, the objective assessment and comparison of WSI methods is crucial. The first effort to evaluate WSI methods under a common framework (evaluation schemes & dataset) was undertaken in the SemEval-2007 WSI task (SWSI) (Agirre and Soroa, 2007), where two separate evaluation schemes were employed. The first one, *unsupervised evaluation*, treats the WSI results as clusters of target word contexts and Gold Standard (GS) senses as classes. The traditional clustering measure of F-Score (Zhao et al., 2005) is used to assess the performance of WSI systems. The second evaluation scheme, *supervised evaluation*, uses the training part of the dataset in order to map the automatically induced clusters to GS senses. In the next step, the testing corpus is used to measure the performance of systems in a Word Sense Disambiguation (WSD) setting.

A significant limitation of F-Score is that it does not evaluate the make up of clusters beyond the majority class (Rosenberg and Hirschberg, 2007). Moreover, F-Score might also fail to evaluate clusters which are not matched to any GS class due to their small size. These two limitations define the *matching problem* of F-Score (Rosenberg and Hirschberg, 2007) which can lead to: (1) identical scores between different clustering solutions, and (2) inaccurate assessment of the clustering quality.

The supervised evaluation scheme employs a method in order to map the automatically induced clusters to GS senses. As a result, this process might change the distribution of clusters by mapping more than one clusters to the same GS sense. The outcome of this process might be more helpful for systems that produce a large number of clusters.

In this paper, we focus on analysing the SemEval-2007 WSI evaluation schemes showing their deficiencies. Subsequently, we present the use of V-



*Proceedings of the NAACL HLT Workshop on Semantic Evaluations: Recent Achievements and Future Directions*, pages 117–122,
Boulder, Colorado, June 2009. 

measure (Rosenberg and Hirschberg, 2007) as an evaluation measure that can overcome the current limitations of F-Score. Finally, we also suggest a small modification on the supervised evaluation scheme, which will possibly allow for a more reliable estimation of WSD performance. The proposed evaluation setting will be applied in the SemEval-2010 WSI task.

## 2 SemEval-2007 WSI evaluation setting

The SemEval-2007 WSI task (Agirre and Soroa, 2007) evaluates WSI systems on 35 nouns and 65 verbs. The corpus consists of texts of the Wall Street Journal corpus, and is hand-tagged with OntoNotes senses (Hovy et al., 2006). For each target word $tw$, the task consists of firstly identifying the senses of $tw$ (e.g. as clusters of target word instances, co-occurring words, etc.), and secondly tagging the instances of the target word using the automatically induced clusters. In the next sections, we describe and review the two evaluation schemes.

### 2.1 SWSI unsupervised evaluation

Let us assume that given a target word $tw$, a WSI method has produced 3 clusters which have tagged 2100 instances of $tw$. Table 1 shows the number of tagged instances for each cluster, as well as the common instances between each cluster and each gold standard sense.

F-Score is used in a similar fashion to Information Retrieval exercises. Given a particular gold standard sense $gs_i$ of size $a_i$ and a cluster $c_j$ of size $a_j$, suppose $a_{ij}$ instances in the class $gs_i$ belong to $c_j$. Precision of class $gs_i$ with respect to cluster $c_j$ is defined as the number of their common instances divided by the total cluster size, i.e. P$(gs_i, c_j) = \frac{a_{ij}}{a_j}$. The recall of class $gs_i$ with respect to cluster $c_j$ is defined as the number of their common instances divided by the total sense size, i.e. R$(gs_i, c_j) = \frac{a_{ij}}{a_i}$. The F-Score of $gs_i$ with respect to $c_j$, $F(gs_i, c_j)$, is then defined as the harmonic mean of $P(gs_i, c_j)$ and $R(gs_i, c_j)$.

The F-Score of class $gs_i$, $F(gs_i)$, is the maximum $F(gs_i, c_j)$ value attained at any cluster. Finally, the F-Score of the entire clustering solution is defined as the weighted average of the F-Scores of each GS sense (Formula 1), where $q$ is the number of GS senses and $N$ is the total number of target word instances. If the clustering is identical to the original classes in the datasets, F-Score will be equal to one. In the example of Table 1, F-Score is equal to 0.714.

| | $gs_1$ | $gs_2$ | $gs_3$ |
|---|---|---|---|
| $cl_1$ | 500 | 100 | 100 |
| $cl_2$ | 100 | 500 | 100 |
| $cl_3$ | 100 | 100 | 500 |

Table 1: Clusters & GS senses matrix.

$$F - Score = \sum_{i=1}^{q} \frac{|gs_i|}{N} F(gs_i) \quad (1)$$

As it can be observed, F-Score assesses the quality of a clustering solution by considering two different angles, i.e. *homogeneity* and *completeness* (Rosenberg and Hirschberg, 2007). Homogeneity refers to the degree that each cluster consists of data points, which primarily belong to a single GS class. On the other hand, completeness refers to the degree that each GS class consists of data points, which have primarily been assigned to a single cluster. A perfect homogeneity would result in a precision equal to 1, while a perfect completeness would result in a recall equal to 1.

Purity and entropy (Zhao et al., 2005) are also used in SWSI as complementary measures. However, both of them evaluate only the homogeneity of a clustering solution disregarding completeness.

### 2.2 SWSI supervised evaluation

In supervised evaluation, the target word corpus is split into a testing and a training part. The training part is used to map the automatically induced clusters to GS senses. In the next step, the testing corpus is used to evaluate WSI methods in a WSD setting.

Let us consider the example shown in Table 1 and assume that this matrix has been created by using the training part of our corpus. Table 1 shows that $cl_1$ is more likely to be associated with $gs_1$, $cl_2$ is more likely to be associated with $gs_2$, and $cl_3$ is more likely to be associated with $gs_3$. This information from the training part is utilised to map the clusters to GS senses.

Particularly, the matrix shown in Table 1 is normalised to produce a matrix $M$, in which each entry depicts the conditional probability $P(gs_i|cl_j)$. Given an instance $I$ of $tw$ from the testing corpus, a row cluster vector $IC$ is created, in which

| System | **F-Sc.** | Pur. | Ent. | # Cl. | **WSD** |
|---|---|---|---|---|---|
| 1c1w-MFS | 78.9 | 79.8 | 45.4 | 1 | 78.7 |
| UBC-AS | 78.7 | 80.5 | 43.8 | 1.32 | 78.5 |
| upv_si | 66.3 | 83.8 | 33.2 | 5.57 | 79.1 |
| UMND2 | 66.1 | 81.7 | 40.5 | 1.36 | 80.6 |
| I2R | 63.9 | 84.0 | 32.8 | 3.08 | 81.6 |
| UOY | 56.1 | 86.1 | 27.1 | 9.28 | 77.7 |
| 1c1inst | 9.5 | 100 | 0 | 139 | N/A |

Table 2: SWSI Unsupervised & supervised evaluation.

each entry $k$ corresponds to the score assigned to $cl_k$ to be the winning cluster for instance $I$. The product of $IC$ and $M$ provides a row sense vector, $IG$, in which the highest scoring entry $a$ denotes that $gs_a$ is the winning sense for instance $I$. For example, if we produce the row cluster vector $[cl_1 = 0.8, cl_2 = 0.1, cl_3 = 0.1]$, and multiply it with the normalised matrix of Table 1, then we would get a row sense vector in which $gs_1$ would be the winning sense with a score equal to 0.6.

### 2.3 SWSI results & discussion

Table 2 shows the unsupervised and supervised performance of systems participating in SWSI. As far as the baselines is concerned, the *1c1w* baseline groups all instances of a target word into a single cluster, while the *1c1inst* creates a new cluster for each instance of a target word. Note that the *1c1w* baseline is equivalent to the *MFS* in the supervised evaluation. As it can be observed, a system with low entropy (high purity) does not necessarily achieve high F-Score. This is due to the fact that entropy and purity only measure the homogeneity of a clustering solution. For that reason, the *1c1inst* baseline achieves a perfect entropy and purity, although its clustering solution is far from ideal.

On the contrary, F-Score has a significant advantage over purity and entropy, since it measures both homogeneity (precision) and completeness (recall) of a clustering solution. However, F-Score suffers from the *matching problem*, which manifests itself either by not evaluating the entire membership of a cluster, or by not evaluating every cluster (Rosenberg and Hirschberg, 2007). The former situation is present, due to the fact that F-Score does not consider the make-up of the clusters beyond the majority class (Rosenberg and Hirschberg, 2007). For example, in Table 3 the F-Score of the clustering solution is 0.714 and equal to the F-Score of the clustering solution shown in Table 1, although these are two significantly different clustering solutions. In fact, the clustering shown in Table 3 should have a better homogeneity than the clustering shown in Table 1, since intuitively speaking each cluster contains fewer classes. Moreover, the second clustering should also have a better completeness, since each GS class contains fewer clusters.

| | $gs_1$ | $gs_2$ | $gs_3$ |
|---|---|---|---|
| $cl_1$ | 500 | 0 | 200 |
| $cl_2$ | 200 | 500 | 0 |
| $cl_3$ | 0 | 200 | 500 |

Table 3: Clusters & GS senses matrix.

An additional instance of the *matching problem* manifests itself, when F-Score fails to evaluate the quality of smaller clusters. For example, if we add in Table 3 one more cluster ($cl_4$), which only tags 50 additional instances of $gs_1$, then we will be able to observe that this cluster will not be matched to any of the GS senses, since $cl_1$ is matched to $gs_1$. Although F-Score will decrease since the recall of $gs_1$ will decrease, the evaluation setting ignores the perfect homogeneity of this small cluster.

In Table 2, we observe that no system managed to outperform the *1c1w* baseline in terms of F-Score. At the same time, some systems participating in SWSI were able to outperform the equivalent of the *1c1w* baseline (MFS) in the supervised evaluation. For example, *UBC-AS* achieved the best F-Score close to the *1c1w* baseline. However, by looking at its supervised recall, we observe that it is below the MFS baseline.

A clustering solution, which achieves high supervised recall, does not necessarily achieve high F-Score. One reason for that stems from the fact that F-Score penalises systems for getting the number of GS classes wrongly, as in *1c1inst* baseline. According to Agirre & Soroa (2007), supervised evaluation seems to be more neutral regarding the number of induced clusters, because clusters are mapped into a weighted vector of senses, and therefore inducing a number of clusters similar to the number of senses is not a requirement for good results.

However, a large number of clusters might also lead to an unreliable mapping of clusters to GS senses. For example, high supervised recall also means high purity and low entropy as in *I2R*, but not vice versa as in *UOY*. *UOY* produces a large number of clean clusters, in effect suffering from an unreliable mapping of clusters to senses due to the lack of adequate training data.

Moreover, an additional supervised evaluation of WSI methods using a different dataset split resulted in a different ranking, in which all of the systems outperformed the MFS baseline (Agirre and Soroa, 2007). This result indicates that the supervised evaluation might not provide a reliable estimation of WSD performance, particularly in the case where the mapping relies on a single dataset split.

## 3 SemEval-2010 WSI evaluation setting

### 3.1 Unsupervised evaluation using V-measure

Let us assume that the dataset of a target word $tw$ comprises of $N$ instances (data points). These data points are divided into two partitions, i.e. a set of automatically generated clusters $C = \{c_j | j = 1 \ldots n\}$ and a set of gold standard classes $GS = \{gs_i | gs = 1 \ldots m\}$. Moreover, let $a_{ij}$ be the number of data points, which are members of class $gs_i$ and elements of cluster $c_j$.

V-measure assesses the quality of a clustering solution by explicitly measuring its homogeneity and its completeness (Rosenberg and Hirschberg, 2007). Recall that homogeneity refers to the degree that each cluster consists of data points which primarily belong to a single GS class. V-measure assesses homogeneity by examining the conditional entropy of the class distribution given the proposed clustering, i.e. $H(GS|C)$. $H(GS|C)$ quantifies the remaining entropy (uncertainty) of the class distribution given that the proposed clustering is known. As a result, when $H(GS|C)$ is 0, we have the perfectly homogeneous solution, since each cluster contains only those data points that are members of a single class. However in an imperfect situation, $H(GS|C)$ depends on the size of the dataset and the distribution of class sizes. As a result, instead of taking the raw conditional entropy, V-measure normalises it by the maximum reduction in entropy the clustering information could provide, i.e. $H(GS)$.

Formulas 2 and 3 define $H(GS)$ and $H(GS|C)$. When there is only a single class ($H(GS) = 0$), any clustering would produce a perfectly homogeneous solution. In the worst case, the class distribution within each cluster is equal to the overall class distribution ($H(GS|C) = H(GS)$), i.e. clustering provides no new information. Overall, in accordance with the convention of 1 being desirable and 0 undesirable, the homogeneity ($h$) of a clustering solution is 1 if there is only a single class, and $1 - \frac{H(GS|C)}{H(GS)}$ in any other case (Rosenberg and Hirschberg, 2007).

$$H(GS) = -\sum_{i=1}^{|GS|} \frac{\sum_{j=1}^{|C|} a_{ij}}{N} \log \frac{\sum_{j=1}^{|C|} a_{ij}}{N} \quad (2)$$

$$H(GS|C) = -\sum_{j=1}^{|C|}\sum_{i=1}^{|GS|} \frac{a_{ij}}{N} \log \frac{a_{ij}}{\sum_{k=1}^{|GS|} a_{kj}} \quad (3)$$

Symmetrically to homogeneity, completeness refers to the degree that each GS class consists of data points, which have primarily been assigned to a single cluster. To evaluate completeness, V-measure examines the distribution of cluster assignments within each class. The conditional entropy of the cluster given the class distribution, $H(C|GS)$, quantifies the remaining entropy (uncertainty) of the cluster given that the class distribution is known.

Consequently, when $H(C|GS)$ is 0, we have the perfectly complete solution, since all the data points of a class belong to the same cluster. Therefore, symmetrically to homogeneity, the completeness $c$ of a clustering solution is 1 if there is only a single cluster ($H(C) = 0$), and $1 - \frac{H(C|GS)}{H(C)}$ in any other case. In the worst case, completeness will be equal to 0, particularly when $H(C|GS)$ is maximal and equal to $H(C)$. This happens when each GS class is included in all clusters with a distribution equal to the distribution of sizes (Rosenberg and Hirschberg, 2007). Formulas 4 and 5 define $H(C)$ and $H(C|GS)$. Finally $h$ and $c$ can be combined and produce V-measure, which is the harmonic mean of homogeneity and completeness.

$$H(C) = -\sum_{j=1}^{|C|} \frac{\sum_{i=1}^{|GS|} a_{ij}}{N} \log \frac{\sum_{i=1}^{|GS|} a_{ij}}{N} \quad (4)$$

$$H(C|GS) = -\sum_{i=1}^{|GS|}\sum_{j=1}^{|C|} \frac{a_{ij}}{N} \log \frac{a_{ij}}{\sum_{k=1}^{|C|} a_{ik}} \quad (5)$$

Returning to our clustering example in Table 1, its V-measure is equal to 0.275. In section 2.3, we also presented an additional clustering (Table 3), which had the same F-Score as the clustering in Table 1, despite the fact that it intuitively had a better completeness and homogeneity. The V-measure of the second clustering solution is equal to 0.45, and higher than the V-measure of the first clustering. This result shows that V-measure is able to discriminate between these two clusterings by considering the make-up of the clusters beyond the majority class. Furthermore, it is straightforward from the description in this section, that V-measure evaluates each cluster in terms of homogeneity and completeness, unlike F-Score which relies on a post-hoc matching.

### 3.2 V-measure results & discussion

Table 4 shows the performance of SWSI participating systems according to V-measure. The last four columns of Table 4 show the weighted average homogeneity and completeness for nouns and verbs. Note that the homogeneity and completeness columns are weighted averages over all nouns or verbs, and are not used for the calculation of the weighted average V-measure (second column). The latter is calculated by measuring for each target word's clustering solution the harmonic mean of homogeneity and completeness separately, and then producing the weighted average.

As it can be observed in Table 4, all WSI systems have outperformed the random baseline which means that they have learned useful information. Moreover, Table 4 shows that on average all systems have outperformed the *1c1w* baseline, which groups the instances of a target word to a single cluster. The completeness of the *1c1w* baseline is equal to 1 by definition, since all instances of GS classes are grouped to a single cluster. However, this solution is as inhomogeneous as possible and causes a homogeneity equal to 0 in the case of nouns. In the verb dataset however, some verbs appear with only one sense, in effect causing the *1c1w* homogeneity to be equal to 1 in some cases, and the average V-measure greater than 0.

In Table 4, we also observe that the *1c1inst* baseline achieves a high performance. In nouns only *I2R* is able to outperform this baseline, while in verbs the *1c1inst* baseline achieves the highest result. By the definition of homogeneity (section 3.1), this baseline is perfectly homogeneous, since each cluster contains one instance of a single sense. However, its completeness is not 0, as one might intuitively expect. This is due to the fact that V-measure considers as the worst solution in terms of completeness the one, in which each class is represented by every cluster, and specifically with a distribution equal to the distribution of cluster sizes (Rosenberg and Hirschberg, 2007). This worst solution is not equivalent to the *1c1inst*, hence completeness of *1c1inst* is greater than 0. Additionally, completeness of this baseline benefits from the fact that around 18% of GS senses have only one instance in the test set. Note however, that on average this baseline achieves a lower completeness than most of the systems.

Another observation from Table 4 is that *upv_si* and *UOY* have a better ranking than in Table 2. Note that these systems have generated a higher number of clusters than the GS number of senses. In verbs *UOY* has been extensively penalised by the F-Score. The inspection of their answers shows that both systems generate highly skewed distributions, in which a small number of clusters tag the majority of instances, while a larger number tag only a few. As mentioned in sections 2.1 and 2.3, these small clusters might not be matched to any GS sense, hence they will decrease the unsupervised recall of a GS class, and consequently the F-Score. However, their high homogeneity is not considered in the calculation of F-Score. On the contrary, V-measure is able to evaluate the quality of these small clusters, and provide a more objective assessment.

Finally, in our evaluation we observe that *I2R* has on average the highest performance among the SWSI methods. This is due to its high V-measure in nouns, but not in verbs. Particularly in nouns, *I2R* achieves a consistent performance in terms of homogeneity and completeness without being biased towards one of them, as is the case for the rest of the systems. For example, *UOY* and *upv_si* achieve on average the highest homogeneity (42.5 & 32.8 resp.) and the worst completeness (11.5 & 13.2 resp.). The opposite picture is present for *UBC-AS* and *UMND2*. Despite that, *UBC-AS* and *UMND2* perform better than *I2R* in verbs, due to the small number of generated clusters (high completeness), and a reasonable homogeneity mainly due to the existence of verbs with one GS sense.

### 3.3 Modified supervised WSI evaluation

In section 2.3, we mentioned that supervised evaluation might favor methods which produce many

| System | V-measure | | | Homogeneity | | Completeness | |
|---|---|---|---|---|---|---|---|
| | **Total** | **Nouns** | **Verbs** | Nouns | Verbs | Nouns | Verbs |
| 1c1inst | 21.6 | 19.2 | 24.3 | 100.0 | 100.0 | 11.3 | 15.8 |
| I2R | 16.5 | 22.3 | 10.1 | 31.6 | 27.3 | 20.0 | 10.0 |
| UOY | 15.6 | 17.2 | 13.9 | 38.9 | 46.6 | 12.0 | 11.1 |
| upv_si | 15.3 | 18.2 | 11.9 | 37.1 | 28.0 | 14.5 | 11.8 |
| UMND2 | 12.1 | 12.0 | 12.2 | 18.1 | 15.3 | 55.8 | 63.6 |
| UBC-AS | 7.8 | 3.7 | 12.4 | 4.0 | 13.7 | 90.6 | 93.0 |
| Rand | 7.2 | 4.9 | 9.7 | 12.0 | 30.0 | 14.1 | 14.3 |
| 1c1w | 6.3 | 0.0 | 13.4 | 0.0 | 13.4 | 100.0 | 100.0 |

Table 4: V-Measure, homogeneity and completeness of SemEval-2007 WSI systems. The range of V-measure, homogeneity & completeness is 0-100.

clusters, since the mapping step can artificially increase completeness. Furthermore, we have shown that generating a large number of clusters might lead to an unreliable mapping of clusters to GS senses due to the lack of adequate training data.

Despite that, the supervised evaluation can be considered as an application-oriented evaluation, since it allows the transformation of unsupervised WSI systems to semi-supervised WSD ones. Given the great difficulty of unsupervised WSD systems to outperform the MFS baseline as well as the SWSI results, which show that some systems outperform the MFS by a significant amount in nouns, we believe that this evaluation scheme should be used to compare against supervised WSD methods.

In section 2.3, we also mentioned that the supervised evaluation on two different test/train splits provided a different ranking of methods, and more importantly a different ranking with regard to the MFS. To deal with that problem, we believe that it would be reasonable to perform $k$-fold cross validation in order to collect statistically significant information.

## 4 Conclusion

We presented and discussed the limitations of the SemEval-2007 evaluation setting for WSI methods. Based on our discussion, we described the use of V-measure as the measure of assessing WSI performance on an unsupervised setting, and presented the results of SWSI WSI methods. We have also suggested a small modification on the supervised evaluation scheme, which will allow for a more reliable estimation of WSD performance. The new evaluation setting will be applied in the SemEval-2010 WSI task.


## Acknowledgements

This work is supported by the European Commission via the EU FP7 INDECT project, Grant No. 218086, Research area: SEC-2007-1.2-01 Intelligent Urban Environment Observation System. The authors would like to thank the anonymous reviewers for their useful comments.


## References


Eneko Agirre and Aitor Soroa. 2007. Semeval-2007 task 02: Evaluating word sense induction and discrimination systems. In *Proceedings of the 4rth International Workshop on Semantic Evaluations*, pages 7–12, Prague, Czech Republic, June. ACL.

Eneko Agirre, Olatz Ansa, David Martinez, and Eduard Hovy. 2001. Enriching wordnet concepts with topic signatures. In *Proceedings of the NAACL workshop on WordNet and Other Lexical Resources: Applications, Extensions and Customizations*. ACL.

Eduard Hovy, Mitchell Marcus, Martha Palmer, Lance Ramshaw, and Ralph Weischedel. 2006. Ontonotes: The 90% solution. In *Proceedings of the Human Language Technology / North American Association for Computational Linguistics conference*, New York, USA.

Andrew Rosenberg and Julia Hirschberg. 2007. V-measure: A conditional entropy-based external cluster evaluation measure. In *Proceedings of the 2007 Joint Conference on Empirical Methods in Natural Language Processing and Computational Natural Language Learning (EMNLP-CoNLL)*, pages 410–420.

Jean Véronis. 2004. Hyperlex: lexical cartography for information retrieval. *Computer Speech & Language*, 18(3):223–252.

Ying Zhao, George Karypis, and Usam Fayyad. 2005. Hierarchical clustering algorithms for document datasets. *Data Mining and Knowledge Discovery*, 10(2):141–168.

# SemEval-2010 Task 17: All-words Word Sense Disambiguation on a Specific Domain


**Eneko Agirre**
IXA NLP group
UBC
Donostia, Basque Country
e.agirre@ehu.es

**Oier Lopez de Lacalle**
IXA NLP group
UBC
Donostia, Basque Country
oier.lopezdelacalle@ehu.es

**Christiane Fellbaum**
Department of Computer Science
Princeton University
Princeton, USA
fellbaum@princeton.edu

**Andrea Marchetti**
IIT
CNR
Pisa, Italy
andrea.marchetti@iit.cnr.it

**Antonio Toral**
ILC
CNR
Pisa, Italy
antonio.toral@ilc.cnr.it

**Piek Vossen**
Faculteit der Letteren
Vrije Universiteit Amsterdam
Amsterdam, Netherlands
p.vossen@let.vu.nl



## Abstract

Domain portability and adaptation of NLP components and Word Sense Disambiguation systems present new challenges. The difficulties found by supervised systems to adapt might change the way we assess the strengths and weaknesses of supervised and knowledge-based WSD systems. Unfortunately, all existing evaluation datasets for specific domains are lexical-sample corpora. With this paper we want to motivate the creation of an all-words test dataset for WSD on the environment domain in several languages, and present the overall design of this SemEval task.


## 1 Introduction

Word Sense Disambiguation (WSD) competitions have focused on general domain texts, as attested in the last Senseval and Semeval competitions (Kilgarriff, 2001; Mihalcea et al., 2004; Pradhan et al., 2007). Specific domains pose fresh challenges to WSD systems: the context in which the senses occur might change, distributions and predominant senses vary, some words tend to occur in fewer senses in specific domains, and new senses and terms might be involved. Both supervised and knowledge-based systems are affected by these issues: while the first suffer from different context and sense priors, the later suffer from lack of coverage of domain-related words and information.

Domain adaptation of supervised techniques is a hot issue in Natural Language Processing, including Word Sense Disambiguation. Supervised Word Sense Disambiguation systems trained on general corpora are known to perform worse when applied to specific domains (Escudero et al., 2000; Martínez and Agirre, 2000), and domain adaptation techniques have been proposed as a solution to this problem with mixed results.

Current research on applying WSD to specific domains has been evaluated on three available lexical-sample datasets (Ng and Lee, 1996; Weeber et al., 2001; Koeling et al., 2005). This kind of dataset contains hand-labeled examples for a handful of selected target words. As the systems are evaluated on a few words, the actual performance of the systems over complete texts can not be measured. Differences in behavior of WSD systems when applied to lexical-sample and all-words datasets have been observed on previous Senseval and Semeval competitions (Kilgarriff, 2001; Mihalcea et al., 2004; Pradhan et al., 2007): supervised systems attain results on the high 80's and beat the most frequent baseline by a large margin for lexical-sample datasets, but results on the all-words datasets were much more modest, on the low 70's, and a few points above the most frequent baseline.

Thus, the behaviour of WSD systems on domain-specific texts is largely unknown. While some words could be supposed to behave in similar ways, and thus be amenable to be properly treated by a generic



*Proceedings of the NAACL HLT Workshop on Semantic Evaluations: Recent Achievements and Future Directions*, pages 123–128,
Boulder, Colorado, June 2009. 

WSD algorithm, other words have senses closely linked to the domain, and might be disambiguated using purpose-built domain adaptation strategies (cf. Section 4). While it seems that domain-specific WSD might be a tougher problem than generic WSD, it might well be that domain-related words are easier to disambiguate.

The main goal of this task is to provide a multilingual testbed to evaluate WSD systems when faced with full-texts from a specific domain, that of environment-related texts. The paper is structured as follows. The next section presents current lexical sample datasets for domain-specific WSD. Section 3 presents some possible settings for domain adaptation. Section 4 reviews the state-of-the art in domain-specific WSD. Section 5 presents the design of our task, and finally, Section 6 draws some conclusions.

## 2 Specific domain datasets available

We will briefly present the three existing datasets for domain-related studies in WSD, which are all lexical-sample.

The most commonly used dataset is the Defense Science Organization (DSO) corpus (Ng and Lee, 1996), which comprises sentences from two different corpora. The first is the Wall Street Journal (WSJ), which belongs to the financial domain, and the second is the Brown Corpus (BC) which is a balanced corpora of English usage. 191 polysemous words (nouns and verbs) of high frequency in WSJ and BC were selected and a total of 192,800 occurrences of these words were tagged with WordNet 1.5 senses, more than 1,000 instances per word in average. The examples from BC comprise 78,080 occurrences of word senses, and examples from WSJ consist on 114,794 occurrences. In domain adaptation experiments, the Brown Corpus examples play the role of general corpora, and the examples from the WSJ play the role of domain-specific examples.

Koeling *et al.* (2005) present a corpus were the examples are drawn from the balanced BNC corpus (Leech, 1992) and the SPORTS and FINANCES sections of the newswire Reuters corpus (Rose et al., 2002), comprising around 300 examples (roughly 100 from each of those corpora) for each of the 41 nouns. The nouns were selected because they were salient in either the SPORTS or FINANCES domains, or because they had senses linked to those domains. The occurrences were hand-tagged with the senses from WordNet version 1.7.1 (Fellbaum, 1998). In domain adaptation experiments the BNC examples play the role of general corpora, and the FINANCES and SPORTS examples the role of two specific domain corpora.

Finally, a dataset for biomedicine was developed by Weeber *et al.* (2001), and has been used as a benchmark by many independent groups. The UMLS Metathesaurus was used to provide a set of possible meanings for terms in biomedical text. 50 ambiguous terms which occur frequently in MEDLINE were chosen for inclusion in the test set. 100 instances of each term were selected from citations added to the MEDLINE database in 1998 and manually disambiguated by 11 annotators. Twelve terms were flagged as "problematic" due to substantial disagreement between the annotators. In addition to the meanings defined in UMLS, annotators had the option of assigning a special tag ("none") when none of the UMLS meanings seemed appropriate.

Although these three corpora are useful for WSD research, it is difficult to infer which would be the performance of a WSD system on full texts. The corpus of Koeling et al., for instance, only includes words which where salient for the target domains, but the behavior of WSD systems on other words cannot be explored. We would also like to note that while the biomedicine corpus tackles scholarly text of a very specific domain, the WSJ part of the DSO includes texts from a financially oriented newspaper, but also includes news of general interest which have no strict relation to the finance domain.

## 3 Possible settings for domain adaptation

When performing supervised WSD on specific domains the first setting is to train on a general domain data set and to test on the specific domain (**source setting**). If performance would be optimal, this would be the ideal solution, as it would show that a generic WSD system is robust enough to tackle texts from new domains, and domain adaptation would not be necessary.

The second setting (**target setting**) would be to train the WSD systems only using examples from the target domain. If this would be the optimal setting, it would show that there is no cost-effective method for domain adaptation. WSD systems would need fresh examples every time they were deployed in new domains, and examples from general domains could be discarded.

In the third setting, the WSD system is trained with examples coming from both the general domain and the specific domain. Good results in this setting would show that **supervised domain adaptation** is working, and that generic WSD systems can be supplemented with hand-tagged examples from the target domain.

There is an additional setting, where a generic WSD system is supplemented with untagged examples from the domain. Good results in this setting would show that **semi-supervised domain adaptation** works, and that generic WSD systems can be supplemented with untagged examples from the target domain in order to improve their results.

Most of current all-words generic supervised WSD systems take SemCor (Miller et al., 1993) as their source corpus, i.e. they are trained on SemCor examples and then applied to new examples. SemCor is the largest publicly available annotated corpus. It's mainly a subset of the Brown Corpus, plus the novel The Red Badge of Courage. The Brown corpus is balanced, yet not from the general domain, as it comprises 500 documents drawn from different domains, each approximately 2000 words long. Although the Brown corpus is balanced, SemCor is not, as the documents were not chosen at random.

## 4 State-of-the-art in WSD for specific domains

Initial work on domain adaptation for WSD systems showed that WSD systems were not able to obtain better results on the source or adaptation settings compared to the target settings (Escudero et al., 2000), showing that a generic WSD system (i.e. based on hand-annotated examples from a generic corpus) would not be useful when moved to new domains.

Escudero et al. (2000) tested the supervised adaptation scenario on the DSO corpus, which had examples from the Brown Corpus and Wall Street Journal corpus. They found that the source corpus did not help when tagging the target corpus, showing that tagged corpora from each domain would suffice, and concluding that hand tagging a large general corpus would not guarantee robust broad-coverage WSD. Agirre and Martínez (2000) used the same DSO corpus and showed that training on the subset of the source corpus that is topically related to the target corpus does allow for domain adaptation, obtaining better results than training on the target data alone.

In (Agirre and Lopez de Lacalle, 2008), the authors also show that state-of-the-art WSD systems are not able to adapt to the domains in the context of the Koeling *et al.* (2005) dataset. While WSD systems trained on the target domain obtained 85.1 and 87.0 of precision on the sports and finances domains, respectively, the same systems trained on the BNC corpus (considered as a general domain corpus) obtained 53.9 and 62.9 of precision on sports and finances, respectively. Training on both source and target was inferior that using the target examples alone.

### Supervised adaptation

Supervised adaptation for other NLP tasks has been widely reported. For instance, (Daumé III, 2007) shows that a simple feature augmentation method for SVM is able to effectively use both labeled target and source data to provide the best domain-adaptation results in a number of NLP tasks. His method improves or equals over previously explored more sophisticated methods (Daumé III and Marcu, 2006; Chelba and Acero, 2004). In contrast, (Agirre and Lopez de Lacalle, 2009) reimplemented this method and showed that the improvement on WSD in the (Koeling et al., 2005) data was marginal.

Better results have been obtained using purpose-built adaptation methods. Chan and Ng (2007) performed supervised domain adaptation on a manually selected subset of 21 nouns from the DSO corpus. They used active learning, count-merging, and predominant sense estimation in order to save target annotation effort. They showed that adding just 30% of the target data to the source examples the same precision as the full combination of target and source data could be achieved. They also showed that using the source corpus significantly improved results when only 10%-30% of the target corpus was used for training. In followup work (Zhong et

*Projections for 2100 suggest that temperature in Europe will have risen by between 2 to 6.3 C above 1990 levels. The sea level is projected to rise, and a greater frequency and intensity of extreme weather events are expected. Even if emissions of greenhouse gases stop today, these changes would continue for many decades and in the case of sea level for centuries. This is due to the historical build up of the gases in the atmosphere and time lags in the response of climatic and oceanic systems to changes in the atmospheric concentration of the gases.*

Figure 1: Sample text from the environment domain.

al., 2008), the feature augmentation approach was combined with active learning and tested on the OntoNotes corpus, on a large domain-adaptation experiment. They significantly reduced the effort of hand-tagging, but only obtained positive domain-adaptation results for smaller fractions of the target corpus.

In (Agirre and Lopez de Lacalle, 2009) the authors report successful adaptation on the (Koeling et al., 2005) dataset on supervised setting. Their method is based on the use of unlabeled data, reducing the feature space with SVD, and combination of features using an ensemble of kernel methods. They report 22% error reduction when using both source and target data compared to a classifier trained on target the target data alone, even when the full dataset is used.

**Semi-supervised adaptation**

There are less works on semi-supervised domain adaptation in NLP tasks, and fewer in WSD task. Blitzer et al. (2006) used Structural Correspondence Learning and unlabeled data to adapt a Part-of-Speech tagger. They carefully select so-called pivot features to learn linear predictors, perform SVD on the weights learned by the predictor, and thus learn correspondences among features in both source and target domains. Agirre and Lopez de Lacalle (2008) show that methods based on SVD with unlabeled data and combination of distinct feature spaces produce positive semi-supervised domain adaptation results for WSD.

**Unsupervised adaptation**

In this context, we take unsupervised to mean Knowledge-Based methods which do not require hand-tagged corpora. The predominant sense acquisition method was succesfully applied to specific domains in (Koeling et al., 2005). The methos has two steps: In the first, a corpus of untagged text from the target domain is used to construct a thesaurus of similar words. In the second, each target word is disambiguated using pairwise WordNet-based similarity measures, taking as pairs the target word and each of the most related words according to the thesaurus up to a certain threshold. This method aims to obtain, for each target word, the sense which is the most predominant for the target corpus. When a general corpus is used, the most predominant sense in general is obtained, and when a domain-specific corpus is used, the most predominant sense for that corpus is obtained (Koeling et al., 2005). The main motivation of the authors is that the most frequent sense is a very powerful baseline, but it is one which requires hand-tagging text, while their method yields similar information automatically. The results show that they are able to obtain good results. In related work, (Agirre et al., 2009) report improved results using the same strategy but applying a graph-based WSD method, and highlight the domain-adaptation potential of unsupervised knowledge-based WSD systems compared to supervised WSD.

## 5 Design of the WSD-domain task

This task was designed in the context of Kyoto (Piek Vossen and VanGent, 2008)[1], an Asian-European project that develops a community platform for modeling knowledge and finding facts across languages and cultures. The platform operates as a Wiki system with an ontological support that social communities can use to agree on the meaning of terms in specific domains of their interest. Kyoto will focus on the environmental domain because it poses interesting challenges for information sharing, but the techniques and platforms will be independent of the application domain. Kyoto

[1] `http://www.kyoto-project.eu/`

will make use of semantic technologies based on ontologies and WSD in order to extract and represent relevant information for the domain, and is thus interested on measuring the performance of WSD techniques on this domain.

The WSD-domain task will comprise comparable all-words test corpora on the environment domain. Texts from the European Center for Nature Conservation[2] and Worldwide Wildlife Forum[3] will be used in order to build domain specific test corpora. We will select documents that are written for a general but interested public and that involve specific terms from the domain. The document content will be comparable across languages. Figure 1 shows an example in English related to global warming.

The data will be available in a number of languages: English, Dutch, Italian and Chinese. The sense inventories will be based on wordnets of the respective languages, which will be updated to include new vocabulary and senses. The test data will comprise three documents of around 2000 words each for each language. The annotation procedure will involve double-blind annotation plus adjudication, and inter-tagger agreement data will be provided. The formats and scoring software will follow those of Senseval-3[4] and SemEval-2007[5] English all-words tasks.

There will not be training data available, but participants are free to use existing hand-tagged corpora and lexical resources (e.g. SemCor and previous Senseval and SemEval data). We plan to make available a corpus of documents from the same domain as the selected documents, as well as wordnets updated to include the terms and senses in the selected documents.

## 6 Conclusions

Domain portability and adaptation of NLP components and Word Sense Disambiguation systems present new challenges. The difficulties found by supervised systems to adapt might change the way we assess the strengths and weaknesses of supervised and knowledge-based WSD systems. Unfortunately, all existing evaluation datasets for specific domains are lexical-sample corpora. With this paper we have motivated the creation of an all-words test dataset for WSD on the environment domain in several languages, and presented the overall design of this SemEval task.

Further details can be obtained from the Semeval-2010[6] website, our task website[7], and in our distribution list[8]

## 7 Acknowledgments

The organization of the task is partially funded by the European Commission (KYOTO FP7 ICT-2007-211423) and the Spanish Research Department (KNOW TIN2006-15049-C03-01).

## References

Eneko Agirre and Oier Lopez de Lacalle. 2008. On robustness and domain adaptation using SVD for word sense disambiguation. In *Proceedings of the 22nd International Conference on Computational Linguistics (Coling 2008)*, pages 17–24, Manchester, UK, August. Coling 2008 Organizing Committee.

Eneko Agirre and Oier Lopez de Lacalle. 2009. Supervised domain adaptation for wsd. In *Proceedings of the 12th Conference of the European Chapter of the Association for Computational Linguistics (EACL-09)*.

E. Agirre, O. Lopez de Lacalle, and A. Soroa. 2009. Knowledge-based WSD and specific domains: Performing over supervised WSD. In *Proceedings of IJ-CAI*, Pasadena, USA.

John Blitzer, Ryan McDonald, and Fernando Pereira. 2006. Domain adaptation with structural correspondence learning. In *Proceedings of the 2006 Conference on Empirical Methods in Natural Language Processing*, pages 120–128, Sydney, Australia, July. Association for Computational Linguistics.

Yee Seng Chan and Hwee Tou Ng. 2007. Domain adaptation with active learning for word sense disambiguation. In *Proceedings of the 45th Annual Meeting of the Association of Computational Linguistics*, pages 49–56, Prague, Czech Republic, June. Association for Computational Linguistics.

Ciprian Chelba and Alex Acero. 2004. Adaptation of maximum entropy classifier: Little data can help a lot. In *Proceedings of the Conference on Empirical Methods in Natural Language Processing (EMNLP)*, Barcelona, Spain.

[2]http://www.ecnc.org

[3]http://www.wwf.org

[4]http://www.senseval.org/senseval3

[5]http://nlp.cs.swarthmore.edu/semeval/

[6]http://semeval2.fbk.eu/

[7]http://xmlgroup.iit.cnr.it/SemEval2010/

[8]http://groups.google.com/groups/wsd-domain

Hal Daumé III and Daniel Marcu. 2006. Domain adaptation for statistical classifiers. *Journal of Artificial Intelligence Research*, 26:101–126.

Hal Daumé III. 2007. Frustratingly easy domain adaptation. In *Proceedings of the 45th Annual Meeting of the Association of Computational Linguistics*, pages 256–263, Prague, Czech Republic, June. Association for Computational Linguistics.

Gerard Escudero, Lluiz Márquez, and German Rigau. 2000. An Empirical Study of the Domain Dependence of Supervised Word Sense Disambiguation Systems. *Proceedings of the joint SIGDAT Conference on Empirical Methods in Natural Language Processing and Very Large Corpora, EMNLP/VLC.*

C. Fellbaum. 1998. *WordNet: An Electronic Lexical Database*. MIT Press.

A. Kilgarriff. 2001. English Lexical Sample Task Description. In *Proceedings of the Second International Workshop on evaluating Word Sense Disambiguation Systems*, Toulouse, France.

R. Koeling, D. McCarthy, and J. Carroll. 2005. Domain-specific sense distributions and predominant sense acquisition. In *Proceedings of the Human Language Technology Conference and Conference on Empirical Methods in Natural Language Processing. HLT/EMNLP*, pages 419–426, Ann Arbor, Michigan.

G. Leech. 1992. 100 million words of English: the British National Corpus. *Language Research*, 28(1):1–13.

David Martínez and Eneko Agirre. 2000. One Sense per Collocation and Genre/Topic Variations. *Conference on Empirical Method in Natural Language.*

R. Mihalcea, T. Chklovski, and Adam Killgariff. 2004. The Senseval-3 English lexical sample task. In *Proceedings of the 3rd ACL workshop on the Evaluation of Systems for the Semantic Analysis of Text (SENSEVAL)*, Barcelona, Spain.

G.A. Miller, C. Leacock, R. Tengi, and R.Bunker. 1993. A Semantic Concordance. In *Proceedings of the ARPA Human Language Technology Workshop. Distributed as* Human Language Technology *by San Mateo, CA: Morgan Kaufmann Publishers.*, pages 303–308, Princeton, NJ.

Hwee Tou Ng and Hian Beng Lee. 1996. Integrating multiple knowledge sources to disambiguate word sense: An exemplar-based approach. In *Proceedings of the 34th Annual Meeting of the Association for Computationla Linguistics (ACL)*, pages 40–47.

Nicoletta Calzolari Christiane Fellbaum Shu-kai Hsieh Chu-Ren Huang Hitoshi Isahara Kyoko Kanzaki Andrea Marchetti Monica Monachini Federico Neri Remo Raffaelli German Rigau Maurizio Tescon Piek Vossen, Eneko Agirre and Joop VanGent. 2008. Kyoto: a system for mining, structuring and distributing knowledge across languages and cultures. In European Language Resources Association (ELRA), editor, *Proceedings of the Sixth International Language Resources and Evaluation (LREC'08)*, Marrakech, Morocco, may.

Sameer Pradhan, Edward Loper, Dmitriy Dligach, and Martha Palmer. 2007. Semeval-2007 task-17: English lexical sample, srl and all words. In *Proceedings of the Fourth International Workshop on Semantic Evaluations (SemEval-2007)*, pages 87–92, Prague, Czech Republic.

Tony G. Rose, Mark Stevenson, and Miles Whitehead. 2002. The Reuters Corpus Volumen 1: from Yesterday's News to Tomorrow's Language Resources. In *Proceedings of the Third International Conference on Language Resources and Evaluation (LREC-2002)*, pages 827–832, Las Palmas, Canary Islands.

Marc Weeber, James G. Mork, and Alan R. Aronson. 2001. Developing a test collection for biomedical word sense disambiguation. In *Proceedings of the AMAI Symposium*, pages 746–750, Washington, DC.

Zhi Zhong, Hwee Tou Ng, and Yee Seng Chan. 2008. Word sense disambiguation using OntoNotes: An empirical study. In *Proceedings of the 2008 Conference on Empirical Methods in Natural Language Processing*, pages 1002–1010, Honolulu, Hawaii, October. Association for Computational Linguistics.

# Relation detection between named entities: report of a shared task

**Cláudia Freitas, Diana Santos**
**Cristina Mota**
SINTEF ICT
claudiafreitas@puc-rio.br
Diana.Santos@sintef.no
cmota@ist.utl.pt

**Hugo Gonçalo Oliveira**
CISUC, DEI - FCTUC
hroliv@dei.uc.pt

**Paula Carvalho**
Univ. Lisbon, FCUL, XLDB
pcc@di.fc.ul.pt

## Abstract

In this paper we describe the first evaluation contest (track) for Portuguese whose goal was to detect and classify relations between named entities in running text, called ReRelEM. Given a collection annotated with named entities belonging to ten different semantic categories, we marked all relationships between them within each document. We used the following fourfold relationship classification: identity, included-in, located-in, and other (which was later on explicitly detailed into twenty different relations). We provide a quantitative description of this evaluation resource, as well as describe the evaluation architecture and summarize the results of the participating systems in the track.

## 1 Motivation

Named entity recognition can be considered the first step towards semantic analysis of texts and a crucial subtask of information extraction systems. Proper names, besides their high frequency in language, do more than just refer – they convey additional information as instances of general semantic categories. But NE recognition is, as just mentioned, only the first step for full language processing. If we want to go beyond the detection of entities, a natural step is establishing semantic relations between these entities, and this is what this paper is about.

There are two fairly independent communities that focus on the task of detecting relations between named entities: the work on anaphora resolution, illustrated by (Mitkov, 2000; Collovini et al., 2007; de Souza et al., 2008) and the work on relation detection in information extraction, see e.g. (Agichtein and Gravano, 2000; Zhao and Grishman, 2005; Culotta and Sorensen, 2004). Although both communities are doing computational semantics, the two fields are largely non-overlapping, and one of the merits of our work is that we tried to merge the two.

Let us briefly describe both traditions: as (Mitkov, 2000) explains, anaphora resolution is concerned with studying the linguistic phenomenon of pointing back to another expression in the text. The semantic relations between the referents of these expressions can be of different types, being co-reference a special case when the relation is identity. The focus of anaphora resolution is determining the antecedent chains, although it implicitly also allows to elicit semantic relations between referents. This task has a long tradition in natural language processing (NLP) since the early days of artificial intelligence (Webber, 1978), and has from the start been considered a key ingredient in text understanding.

A different tradition, within information extraction and ontology building, is devoted to fact extraction. The detection of relations involving named entities is seen as a step towards a more structured model of the meaning of a text. The main concerns here (see e.g. (Zhao and Grishman, 2005)) are the extraction of large quantities of facts, generally coupled with machine learning approaches.[1]

Although mentions of named entities may ex-

[1]Other authors use the term *relation detection* in still other ways: for example, (Roth and tau Yih, 2004) use it for the translation of any natural language sentences into "logical form", as in *kill (x,y)*. This task does not concern us here.



*Proceedings of the NAACL HLT Workshop on Semantic Evaluations: Recent Achievements and Future Directions*, pages 129–137,
Boulder, Colorado, June 2009. 

| Relations | Works |
|---|---|
| orgBased-in, Headquarters, Org-Location, Based-in | RY, AG, DI, Sn, CS, ACE07, ACE04, ZG |
| live-in, Citizen-or-Resident | RY, ACE04, ZG, ACE07,CS |
| Employment, Membership, Subsidiary | ZG, CS, ACE04, ACE07 |
| located(in), residence, near | ACE04, ACE07,CS, ZG |
| work-for, Affiliate, Founder, Management, Client, Member, Staff | CS, ACE04, ACE07, RY, ZG |
| Associate, Grandparent, Parent, Sibling, Spouse, Other-professional, Other-relative, Other-personal | CS, ACE04, ACE07 |
| User, Owner,Inventor, Manufacturer | ACE04,ACE07, ZG, CS |
| DiseaseOutbreaks | AG |
| Metonymy | ACE07 |
| identity | ARE |
| synonym | ARE |
| generalisation | ARE |
| specialisation | ARE |

Table 1: Relations used in other works or evaluation contests.

press semantic relations other than identity or dependency, the main focus of the first school has been limited to co-reference. Yet, relations such as `part-of` have been considered under the label of indirect anaphora, also known as associative or bridging anaphora.

Contrarywise, the list of relations of interest for the second school is defined simply by world knowledge (not linguistic clues), and typical are the relations between an event and its location, or an organization and its headquarters. Obviously, these relations do occur between entities that do not involve (direct or indirect) anaphora in whatever broad understanding of the term.

Also, relation detection in the second school does not usually cover identity (cf. ACE's seven relation types): identity or co-reference is often considered an intermediate step before relation extraction (Culotta and Sorensen, 2004).

Table 1 displays a non-exhaustive overview of the different relations found in the literature.[2]

In devising the ReRelEM[3] pilot track, our goal was twofold: to investigate which relations could be found between named entities in Portuguese text, and how could a pilot task be devised that compared the performance of different automatic systems supposed to identify them. It should be emphasized that both MUC and ACE were key inspiration sources for ReRelEM, which stems from Linguateca's emphasis on evaluation.

In fact, we were conversant with MUC co-reference track and the way it was scored, as well as aware of two other related evaluation contests: ACE (Doddington et al., 2004; NIST and ACE, 2007), which extended MUC by dropping the requirement that entities had to be named, and ARE (Orăsan et al., 2008), which requested the identification of an anaphoric relation in certain types of pre-defined relations (identity, synonymy, generalization and specification), but which ignored indirect anaphora (that may convey meronymy, or inclusion, in a broad sense).

ReRelEM, although maintaining (or adding) the restriction to named entitites, is, from our point of view, an advance in the field of relation detection, since we proposed the detection (and classification) of all (relevant) kinds of relations between NEs in a document, providing thus both a merge and an extension of the previous evaluation campaigns.

[2]There is overlap between ACE 2007 and 2004 types of relations. In order to ease the comparison, we used the names of subtypes for ACE relations.

[3]ReRelEM stands for *Reconhecimento de Relações entre Entidades Mencionadas*, Portuguese for "recognition of relations between named entities", see (Freitas et al., 2008).

| Category/gloss | # |
|---|---|
| PESSOA/person | 196 |
| LOCAL/place | 145 |
| ORGANIZACAO/org | 102 |
| TEMPO/time | 84 |
| OBRA/title | 33 |
| VALOR/value | 33 |
| ACONTECIMENTO/event | 21 |
| ABSTRACCAO/abstraction | 17 |
| OUTRO/other | 6 |
| COISA/thing | 5 |

Table 2: Category distribution in the golden collection

## 2 Track description

The purpose of ReRelEM is to assess systems that try to recognize the most relevant relations between named entities, even if those relations do not involve coreference or anaphora.

### 2.1 Context

In order for it to be feasible in the short time we had, the track definition required that both referring expression and their semantic referent were named entities. Pronouns and definite descriptions were hence excluded. Note also that ReRelEM was defined in the context of the second edition of a larger evaluation contest dealing with NE detection and classification in Portuguese, HAREM (Santos et al., 2008) (for a detailed description of HAREM, in Portuguese, see also (Santos and Cardoso, 2007; Mota and Santos, 2008)). HAREM required systems to choose among ten categories (see Table 2), 43 types and 21 subtypes, the later concerning the categories TEMPO (time) and LOCAL (place).

So, it should be emphasized that ReRelEM focuses only on the classification and detection of the relations, not limiting in any way the kinds of (named) entities that can be related (as usualy done in other detection tasks). It only enforces the kinds of relations that must be identified.

### 2.2 Relation inventory

The establishment of an inventory of the most relevant relations between NEs is ultimately subjective, depending on the kind of information that each participant aims to extract. We have nevertheless done an exploratory study and annotated exhaustively a few texts to assess the most frequent and less controversial (or easier to assign) relations, and came up with just the following relation types for the task proposal:

- identity (`ident`);
- inclusion (`inclui` (includes) or `incluido` (included));
- placement (`ocorre-em` (occurs-in) or `sede-de` (place-of));
- other (`outra`)

For further description and examples see section 3.

However, during the process of building ReRelEM's golden collection (a subset of the HAREM collection used as gold standard), human annotation was felt to be more reliable – and also more understandable – if one specified what "other" actually meant, and so a further level of detail (twenty new relations) was selected and marked, see Table 3. (In any case, since this new refinement did not belong to the initial task description, all were mapped back to the coarser `outra` relation for evaluation purposes.)

### 2.3 ReRelEM features and HAREM requirements

The annotation process began after the annotation of HAREM's golden collection, that is, the relations started to be annotated after all NE had been tagged and totally revised. For ReRelEM, we had therefore no say in that process – again, ReRelEM was only concerned with the relations between the classified NEs. However, our detailed consideration of relations helped to uncover – and correct some mistakes in the original classification.

In order to explain the task(s) at hand, let us describe shortly ReRelEM's syntax: In ReRelEM's golden collection, each NE has a unique ID. A relation between NE is indicated by the additional attributes COREL (filled with the ID of the related entity) and TIPOREL (filled with the name of the relation) present in the NE that corresponds to one of the arguments of the relation. (Actually, there's no difference if the relation is marked in the first or in the second argument.)

One referring expression can be associated with one or more NEs through several semantic relations. In such cases, all possible relations must be assigned to the referring expression, in the form of a list, as illustrated by *UTAD* in Figure 1.

In this example, the NE with name *UTAD* (and id `ex1-42`) corresponds to an acronym of *Universidade de Trás-os-Montes e Alto Douro* (a university in Portugal), maintaining with this entity an identity relation (`ident`). The TIPOREL field of `ex1-42` contains another relation, `inclui`, which stands for the relation of inclusion, this time with the previously mentioned *Serviços Administrativos* (`ex1-40`), a specific department of the university.

In order to minimize human labour and also to let systems mark relations the way it would better suit them, we have postulated from the start that, for all purposes, it would be equivalent to annotate everything or just enough relations so that all others can be automatically computed. So, the evaluation programs, in an obvious extension of what was proposed in (Vilain et al., 1995) for identity,

1. add/expand all relations with their inverses (e.g., "A includes B" entails "B is included in A"), and

2. apply a set of expansion rules (see examples in Table 4) to compute the closure

As a consequence, different systems may tag the same text in different ways, but encoding the same knowledge.

### 2.4 What is a relevant relation?

An important difference as to what we expect as relevant relations should be pointed out: instead of requiring explicit (linguistic) clues, as in traditional research on anaphor, we look for all relations that may make sense in the specific context of the whole document. Let us provide two arguments supporting this decision:

- the first one is philosophical: the borders between world knowledge and contextual inference can be unclear in many cases, so it is not easy to distinguish them, even if we did believe in that separation in the first place;
- the second is practical: marking all possible relations is a way to also deal with unpredictable informational needs, for example for text mining applications. Take a sentence like "When I lived in Peru, I attended a horse show and was able to admire breeds I had known only from pictures before, like Falabella and Paso.". From this sentence, few people would infer that Paso is a Peruvian breed, but a horse specialist might at once see the connection. The question is: should one identify a relation between Peru and Paso in this document? We took the affirmative decision, assuming the existence of users interested in the topic: "relation of breeds to horse shows: are local breeds predominant?".

However, and since this was the first time such evaluation contest was run, we took the following measure: we added the attribute INDEP to the cases where the relation was not possible to be inferred by the text. In this way, it is possible to assess the frequency of these cases in the texts, and one may even filter them out before scoring the system runs to check their weight in the ranking of the systems. Interestingly, there were very few cases (only 6) marked INDEP in the annotated collection.

## 3 Qualitative relation description

Identity (or co-reference) does not need to be explained, although we should insist that this is not identity of expression, but of meaning. So the same string does not necessarily imply identity, cf.:

> Os adeptos do **Porto** invadiram a cidade do **Porto** em júbilo.[4]

Interestingly, even though organization is only the third most frequent category, Figure 2 shows that we found more co-reference among organizations than among any other category.

As to inclusion (see Figure 3), it was defined between NEs of the same sort, as the folowing examples, respectively illustrating LOCAL, PESSOA, OBRA and ORGANIZACAO, show:

> Centenas de pessoas recepcionaram no **Aeroporto da Portela** num clima de enorme entusiasmo e euforia, a selecção

[4]The (FC) Porto fans invaded the (city of) **Porto**, very happy

```
<EM ID="ex1-39" CATEG="PESSOA" TIPO="INDIVIDUAL"> Miguel Rodrigues</EM>
, chefe dos <EM ID="ex1-40" CATEG="ORGANIZACAO" TIPO="INSTITUICAO"
COREL="ex1-39" TIPOREL="outra">Serviços Administrativos</EM> da <EM
ID="ex1-41" CATEG="ORGANIZACAO" TIPO="INSTITUICAO" COREL="ex1-40"
TIPOREL="inclui"> Universidade de Trás-os-Montes e Alto Douro</EM> <EM
ID="ex1-42" CATEG="ORGANIZACAO" TIPO="INSTITUICAO" COREL="ex1-41 ex1-40"
TIPOREL="ident inclui">UTAD</EM>
```

Figure 1: Full example of ReRelEM syntax.

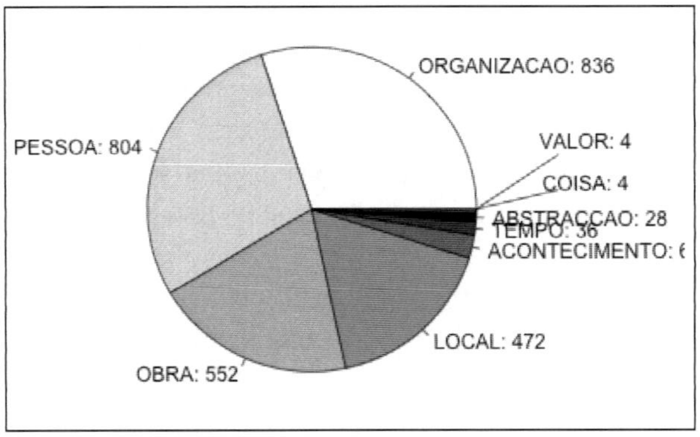


Figure 2: Distribution of NE categories for identity.

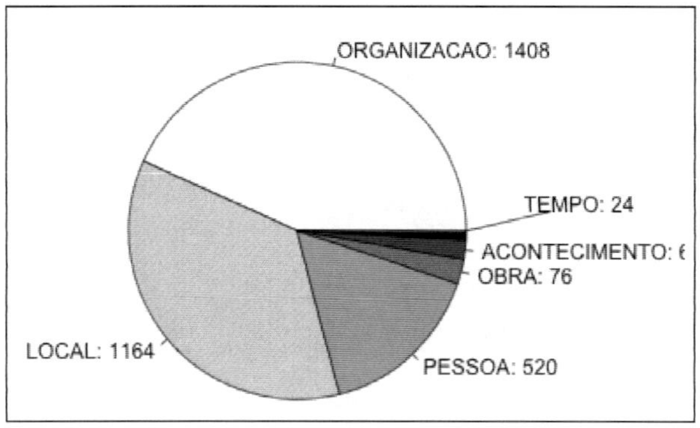


Figure 3: NE categories related by inclusion.

portuguesa de râguebi. A boa prestação global da equipa (...) não passou despercebida em **Portugal**.[5]

**Lewis Hamilton**, colega de Alonso na **McLaren**[6]

da assinatura do **Tratado de Lisboa** (...) de ver reconhecido o valor juridicamente vinculativo da **Carta** um passo "essencial no quadro de reforma dos **Tratados**[7]

por participar na cerimónia de proclamação da Carta dos Direitos Fundamentais da **UE** (...) salientou ainda o compromisso assumido pelas três instituições - **PE**[8]

Placement is clearly skewed towards placement of organizations (518 cases) as opposed to occurrence of events (just 98 instances). However, if we consider the relative distribution of organizations and events (see Table 2), we can state that, relative to their places, events have 4.8 relations in average and organizations 5.0, which is a far more interesting result, not favouring any of the NE classes.

Examples of this relation are:

**GP Brasil** – Não faltou emoção em Interlagos no **Circuito José Carlos Pace**[9]

As to the refinement of `outra`, Table 3 presents the relations found in the material.

### 3.1 Vague categories

It is important to stress that the basic tenets of HAREM had to be followed or reckoned with, not only the classification grid (see Table 2) but particularly the fact that some named entities are considered to be vague among different categories in

[5]Hundreds of people waited with enthusiasm and euphoria at the **Portela Airport** for the Portuguese national rugby team.(...) The team's good performance did not go unnoticed in **Portugal**

[6]**Lewis Hamilton**, Alonso's team-mate in **McLaren** – Note that, in HAREM, teams are considered groups of people, therefore an individual and a team have the same category PESSOA (person), but differ in the type.

[7]the signing of the **Lisbon Treaty** (...) juridically vinculative value of the **Charter**, a crucial step for the **Treaties** reform policy

[8]to participate in the proclamation ceremony of the Charter of Fundamental Rights of the **EU** (...) stressed the commitment assumed by the three institutions - **EP**

[9]**GP Brasil** – There was no lack of excitement in Interlagos at the **José Carlos Pace Circuit**.

| Relation / gloss | Number |
|---|---|
| vinculo-inst / inst-commitment | 936 |
| obra-de / work-of | 300 |
| participante-em / participant-in | 202 |
| ter-participacao-de / has-participant | 202 |
| relacao-familiar / family-tie | 90 |
| residencia-de / home-of | 75 |
| natural-de / born-in | 47 |
| relacao-profissional / professional-tie | 46 |
| povo-de / people-of | 30 |
| representante-de / representative-of | 19 |
| residente-de / living-in | 15 |
| personagem-de / character-of | 12 |
| periodo-vida / life-period | 11 |
| propriedade-de / owned-by | 10 |
| proprietario-de / owner-of | 10 |
| representado-por / represented-by | 7 |
| praticado-em / practised-in | 7 |
| outra-rel/other | 6 |
| nome-de-ident / name-of | 4 |
| outra-edicao / other-edition | 2 |

Table 3: Frequency of `other` relations.

HAREM.[10]

This last property, namely that named entities could belong to more than one category, posed some problems, since it was not straightforward whether different relations would involve all or just some (or one) category. So, in order to specify clearly the relations between vague NEs, we decided to specify separate relations between facets of vague named entities. Cf. the following example, in which vagueness is conveyed by a slash:

> (...) a ideia de uma **Europa** (LOCAL/PESSOA) unida. (...) um dia feliz para as cidadãs e os cidadãos da **União Europeia** (LOCAL). (...) Somos essencialmente uma comunidade de valores – são estes valores comuns que constituem o fundamento da **União Europeia** (ABSTRACCAO/ORG/LOCAL).[11]

The several relations between the three bold-faced NEs have been found to be as follows: The LOCAL facet of the first NE is identical with the LOCAL facets of the second and third NEs, while the ORG(ANIZACAO) facet of the third NE is located in the LOCAL facet of the second and first NEs. (Two kinds of relations are therefore involved here: `ident` and `inclui`.)

## 4 Evaluation: architecture and measures

Our first concern in this pilot track was to make a clear separation between the evaluation of relations and the evaluation of NE detection, which was the goal of HAREM. So, ReRelEM 's evaluation uses as a starting point the set of alignments that correspond to a mapping of the NE in the golden collection (GC) to a (candidate) NE in the participation.

Evaluation has the following stages:

- Maximization: the sets of relations annotated in both the GC and in the participation are maximized, applying the rules in Table 4;
- Selection: the alignments where the NE in the GC is different from the corresponding one in the participation are removed, and so are all relations held between removed NEs;
- Normalization: The identifiers of the NE in the participation are normalized in order to make it possible to compare the relations in both sides, given that each system uses its own identifiers.
- Translation: The alignments are translated to triples: `arg1 relation arg2`, where the arguments consist of the identifiers of the NE together with the facet, for example `x67 LOCAL sede-de ty45 ORGANIZACAO`.
- Filtering: removing relations of types not being evaluated (because HAREM, and therefore ReRelEM, allows for partial participation – and evaluation – scenarios[12]).
- Individual evaluation: the triples in the GC are compared to the triples in the participation.

[10] This is different from considering metonymy classes, in that no classifications are considered more basic than others, see (Santos, 2006) for vagueness as an intrinsic property of natural language.

[11] the idea of a united **Europe** (...) a happy day for the citizens of the **European Union** (...) We are mainly a community of values and these common values constitute the foundation of the **European Union**.

[12] In other words, it is possible to select a subset of the classification hierarchy.

| |
|---|
| $\mathrm{A}\ \texttt{ident}\ \mathrm{B} \wedge \mathrm{B}\ \texttt{ident}\ \mathrm{C} \Rightarrow \mathrm{A}\ \texttt{ident}\ \mathrm{C}$ |
| $\mathrm{A}\ \texttt{inclui}\ \mathrm{B} \wedge \mathrm{B}\ \texttt{inclui}\ \mathrm{C} \Rightarrow \mathrm{A}\ \texttt{inclui}\ \mathrm{C}$ |
| $\mathrm{A}\ \texttt{inclui}\ \mathrm{B} \wedge \mathrm{B}\ \texttt{sede\_de}\ \mathrm{C} \Rightarrow \mathrm{A}\ \texttt{sede\_de}\ \mathrm{C}$ |
| $\mathrm{A}\ \texttt{ident}\ \mathrm{B} \wedge \mathrm{B}\ \texttt{any\_rel}\ \mathrm{C} \Rightarrow \mathrm{A}\ \texttt{any\_rel}\ \mathrm{C}$ |

Table 4: Maximization rules

| System | NE task | Relations |
|---|---|---|
| Rembr. | all | all |
| SeRelEP | only identification | all but outra |
| SeiGeo | only LOCAL detection | inclusion |

Table 5: Participant systems

- Global evaluation: measures (precision, recall and F-measure) are calculated based on the score of each triple.

Each triple is scored as correct, missing or incorrect. We only considered as correct triples (and correct relations) those which linked the correct NEs and whose relation was well classified. So, a system doesn't score if it correctly matches the NEs to be related, but fails to recognize the kind of relation. We assign one point to each correct relation and none to incorrect or missing relations, and then we compute precision, recall and F-measure.

ReRelEM's golden collection includes 12 texts with 4,417 words and 573 NEs (corresponding to 642 different facets). In all we annotated 6,790 relations (1436 identity; 1612 inclusion; 1232 placement; 2510 other).

## 5 Participation and results

For this first edition, only three systems (totalling nine runs) participated, namely REMBRANDT (Cardoso, 2008), SEI-Geo (Chaves, 2008), and SeRelEP (Bruckschen et al., 2008), whose results are found in Figure 4. However, they did not compare well: they selected different NER tasks and different relation types, as shown in Table 5. So, given the little and diverse participation in ReRelEM, we cannot do a useful state of the art, but we were definitely able to provide an interesting and important resource for empirical studies and for training of future systems, as well as a set of publicly available programs to manipulate, evaluate and display this kind of semantic data[13].

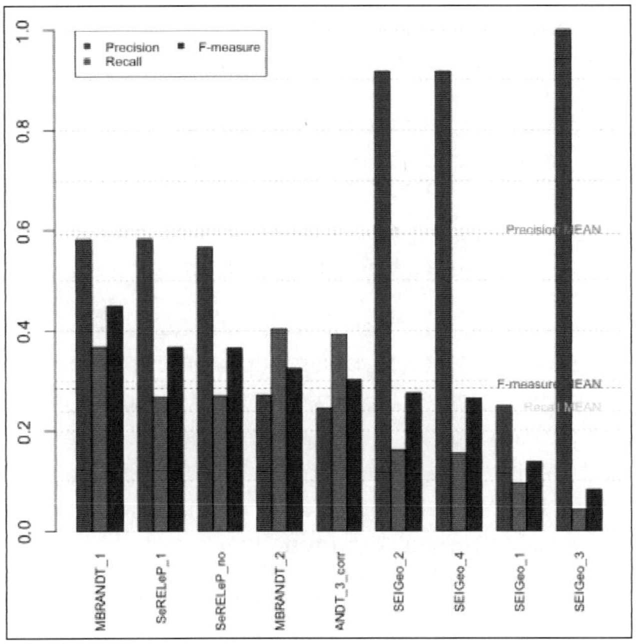


Figure 4: ReRelEM results: F-measure, all relations

## 6 Discussion and further work

Although this was just a pilot, a lot of knowledge about the task and the problems to be dealt with were gathered for the future, and important resources were offered to the community.

We intend to annotate further sections of the HAREM golden collection (as well as other kinds of texts and materials) with more relations in order to have more quantitative empirical data for studying the semantic fabric of Portuguese.

Although from an organization point of view it made sense to couple ReRelEM with HAREM, one should reflect over the consequences of inheriting a lot of decisions taken in HAREM, somehow going counter the intuitive and easier task of just annotating relations in a first round. However, despite initial fears to the contrary, we found out that the considerably fine-grained HAREM grid was in fact beneficial to the task of specifying relations: it is, after all, much more informative to have a relation of inclusion between a COISA-MEMBROCLASSE (concrete instance of a class of objects) and a COISA-CLASSE (a class of objects), than just a relation of inclusion

[13] http://www.linguateca.pt/HAREM/

tout court. In fact, in the next sentence, a kind of specialization relation can be uncovered.

> Astrônomos brasileiros esperam fotografar os primeiros planetas fora do Sistema Solar com a ajuda do maior telescópio do mundo, o *Gemini* (...) os telescópios Gemini têm capacidade científica...[14]

Likewise, an inclusion relation held between PESSOA-GRUPOCARGO (a group of roles performed by people) and PESSOA-INDIVIDUAL (an individual person) , as in the following example, is more informative than a simple relation of inclusion between NEs, or even inclusion between PESSOA entities without further discrimination.

> *Pöttering*, *Sócrates* e *Barroso* assinam Carta dos Direitos Fundamentais da UE. Depois de a Carta ser assinada pelos Presidentes das três instituições, ouviu-se o hino europeu...[15]

Furthermore, this relation is also different from an inclusion relation held between PESSOA-INDIVIDUAL (an individual) and PESSOA-GRUPOMEMBRO (a group of people):

> *Lobos* recebidos em apoteose. (...) o capitão Vasco Uva explicou por que houve uma empatia tão grande entre... [16]

Conversely, the specification of relations between different NEs in a text may help in detecting and justifying different facets of a particular NE, i.e., multiple semantic categories that should be assigned to it.

This illustrates the often observed case that it may be easier for a human annotator to decide and choose a specific issue than a too general one, and that therefore categories or choices should be more dependent on ease of human interpretation than quantitative factors (such as few categories or balanced ones).

[14]Brazilian astronomers expect to take the first pictures of planets beyond the solar system with the help of the largest telescope in the world, **Gemini** (...) **Gemini** telescopes have a capacity...

[15]**Pöttering**, **Sócrates** e **Barroso** sign the declaration... After being signed by the **Presidents** of the three institutions, ...

[16]**Lobos** received apoteothically. (...) Captain **Vasco Uva** explained why ...

For future work, we obviously intend to increase the size of the annotated collection (to the whole HAREM collection and even beyond), and investigate a couple of issues that interest us: which strategies are used to avoid repetition of proper names and establish textual cohesion? How do relations between noun phrases in general compare with relations between entities?

We would also like to investigate closer relationships between different relations: for example, is it more appropriate to also develop a hierarchy of relations, reconsidering, for example, `affiliation` (currently one of the `other`) as a kind of `inclusion`?

In order to understand better what this task is about, we would also like to investigate whether there are interesting correlations between NE categories and relations, as well as text genre and this sort of connectivity. Even though we only studied and annotated in depth 12 different texts, it was at once obvious that they had quite different properties as far as the number and kinds of relations was concerned.

From an evaluation point of view, we would like to improve our inconsistency detection programs and be able to reason about possible contradictions (of the annotation or of the interpretation) as well as experiment with different weights and evaluation measures, taking into account criteria such as predictability of relationships between NEs.

In any case, we believe this was an important first step to understand a number of issues and to reflect about what computational systems should be doing to harvest semantic knowledge. We would like to receive feedback on whether the task design seems sound to the rest of the community, and whether systems which would perform well in such task could be put to good use in real world applications.

## Acknowledgments

This work was done in the scope of the Linguateca project, jointly funded by the Portuguese Government and the European Union (FEDER and FSE) under contract ref. POSC/339/1.3/C/NAC.

## References


Eugene Agichtein and Luis Gravano. 2000. Snowball: Extracting Relations from Large Plain-Text Collections. In *Proc. of the 5th ACM International Conference on Digital Libraries (ACM DL)*, pages 85–94, San Antonio, Texas, USA, June, 2-7.

Mírian Bruckschen, José Guilherme Camargo de Souza, Renata Vieira, and Sandro Rigo. 2008. Sistema SeRELeP para o reconhecimento de relações entre entidades mencionadas. In Mota and Santos (Mota and Santos, 2008).

Nuno Cardoso. 2008. REMBRANDT - Reconhecimento de Entidades Mencionadas Baseado em Relações e ANálise Detalhada do Texto. In Mota and Santos (Mota and Santos, 2008).

Marcírio Chaves. 2008. Geo-ontologias e padrões para reconhecimento de locais e de suas relações em textos: o SEI-Geo no Segundo HAREM. In Mota and Santos (Mota and Santos, 2008).

Sandra Collovini, Thiago Ianez Carbonel, Juliana Thiesen Fuchs, Jorge César Coelho, Lucia Helena Machado Rino, and Renata Vieira. 2007. Summ-it: Um corpus anotado com informações discursivas visando à sumarização automática. In *Anais do XXVII Congresso da SBC: V Workshop em Tecnologia da Informação e da Linguagem Humana - TIL*, pages 1605–1614, Rio de Janeiro, RJ, Brazil, junho/julho.

Aron Culotta and Jeffrey Sorensen. 2004. Dependency tree kernels for relation extraction. In *Proceedings of the 42rd Annual Meeting of the Association for Computational Linguistics (ACL'04)*, pages 423–429. Association for Computational Linguistics, July.

José Guilherme Camargo de Souza, Patrícia Nunes Gonçalves, and Renata Vieira. 2008. Learning coreference resolution for portuguese texts. In António Teixeira, Vera Lúcia Strube de Lima, Luís Caldas de Oliveira, and Paulo Quaresma, editors, *PROPOR*, volume 5190 of *Lecture Notes in Computer Science*, pages 153–162. Springer.

Georde Doddington, Alexis Mitchell, Mark Przybocki, Lance Ramshaw, Stephanie Strassel, and Ralph Weischedel. 2004. The automatic content extraction (ace) programm. tasks, data and evaluation. In *Proceedings of the Fourth International Conference on Language Resources and Evaluation*, pages 837–840, Lisbon, Portugal.

Cláudia Freitas, Diana Santos, Hugo Gonçalo Oliveira, Paula Carvalho, and Cristina Mota. 2008. Relações semânticas do ReRelEM: além das entidades no Segundo HAREM. In Mota and Santos (Mota and Santos, 2008).

Ruslan Mitkov. 2000. Towards a more consistent and comprehensive evaluation of anaphora resolution algorithms and systems. In *Proceedings of the Discourse Anaphora and Anaphora Resolution Colloquium (DAARC-2000)*, pages 96–107, Lancaster, UK.

Cristina Mota and Diana Santos, editors. 2008. *Desafios no reconhecimento de entidades mencionadas: O Segundo HAREM*. Linguateca.

NIST and ACE. 2007. Automatic Content Extraction 2008 Evaluation Plan (ACE08) – Assessment of Detection and Recognition of Entities and Relations within and across Documents. Technical report, NIST.

Constantin Orăsan, Dan Cristea, Ruslan Mitkov, and Antonio Branco. 2008. Anaphora resolution exercise: An overview. In *Proceedings of the Sixth International Language Resources and Evaluation (LREC'08)*, Marrakech, Morocco, May, 28 - 30.

Dan Roth and Wen tau Yih. 2004. A linear programming formulation for global inference in natural language tasks. In *Proceedings of CoNLL-2004*, pages 1–8.

Diana Santos and Nuno Cardoso, editors. 2007. *Reconhecimento de entidades mencionadas em português: Documentação e actas do HAREM, a primeira avaliação conjunta na área*. Linguateca, Portugal.

Diana Santos, Cláudia Freitas, Hugo Gonçalo Oliveira, and Paula Carvalho. 2008. Second HAREM: new challenges and old wisdom. In António Teixeira, Vera Lúcia Strube de Lima, Luís Caldas de Oliveira, and Paulo Quaresma, editors, *Computational Processing of the Portuguese Language, 8th International Conference, Proceedings (PROPOR 2008)*, volume LNAI 5190, pages 212–215. Springer Verlag.

Diana Santos. 2006. What is natural language? Differences compared to artificial languages, and consequences for natural language processing, 15 May. Invited lecture, SBLP2006 and PROPOR'2006.

Marc Vilain, John Burger, John Aberdeen, Dennis Connolly, and Lynette Hirschman. 1995. A model-theoretic coreference scoring scheme. In *Proceedings of the Sixth Message Understanding Conference (MUC-6)*, pages 45–52. Morgan Kaufmann.

Bonnie Lynn Webber. 1978. *A formal approach to discourse anaphora*. Outstanding dissertations in linguistics. Garland Publishing, New York, NY, USA.

Shubin Zhao and Ralph Grishman. 2005. Extracting relations with integrated information using kernel methods. In *Proceedings of the 43rd Annual Meeting on Association for Computational Linguistics (ACL 2005)*, pages 419–426, Morristown, NJ, USA. Association for Computational Linguistics.

# Error Analysis of the TempEval Temporal Relation Identification Task

**Chong Min Lee**
Linguistics Department
Georgetown University
Washington, DC 20057, USA
cml54@georgetown.edu

**Graham Katz**
Linguistics Department
Georgetown University
Washington, DC 20057, USA
egk7@georgetown.edu

## Abstract

The task to classify a temporal relation between temporal entities has proven to be difficult with unsatisfactory results of previous research. In TempEval07 that was a first attempt to standardize the task, six teams competed with each other for three simple relation-identification tasks and their results were comparably poor. In this paper we provide an analysis of the TempEval07 competition results, identifying aspects of the tasks which presented the systems with particular challenges and those that were accomplished with relative ease.

## 1 Introduction

The automatic temporal interpretation of a text has long been an important area computational linguistics research (Bennett and Partee, 1972; Kamp and Reyle, 1993). In recent years, with the advent of the TimeML markup language (Pustejovsky et al., 2003) and the creation of the TimeBank resource (Pustejovsky et al., 2003) interest has focussed on the application of a variety of automatic techniques to this task (Boguraev and Ando, 2005; Mani et al., 2006; Bramsen et al., 2006; Chambers et al., 2007; Lee and Katz, 2008). The task of identifying the events and times described in a text and classifying the relations that hold among them has proven to be difficult, however, with reported results for relation classification tasks ranging in F-score from 0.52 to 0.60.

Variation in the specifics has made comparison among research methods difficult, however. A first attempt to standardize this task was the 2007 TempEval competition(Verhagen et al., 2007). This competition provided a standardized training and evaluation scheme for automatic temporal interpretation systems. Systems were pitted against one another on three simple relation-identification tasks. The competing systems made use of a variety of techniques but their results were comparable, but poor, with average system performance on the tasks ranging in F-score from 0.74 on the easiest task to 0.51 on the most difficult. In this paper we provide an analysis of the TempEval 07 competition, identifying aspects of the tasks which presented the systems with particular challenges and those that were accomplished with relative ease.

## 2 TempEval

The TempEval competition consisted of three tasks, each attempting to model an important subpart of the task of general temporal interpretation of texts. Each of these tasks involved identifying in running text the temporal relationships that hold among events and times referred to in the text.

- **Task A** was to identify the temporal relation holding between an event expressions and a temporal expression occurring in the same sentence.
- **Task B** was to identify the temporal relations holding between an event expressions and the Document Creation Time (DCT) for the text.
- **Task C** was to identify which temporal relation held between main events of described by sen-



*Proceedings of the NAACL HLT Workshop on Semantic Evaluations: Recent Achievements and Future Directions*, pages 138–145,
Boulder, Colorado, June 2009. ©2009 Association for Computational Linguistics

tences adjacent in text.

For the competition, training and development data—newswire files from the TimeBank corpus (Pustejovsky et al., 2003) —was made available in which the events and temporal expressions of interest were identified, and the gold-standard temporal relation was specified (a simplified set of temporal relations was used: BEFORE, AFTER, OVERLAP, OVERLAP-OR-BEFORE,AFTER-OR-OVERLAP and VAGUE.[1]). For evaluation, a set of newswire texts was provided in which the event and temporal expressions to be related were identified (with full and annotated in TimeML markup) but the temporal relations holding among them withheld. The task in was to identify these relations.

The text below allows illustrates the features of the TimeML markup that were made available as part of the training texts and which will serve as the basis for our analysis below:

```
<TIMEX3 tid="t13" type="DATE"
value="1989-11-02"
temporalFunction="false"
functionInDocument="CREATION_TIME">11/02/89
</TIMEX3> <s> Italian chemical giant
Montedison S.p.A. <TIMEX3 tid="t19"
type="DATE" value="1989-11-01"
temporalFunction="true"
functionInDocument="NONE"
anchorTimeID="t13">yesterday</TIMEX3
<EVENT eid="e2" class="OCCURRENCE"
stem="offer" aspect="NONE"
tense="PAST" polarity="POS"
pos="NOUN">offered</EVENT>
$37-a-share for all the common shares
outstanding of Erbamont N.V.</s>
<s>Montedison <TIMEX3 tid="t17"
type="DATE" value="PRESENT_REF"
temporalFunction="true"
functionInDocument="NONE"
anchorTimeID="t13">currently</TIMEX3>
<EVENT eid="e20" class="STATE"
stem="own" aspect="NONE"
tense="PRESENT" polarity="POS"
pos="VERB">owns</EVENT> about
72%of Erbamont's common shares
outstanding.</s>
```

TimeML annotation associates with temporal expression and event expression identifiers (tid and eid, respectively). Task A was to identify the temporal relationships holding between time t19 and event e2 and between t17 and e20 (OVERLAP was the gold-standard answer for both). Task B was to identify the relationship between the events and the document creation time t13 (BEFORE for e2 and OVERLAP for e20). Task C was to identify the relationship between e2 and e20 (OVERLAP-OR-BEFORE). The TempEval07 training data consisted of a total of 162 document. This amounted to a total of 1490 total relations for Task A, 2556 for task B, and 1744 for Task C. The 20 documents of testing data had 169 Task A relations, 337 Task B relations, and 258 Task C relations. The distribution of items by relation type in the training and test data is given in Table 1.

[1]This contrasts with the 13 temporal relations supported by TimeML. The full TimeML markup of event and temporal expressions was maintained.

| | Task A | Task B | Task C |
|---|---|---|---|
| CU-TMP | 60.9 | 75.2 | 53.5 |
| LCC-TE | 57.4 | 71.3 | 54.7 |
| NAIST | 60.9 | 74.9 | 49.2 |
| TimeBandits | 58.6 | 72.5 | 54.3 |
| WVALI | 61.5 | 79.5 | 53.9 |
| XRCE-T | 24.9 | 57.4 | 42.2 |
| average | 54.0 | 71.8 | 51.3 |

Table 2: TempEval Accuracy (%)

Six teams participated in the TempEval competition. They made use of a variety of techniques, from the application of off-the shelf machine learning tools to "deep" NLP. As indicated in Table 2[2], while the tasks varied in difficulty, within each task the results of the teams were, for the most part, comparable.[3]

The systems (other than XRCE-T) did somewhat to quite a bit better than baseline on the tasks.

Our focus here is on identifying features of the task that gave rise to difficult, using overall performance of the different systems as a metric. Of the 764 test items, a large portion were either 'easy'—meaning that all the systems provided correct output—or 'hard'—meaning none did.

| | Task A | Task B | Task C |
|---|---|---|---|
| All systems correct | 24 (14%) | 160 (45%) | 35 (14%) |
| No systems correct | 33 (20%) | 36 (11%) | 40 (16%) |

In task A, the cases (24/14%) that all participants make correct prediction are when the target relation is *overlap*. And, the part-of-speeches of most events

[2]TempEval was scored in a number of ways; we report accuracy of relation identification here as we will use this measure, and ones related to it below

[3]The XRCE-T team, which made use of the deep analysis engine XIP lightly modified for the competition, was a clear outlier.

| | Task A | Task B | Task C |
|---|---|---|---|
| BEFORE | 276(19%)/21(12%) | 1588(62%)/186(56%) | 434(25%)/59(23%) |
| AFTER | 369(25%)/30(18%) | 360(14%)/48(15%) | 306(18%)/42(16%) |
| OVERLAP | 742(50%)/97(57%) | 487(19%)/81(25%) | 732(42%)/122(47%) |
| BEFORE-OR-OVERLAP | 32(2%)/2(1%) | 47(2%)/8(2%) | 66(4%)/12(5%) |
| OVERLAP-OR-AFTER | 35(2%)/5(3%) | 35(1%)/2(1%) | 54(3%)/7(3%) |
| VAGUE | 36(2%)/14(8%) | 39(2%)/5(2%) | 152(9%)/16(6%) |

Table 1: Relation distribution of training/test sets

in the cases are verbs (19 cases), and their tenses are *past* (13 cases). In task B, among 160 cases for that every participant predicts correct temporal relation, 159 cases are *verbs*, 122 cases have *before* as target relation, and 112 cases are simple past tenses. In task C, we find that 22 cases among 35 cases are *reporting:reporting* with *overlap* as target relation. In what follows we will identify aspects of the tasks that make some items difficult and some not so much so.

## 3 Analysis

In order to make fine-grained distinctions and to compare arbitrary classes of items, our analysis will be stated in terms of a summary statistic: the *success measure* (SM).

(1) Success measure

$$\frac{\sum_{k=0}{}^{6} kC_k}{6(\sum_{k=0}{}^{6} C_k)}$$

where $C_k$ is the number of items $k$ systems got correct. This simply the proportion of total correct responses to items in a class (for all systems) divided by the total number of items in that class (a success measure of 1.0 is easy and of 0.0 is hard). For example, let's suppose *before* relation have 10 instances. Among the instances, three cases are correct by all teams, four by three teams, two by two teams, and one by no teams. Then, SM of *before* relation is 0.567 ($\frac{(3\times6)+(4\times3)+(2\times2)+(1\times0)}{6\times(1+2+4+3)}$).

In addition, we would like to keep track of how important each class of errors is to the total evaluation. To indicate this, we compute the *error proportion* (ER) for each class: the proportion of total errors attributable to that class.

(2) Error proportion

$$\frac{\sum_{k=0}{}^{6}(6-k)C_k}{AllErrorsInTask \times NumberOfTeams}$$

| | TaskA | TaskB | TaskC |
|---|---|---|---|
| BEFORE | 0.26/21% | 0.89/23% | 0.47/25% |
| AFTER | 0.42/24% | 0.56/23% | 0.48/17% |
| OVERLAP | 0.75/33% | 0.56/39% | 0.68/31% |
| BEFORE-OR-OVERLAP | 0.08/9% | 0/3% | 0.06/9% |
| OVERLAP-OR-AFTER | 0.03/2% | 0/1% | 0.10/5% |
| VAGUE | 0/19% | 0/5% | 0.02/12% |

Table 3: Overall performance by relation type (SM/ER)

When a case shows high SM and high ER, we can guess that the case has lots of instances. With low SM and low ER, it says there is little instances. With high SM and low ER, we don't need to focus on the case because the case show very good performance. Of particular interest are classes in which the SM is low and the ER is high because it has a room for the improvement.

### 3.1 Overall analysis

Table 3 provides the overall analysis by relation type. This shows that (as might be expected) the systems did best on the relations that were the majority class for each task: *overlap* in Task A, *before* in Task B, and *overlap* in Task C.

Furthermore systems do poorly on all of the disjunctive classes, with this accounting for between 1% and 9% of the task error. In what follows we will ignore the disjunctive relations. Performance on the *before* relation is low for Task A but very good for Task B and moderate for Task C. For more detailed analysis we treat each task separately.

### 3.2 Task A

For Task A we analyze the results with respect to the attribute information of the EVENT and TIMEX3 TimeML tags. These are the event class (*aspectual, i_action, i_state, occurrence, perception, reporting,* and *state*)[4] part-of-speech (basically *noun* and *verb*),

[4]The detailed explanations on the event classes can be found in the TimeML annotation guideline at

| | NOUN | VERB |
|---|---|---|
| BEFORE | 0/5% | 0.324/15% |
| AFTER | 0.119/8% | 0.507/15% |
| OVERLAP | 0.771/7% | 0.747/24% |
| VAGUE | 0/8% | 0/10% |

Table 4: POS of EVENT in Task A

and tense&aspect marking for event expressions. Information about the temporal expression turned out not to be a relevant dimension of analysis.

As we seen in Table 4, verbal event expressions make for easier classification for *before* and *after* (there is a 75%/25% verb/noun split in the data). When the target relation is *overlap*, nouns and verbs have similar SMs.

One reason for this difference, of course, is that verbal event expressions have tense and aspect marking (the tense and aspect marking for nouns is simply none).

In Table 5 we show the detailed error analysis with respect to tense and aspect values of the event expression. The combination of tense and aspect values of verbs generates 10 possible values: *future, infinitive, past, past-perfective, past-progressive (pastprog), past-participle (pastpart), present, present-perfective (presperf), present-progressive (presprog),* and *present-participle (prespart).* Among them, only five cases (*infinitive, past, present, presperf,* and *prespart*) have more than 2 examples in test data. *Past* takes the biggest portions (40%) in test data and in errors (33%). *Overlap* seems less influenced with the values of tense and aspect than *before* and *after* when the five cases are considered. *Before* and *after* show 0.444 and 0.278 differences between *infinitive* and *present* and between *infinitive* and *present*. But, *overlap* scores 0.136 differences between *present* and *past*. And a problem case is *before* with *past* tense that shows 0.317 SM and 9% EP.

When we consider simultaneously SM and EP of the semantic class of events in Table 6, we can find three noticeable cases: *occurrence* and *reporting* of *before*, and *occurrence* of *after*. All of them have over 5% EP and under 0.4 SM. In case of *reporting* of *after*, its SM is over 0.5 but its EP shows some room for the improvement.

`http://www.timeml.org/.`

| | BEFORE | AFTER | OVERLAP | VAGUE |
|---|---|---|---|---|
| FUTURE | 0/0% | 0.333/1% | 0.833/0% | 0/0% |
| INFINITIVE | 0/3% | 0.333/3% | 0.667/2% | 0/1% |
| NONE | 0/5% | 0.119/8% | 0.765/7% | 0/8% |
| PAST | **0.317/9%** | 0.544/9% | 0.782/10% | 0/5% |
| PASTPERF | 0/0% | 0.333/1% | 0.833/0% | 0/0% |
| PASTPROG | 0/0% | 0/0% | 0.500/1% | 0/0% |
| PRESENT | 0.444/2% | 0.611/2% | 0.646/4% | 0/1% |
| PRESPERF | 0.833/0% | 0/0% | 0.690/3% | 0/0% |
| PRESPROG | 0/0% | 0/0% | 0.833/0% | 0/0% |
| PRESPART | 0/0% | 0/0% | 0.774/4% | 0/1% |

Table 5: Tense & Aspect of EVENT in Task A

| | $\leq 4$ | $\leq 16$ | $> 16$ |
|---|---|---|---|
| BEFORE | 0/1% | **0.322/13%** | 0.133/6% |
| AFTER | 0.306/5% | **0.422/13%** | 0.500/5% |
| OVERLAP | 0.846/10% | 0.654/17% | 0.619/3% |
| VAGUE | 0/0% | 0/5% | **0/13%** |

Table 7: Distance in Task A

Boguraev and Ando (2005) report a slight increase in performance in relation identification based on proximity of the event expression to the temporal expression. We investigated this in Table 7, looking at the distance in word tokens.

We can see noticeable cases in *before* and *after* of $\leq$ 16 row. Both cases show over 13% EP and under 0.5 SM. The participants show good SM in *overlap* of $\leq$ 4. *Overlap* of $\leq$ 16 has the biggest EP (17%). When its less satisfactory SM (0.654) is considered, it seems to have a room for the improvement. One of the cases that have 13% EP is *vague* of $\geq$ 16. It says that it is difficult even for humans to make a decision on a temporal relation when the distance between an event and a temporal expression is greater than and equal to 16 words.

### 3.3 Task B

Task B is to identify a temporal relation between an EVENT and DCT. We analyze the participants performance with part-of-speech. This analysis shows how poor the participants are on *after* and *overlap* of nouns (0.167 and 0.115 SM). And the EM of *overlap* of verbs (26%) shows that the improvement is needed on it.

In test data, *occurrence* and *reporting* have similar number of examples: 135 (41%) and 106 (32%) in 330 examples. In spite of the similar distribution, their error rates show difference. It suggests that *reporting* is easier than *occurrence*. Moreover,

| | ASPECTUAL | I_ACTION | I_STATE | OCCURRENCE | PERCEPTION | REPORTING | STATE |
|---|---|---|---|---|---|---|---|
| BEFORE | 0.167/1% | 0/0% | 0.333/3% | **0.067/6%** | 0/0% | **0.364/9%** | 0/1% |
| AFTER | 0.111/3% | 0/0% | 0/0% | **0.317/9%** | 0/0% | **0.578/8%** | 0.167/2% |
| OVERLAP | 0.917/0% | 0.778/1% | 0.583/3% | 0.787/15% | 0.750/1% | 0.667/9% | 0.815/2% |
| VAGUE | 0/1% | 0/1% | 0/0% | 0/9% | 0/0% | 0/6% | 0/0% |

Table 6: EVENT Class in Task A

| | ASPECTUAL | I_ACTION | I_STATE | OCCURRENCE | PERCEPTION | REPORTING | STATE |
|---|---|---|---|---|---|---|---|
| BEFORE | 1/0% | 0.905/1% | 0.875/1% | **0.818/13%** | 0.556/1% | **0.949/5%** | 0.750/1% |
| AFTER | 0.500/3% | 0.500/1% | 0/0% | **0.578/15%** | 0.778/1% | 0.333/1% | 0.444/2% |
| OVERLAP | 0.625/2% | 0.405/5% | 0.927/1% | 0.367/17% | 0.500/1% | 0.542/6% | 0.567/7% |
| VAGUE | 0/1% | 0/0% | 0/0% | 0/4% | 0/0% | 0/0% | 0/0% |

Table 9: EVENT Class in Task B

| | NOUN | VERB |
|---|---|---|
| BEFORE | 0.735/6% | 0.908/16% |
| AFTER | 0.167/8% | 0.667/14% |
| OVERLAP | 0.115/13% | 0.645/26% |
| VAGUE | 0/4% | 0/1% |

Table 8: POS of EVENT in Task B

Table 9 shows most errors in *after* occur with *occurrence* class 65% (15%/23%) when we consider 23% EP in Table 3. *Occurrence* and *reporting* of *before* show noticeably good performance (0.818 and 0.949). And *occurrence* of *overlap* has the biggest error rate (17%) with 0.367 of SM.

In case of *state*, it has 22 examples (7%) but takes 10% of errors. And it is interesting that the most errors are concentrated in *state*. In our intuition, it is not a difficult task to identify *overlap* relation of *state* class.

Table 9 does not clearly show what causes the poor performance of nouns in *after* and *overlap*. In the additional analysis of nouns with class information, *occurrence* shows poor performance in *after* and *overlap*: 0.111/6% and 0.083/8%. And other noticeable case in nouns is *state* of *overlap*: 0.125/4%. We can see the low performance of nouns in *overlap* is due to the poor performance of *state* and *occurrence*, but only *occurrence* is a cause of the poor performance in *after*.

DCT can be considered as speech time. Then, tense and aspect of verb events can be a cue in predicting temporal relations between verb events and DCT. The better performance of the participants in verbs can be an indirect evidence. The analysis with tense & aspect can tell us which tense & aspect information is more useful. A problem with the information is sparsity. Most cases appear less than 3 times. The cases that have more than or equal to three instances are 13 cases among the possible combinations of 7 tenses and 4 aspects in TimeML. Moreover, only two cases are over 5% of the whole data: *past* with *before* (45%) and *present* with *overlap* (15%). In Table 10, tense and aspect information seems valuable in judging a relation between a verb event and DCT. The participants show good performances in the cases that seem easy intuitively: *past* with *before*, *future* with *after*, and *present* with *overlap*. Among intuitively obvious cases that are *past*, *present*, or *future* tense, present tense makes large errors (20% of verb errors). And *present* shows 7% EP in *before*.

When events has no cue to infer a relation like *infinitive*, *none*, *pastpart*, and *prespart*, their SMs are lower than 0.500 except *infinitive* and *none* of *after*. *infinitive* of *overlap* shows poor performance with the biggest error rate (0.125/12%).

### 3.4 Task C

The task is to identify the relation between consecutive main events. There are four part-of-speeches in Task C: *adjective*, *noun*, *other*, and *verb*. Among eight possible pairs of part-of-speeches, only three pairs have over 1% in 258 TLINKs: *noun* and *verb* (4%), *verb* and *noun* (4%), and *verb* and *verb* (85%). When we see the distribution of *verb* and *verb* by three relations (*before, after,* and *overlap*), the relations show 19%, 14%, and 41% distribution each. In Table 11, the best SM is *verb:verb* of *overlap* (0.690). And *verb:verb* shows around 0.5 SM in *before* and *after*.

Tense & aspect pairs of main event pairs show

| | BEFORE | AFTER | OVERLAP | VAGUE |
|---|---|---|---|---|
| FUTURE | 0/0% | 0.963/1% | 0.333/2% | 0/0% |
| FUTURE-PROGRESSIVE | 0/0% | 0/0% | 0.167/1% | 0/0% |
| INFINITIVE | 0.367/5% | 0.621/7% | 0.125/12% | 0/2% |
| NONE | 0/0% | 0.653/7% | 0/2% | 0/0% |
| PAST | **0.984/3%** | 0.333/1% | 0.083/3% | 0/0% |
| PASTPERF | 1.000/0% | 0/0% | 0/0% | 0/0% |
| PASTPROG | 1.000/0% | 0/0% | 0/0% | 0/0% |
| PASTPART | 0.583/1% | 0/0% | 0/0% | 0/0% |
| PRESENT | 0.429/7% | 0.167/3% | **0.850/10%** | 0/0% |
| PRESPERP | 0.861/3% | 0/0% | 0/2% | 0/0% |
| PRESENT-PROGRESIVE | 0/0% | 0/0% | 0.967/0% | 0/0% |
| PRESPART | 0/0% | 0.444/3% | 0.310/8% | 0/0% |

Table 10: Tense & Aspect of EVENT in Task B

| | BEFORE | AFTER | OVERLAP | VAGUE |
|---|---|---|---|---|
| NOUN:VERB | 0.250/2% | 0/0% | 0.625/1% | 0/0% |
| VERB:NOUN | 0.583/1% | 0.500/2% | 0.333/1% | 0/1% |
| VERB:VERB | 0.500/20% | 0.491/15% | **0.690/26%** | 0.220/12% |

Table 11: POS pairs in Task C

skewed distribution, too. The cases that have over 1% data are eight: *past:none, past:past, past:present, present:past, present:present, present:past, presperf:present,* and *presperf:presperf.* Among them, *past* tense pairs show the biggest portion (40%). The performance of the eight cases is reported in Table 12. As we can guess with the distribution of tense&aspect, most errors are from *past:past (40%)*. When the target relation of *past:past* is *overlap*, the participants show reasonable SM (0.723). But, their performances are unsatisfactory in *before* and *after*.

When we consider cases over 1% of test data in main event class pairs, we can see eleven cases as Table 13. Among the eleven cases, four pairs have over 5% data: *occurrence:occurrence* (13%), *occurrence:reporting* (14%), *reporting:occurrence* (9%), and *reporting:reporting* (17%). *Reporting:reporting* shows the best performance (0.934/2%) in *overlap*. Two class pairs have over 10% EP: *occurrence:occurrence* (15%), and *occurrence:reporting* (14%). In addition, *occurrence* pairs seem difficult tasks when target relations are *before* and *after* because they show low SMs (0.317 and 0.200) with 5% and 3% error rates.

## 4 Discussion and Conclusion

Our analysis shows that the participants have the difficulty in predicting a relation of a noun event when its target relation is *before* and *after* in Task A, and *after* and *overlap* in Task B. When the distance is in the range from 5 to 16 in Task A, more effort seems to be needed.

In Task B, tense and aspect information seems valuable. Six teams show good performance when simple tenses such as *past*, *present*, and *future* appear with intuitively relevant target relations such as *before*, *overlap*, and *after*. Their poor performance with *none* and *infinitive* tenses, and nouns can be another indirect evidence.

A difficulty in analyzing Task C is sparsity. So, this analysis is focused on *verb:verb* pair. When we can see in (12), *past* pairs still show the margin for the improvement. But, a lot of *reporting* events are used as main events. When we consider that important events in news paper are cited, the current TempEval task can miss useful information.

Six participants make very little correct predictions on *before-or-overlap, overlap-or-after,* and *vague*. A reason on the poor prediction can be small distribution in the training data as we can see in Table 1. Data sparsity problem is a bottleneck in natural language processing. The addition of the disjunctive relations and *vague* to the target labels can make the sparsity problem worse. When we consider the participants' poor performance on the labels, we suggest to use three labels (*before*, *overlap*, and *after*) as the target labels.

| | BEFORE | AFTER | OVERLAP | VAGUE |
|---|---|---|---|---|
| PAST:NONE | 0.750/1% | 0.167/1% | 0.167/3% | 0/0% |
| PAST:PAST | 0.451/12% | 0.429/10% | **0.723/11%** | 0.037/7% |
| PAST:PRESENT | 0.667/1% | 0/0% | 0.708/2% | 0/0% |
| PRESENT:PAST | 0/0% | 0.292/2% | 0.619/2% | 0/1% |
| PRESENT:PRESENT | 0.056/2% | 0/0% | 0.939/1% | 0/1% |
| PRESPERF:PAST | 0.500/0% | 0/0% | 0.542/1% | 0/0% |
| PRESPERF:PRESENT | 0/1% | 0/0% | 0.583/1% | 0/0% |
| PRESPERF:PRESPERF | 0/0% | 0/0% | 0.600/2% | 0/0% |

Table 12: Tense&Aspect Performance in Task C

| | BEFORE | AFTER | OVERLAP | VAGUE |
|---|---|---|---|---|
| I_ACTION:OCCURRENCE | 0.524/1% | 0.400/2% | 0.500/1% | 0/0% |
| I_STATE:OCCURRENCE | 0.250/1% | 0.500/1% | 0.833/0% | 0/0% |
| I_STATE:ASPECTUAL | 0/0% | 0.333/1% | 0.500/0% | 0/0% |
| OCCURRENCE:I_ACTION | 0.583/1% | 0.417/1% | 0.300/3% | 0/0% |
| OCCURRENCE:OCCURRENCE | 0.317/5% | 0.200/3% | 0.600/5% | 0/2% |
| OCCURRENCE:REPORTING | 0.569/4% | 0.367/3% | 0.594/5% | 0.111/2% |
| OCCURRENCE:STATE | 0.333/1% | 0/0% | 0.583/1% | 0/0% |
| REPORTING:I_STATE | 0.167/1% | 0.583/1% | 0.867/1% | 0/0% |
| REPORTING:OCCURRENCE | 0.625/1% | 0.611/3% | 0.542/3 | 0/2% |
| REPORTING:REPORTING | 0.167/1% | 0.167/2% | **0.934/2%** | 0/4% |

Table 13: Event class in Task C

Our analysis can be used as a cue in adding an additional module for weak points. When a pair of a noun event and a temporal expression appears in a sentence, a module can be added based on our study.

## References


Branimir Boguraev and Rie Kubota Ando. 2005. TimeML-Compliant Text Analysis for Temporal Reasoning. *Preceedings of IJCAI-05*, 997–1003.

James Pustejovsky, Patrick Hanks, Roser Sauri, Andrew See, David Day, Lisa Ferro, Robert Gaizauska, Marcia Lazo, Andrea Setzer, and Beth Sundheim. 2003. The TIMEBANK corpus. *Proceedings of Corpus Linguistics 2003*, 647–656.

Michael Bennett and Barbara Partee. 1972. Toward the logic of tense and aspect in English. *Technical report, System Development Corporation.* Santa Monica, CA

Philip Bramsen, Pawan Deshpande, Yoong Keok Lee, and Regina Barzilay. 2006. Inducing Temporal Graphs *Proceedings of EMNLP 2006*, 189–198.

Nathanael Chambers, Shan Wang, and Dan Jurafsky. 2007. Classifying Temporal Relations Between Events *Proceedings of ACL 2007*, 173–176.

Inderjeet Mani, Marc Verhagen, Ben Wellner, Chong Min Lee, and James Pustejovsky. 2006. Machine Learning of Temporal Relations. *Proceedings of ACL-2006*, 753–760.

Chong Min Lee and Graham Katz. 2008. Toward an Automated Time-Event Anchoring System. *The Fifth Midwest Computational Linguistics Colloquium.*

Hans Kamp and Uwe Reyle. 1993. *From Discourse to Logic: Introduction to modeltheoretic semantics of natural language.* Kluwer Academic, Boston.

James Pustejovsky, José Castaño, Robert Ingria, Roser Saurí, Robert Gaizauskas, Andrea Setzer, and Graham Katz. 2003. TimeML: Robust Specification of Event and Temporal Expressions in Text. *IWCS-5, Fifth International Workshop on Computational Semantics.*

Marc Verhagen, Robert Gaizauskas, Frank Schilder, Mark Hepple, Graham Katz, James Pustejovsky. 2007. SemEval-2007 Task 15: TempEval Temporal Relation Identification. *Proceedings of SemEval-2007*, 75–80.

Caroline Hagège and Xavier Tannier. 2007 XRCE-T: XIP Temporal Module for TempEval campaign. *Proceedings of the Fourth International Workshop on Semantic Evaluations (SemEval-2007)*, 492–495.

Steven Bethard and James H. Martin. 2007. CU-TMP: Temporal Relation Classification Using Syntactic and Semantic Features. *Proceedings of the Fourth International Workshop on Semantic Evaluations (SemEval-2007)*, 129–132.

Congmin Min, Munirathnam Srikanth, and Abraham Fowler. 2007. LCC-TE: A Hybrid Approach to Temporal Relation Identification in News Text. *Proceedings of the Fourth International Workshop on Semantic Evaluations (SemEval-2007)*, 219–222.

Yuchang Cheng, Masayuki Asahara, and Yuji Matsumoto. 2007. NAIST.Japan: Temporal Relation

Identification Using Dependency Parsed Tree. *Proceedings of the Fourth International Workshop on Semantic Evaluations (SemEval-2007)*, 245–248.

Georgiana Puşcaşu. 2007. WVALI: Temporal Relation Identification by Syntactico-Semantic Analysis *Proceedings of the Fourth International Workshop on Semantic Evaluations (SemEval-2007)*, 484–487.

Mark Hepple, Andrea Setzer, and Robert Gaizauskas. 2007. USFD: Preliminary Exploration of Features and Classifiers for the TempEval-2007 Task. *Proceedings of the Fourth International Workshop on Semantic Evaluations (SemEval-2007)*, 438–441.

# Automatic Recognition of Logical Relations for English, Chinese and Japanese in the GLARF Framework

**Adam Meyers**[†], **Michiko Kosaka**[‡], **Nianwen Xue**[◇], **Heng Ji**[⋆], **Ang Sun**[†], **Shasha Liao**[†] **and Wei Xu**[†]
[†] New York University, [‡]Monmouth University, [◇]Brandeis University, [⋆] City University of New York

## Abstract

We present GLARF, a framework for representing three linguistic levels and systems for generating this representation. We focus on a logical level, like LFG's F-structure, but compatible with Penn Treebanks. While less fine-grained than typical semantic role labeling approaches, our logical structure has several advantages: (1) it includes all words in all sentences, regardless of part of speech or semantic domain; and (2) it is easier to produce accurately. Our systems achieve 90% for English/Japanese News and 74.5% for Chinese News – these F-scores are nearly the same as those achieved for treebank-based parsing.

## 1 Introduction

For decades, computational linguists have paired a surface syntactic analysis with an analysis representing something "deeper". The work of Harris (1968), Chomsky (1957) and many others showed that one could use these deeper analyses to regularize differences between ways of expressing the same idea. For statistical methods, these regularizations, in effect, reduce the number of significant differences between observable patterns in data and raise the frequency of each difference. Patterns are thus easier to learn from training data and easier to recognize in test data, thus somewhat compensating for the spareness of data. In addition, deeper analyses are often considered semantic in nature because conceptually, two expressions that share the same regularized form also share some aspects of meaning. The specific details of this "deep" analysis have varied quite a bit, perhaps more than surface syntax.

In the 1970s and 1980s, Lexical Function Grammar's (LFG) way of dividing C-structure (surface) and F-structure (deep) led to parsers such as (Hobbs and Grishman, 1976) which produced these two levels, typically in two stages. However, enthusiasm for these two-stage parsers was eclipsed by the advent of one stage parsers with much higher accuracy (about 90% vs about 60%), the now-popular treebank-based parsers including (Charniak, 2001; Collins, 1999) and many others. Currently, many different "deeper" levels are being manually annotated and automatically transduced, typically using surface parsing and other processors as input. One of the most popular, semantic role labels (annotation and transducers based on the annotation) characterize relations anchored by select predicate types like verbs (Palmer et al., 2005), nouns (Meyers et al., 2004a), discourse connectives (Miltsakaki et al., 2004) or those predicates that are part of particular semantic frames (Baker et al., 1998). The CONLL tasks for 2008 and 2009 (Surdeanu et al., 2008; Hajič et al., 2009) has focused on unifying many of these individual efforts to produce a logical structure for multiple parts of speech and multiple languages.

Like the CONLL shared task, we link surface levels to logical levels for multiple languages. However, there are several differences: (1) The logical structures produced automatically by our system can be expected to be more accurate than the comparable CONLL systems because our task involves predicting semantic roles with less fine-grained distinctions. Our English and Japanese results were higher than the CONLL 2009 SRL systems. Our English F-scores range from 76.3% (spoken) to 89.9% (News):



*Proceedings of the NAACL HLT Workshop on Semantic Evaluations: Recent Achievements and Future Directions*, pages 146–154,
Boulder, Colorado, June 2009. 

the best CONLL 2009 English scores were 73.31% (Brown) and 85.63% (WSJ). Our Japanese system scored 90.6%: the best CONLL 2009 Japanese score was 78.35%. Our Chinese system 74.5%, 4 points lower than the best CONLL 2009 system (78.6%), probably due to our system's failings, rather than the complexity of the task; (2) Each of the languages in our system uses the same linguistic framework, using the same types of relations, same analyses of comparable constructions, etc. In one case, this required a conversion from a different framework to our own. In contrast, the 2009 CONLL task puts several different frameworks into one compatible input format. (3) The logical structures produced by our system typically connect all the words in the sentence. While this is true for some of the CONLL 2009 languages, e.g., Czech, it is not true about all the languages. In particular, the CONLL 2009 English and Chinese logical structures only include noun and verb predicates.

In this paper, we will describe the GLARF framework (Grammatical and Logical Representation Framework) and a system for producing GLARF output (Meyers et al., 2001; Meyers, 2008). GLARF provides a logical structure for English, Chinese and Japanese with an F-score that is within a few percentage points of the best parsing results for that language. Like LFG's (LFG) F-structure, our logical structure is less fine-grained than many of the popular semantic role labeling schemes, but also has two main advantages over these schemes: it is more reliable and it is more comprehensive in the sense that it covers all parts of speech and the resulting logical structure is a connected graph. Our approach has proved adequate for three genetically unrelated natural languages: English, Chinese and Japanese. It is thus a good candidate for additional languages with accurate parsers.

## 2 The GLARF framework

Our system creates a multi-tiered representation in the GLARF framework, combining the theory underlying the Penn Treebank for English (Marcus et al., 1994) and Chinese (Xue et al., 2005) (Chomskian linguistics of the 1970s and 1980s) with: (2) Relational Grammar's graph-based way of representing "levels" as sequences of relations; (2) Feature structures in the style of Head-Driven Phrase Structure Grammar; and (3) The Z. Harris style goal of attempting to regularize multiple ways of saying the same thing into a single representation. Our approach differs from LFG F-structure in several ways: we have more than two levels; we have a different set of relational labels; and finally, our approach is designed to be compatible with the Penn Treebank framework and therefore, Penn-Treebank-based parsers. In addition, the expansion of our theory is governed more by available resources than by the underlying theory. As our main goal is to use our system to regularize data, we freely incorporate any analysis that fits this goal. Over time, we have found ways of incorporating Named Entities, PropBank, NomBank and the Penn Discourse Treebank. Our agenda also includes incorporating the results of other research efforts (Pustejovsky et al., 2005).

For each sentence, we generate a feature structure (FS) representing our most complete analysis. We distill a subset of this information into a dependency structure governed by theoretical assumptions, e.g., about identifying *functors* of phrases. Each GLARF dependency is between a functor and an argument, where the functor is the head of a phrase, conjunction, complementizer, or other function word. We have built applications that use each of these two representations, e.g., the dependency representation is used in (Shinyama, 2007) and the FS representation is used in (K. Parton and K. R. McKeown and R. Coyne and M. Diab and R. Grishman and D. Hakkani-Tür and M. Harper and H. Ji and W. Y. Ma and A. Meyers and S. Stolbach and A. Sun and G. Tür and W. Xu and S. Yarman, 2009).

In the dependency representation, each sentence is a set of 23 tuples, each 23-tuple characterizing up to three relations between two words: (1) a SURFACE relation, the relation between a functor and an argument in the parse of a sentence; (2) a LOGIC1 relation which regularizes for lexical and syntactic phenomena like passive, relative clauses, deleted subjects; and (3) a LOGIC2 relation corresponding to relations in PropBank, NomBank, and the Penn Discourse Treebank (PDTB). While the full output has all this information, we will limit this paper to a discussion of the LOGIC1 relations. Figure 1 is a 5 tuple subset of the 23 tuple GLARF analysis of the sentence *Who was eaten by Grendel?* (The full

| L1 | Surf | L2 | Func | Arg |
|---|---|---|---|---|
| NIL | SENT | NIL | Who | was |
| PRD | PRD | NIL | was | eaten |
| COMP | COMP | ARG0 | eaten | by |
| OBJ | NIL | ARG1 | eaten | Who |
| NIL | OBJ | NIL | by | Grendel |
| SBJ | NIL | NIL | eaten | Grendel |

Figure 1: 5-tuples: *Who was eaten by Grendel*

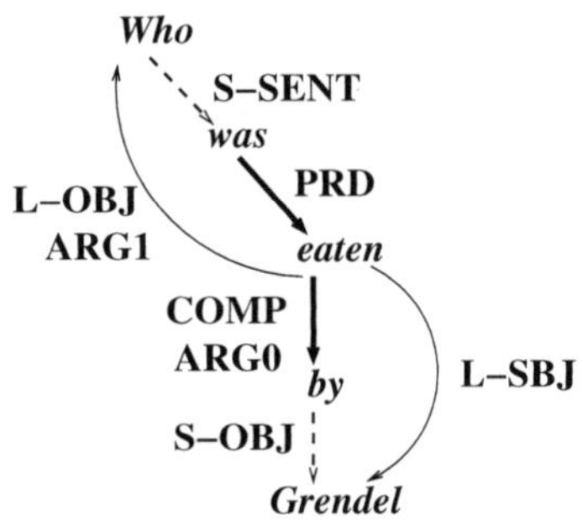


Figure 2: Graph of *Who was eaten by Grendel*

23 tuples include unique ids and fine-grained linguistic features). The fields listed are: logic1 label (L1), surface label (Surf), logic2 label (L2), functor (Func) and argument (Arg). NIL indicates that there is no relation of that type. Figure 2 represents this as a graph. For edges with two labels, the ARG0 or ARG1 label indicates a LOGIC2 relation. Edges with an L- prefix are LOGIC1 labels (the edges are curved); edges with S-prefixes are SURFACE relations (the edges are dashed); and other (thick) edges bear unprefixed labels representing combined SURFACE/LOGIC1 relations. Deleting the dashed edges yields a LOGIC1 representation; deleting the curved edges yields a SURFACE representation; and a LOGIC2 consists of the edges labeled ARGO and ARG1 relations, plus the surface subtrees rooted where the LOGIC2 edges terminate. Taken together, a sentence's SURFACE relations form a tree; the LOGIC1 relations form a directed acyclic graph; and the LOGIC2 relations form directed graphs with some cycles and, due to PDTB relations, may connect sentences to previous ones, e.g., adverbs like *however*, take the previous sentence as one of their arguments.

LOGIC1 relations (based on Relational Grammar) regularize across grammatical and lexical alternations. For example, subcategorized verbal arguments include: SBJect, OBJect and IND-OBJ (indirect Object), COMPlement, PRT (Particle), PRD (predicative complement). Other verbal modifiers include AUXilliary, PARENthetical, ADVerbial. In contrast, FrameNet and PropBank make finer distinctions. Both PP arguments of *consulted* in *John consulted with Mary about the project* bear COMP relations with the verb in GLARF, but would have distinct labels in both PropBank and FrameNet. Thus Semantic Role Labeling (SRL) should be more difficult than recognizing LOGIC1 relations.

Beginning with Penn Treebank II, Penn Treebank annotation includes Function tags, hyphenated additions to phrasal categories which indicate their function. There are several types of function tags:

- **Argument Tags** such as SBJ, OBJ, IO (IND-OBJ), CLR (COMP) and PRD–These are limited to verbal relations and not all are used in all treebanks. For example, OBJ and IO are used in the Chinese, but not the English treebank. These labels can often be directly translated into GLARF LOGIC1 relations.
- **Adjunct Tags** such as ADV, TMP, DIR, LOC, MNR, PRP–These tags often translate into a single LOGIC1 tag (ADV). However, some of these also correspond to LOGIC1 arguments. In particular, some DIR and MNR tags are realized as LOGIC1 COMP relations (based on dictionary entries). The fine grained semantic distinctions are maintained in other features that are part of the GLARF description.

In addition, GLARF treats Penn's PRN phrasal category as a relation rather than a phrasal category. For example, given a sentence like, *Banana ketchup, the agency claims, is very nutritious*, the phrase *the agency claims* is analyzed as an S(entence) in GLARF bearing a (surface) PAREN relation to the main clause. Furthermore, the whole sentence is a COMP of the verb *claims*. Since PAREN is a SURFACE relation, not a LOGIC1 relation, there is no LOGIC1 cycle as shown by the set of 5-tuples in Figure 3– a cycle only exists if you include both SURFACE and LOGIC1 relations in a single graph.

Another important feature of the GLARF framework is *transparency*, a term originating from N.

| L1 | Surf | L2 | Func | Arg |
|---|---|---|---|---|
| NIL | SBJ | ARG1 | is | ketchup |
| PRD | PRD | ARG2 | is | nutritious |
| SBJ | NIL | NIL | nutritious | Ketchup |
| ADV | ADV | NIL | nutritious | very |
| N-POS | N-POS | NIL | ketchup | Banana |
| NIL | PAREN | NIL | is | claims |
| SBJ | SBJ | ARG0 | claims | agency |
| Q-POS | Q-POS | NIL | agency | the |
| COMP | NIL | ARG1 | claims | is |

Figure 3: 5-tuples: *Banana Ketchup, the agency claims, is very nutritious*

| L1 | Surf | L2 | Func | Arg |
|---|---|---|---|---|
| SBJ | SBJ | ARG0 | ate | and |
| OBJ | OBJ | ARG1 | ate | box |
| CONJ | CONJ | NIL | and | John |
| CONJ | CONJ | NIL | and | Mary |
| COMP | COMP | NIL | box | of |
| Q-POS | Q-POS | NIL | box | the |
| OBJ | OBJ | NIL | of | cookies |

Figure 4: 5-tuples: *John and Mary ate the box of cookies*

Sager's unpublished work. A relation between two words is transparent if: the functor fails to characterize the selectional properties of the phrase (or subgraph in a Dependency Analysis), but its argument does. For example, relations between conjunctions (e.g., *and, or, but*) and their conjuncts are transparent CONJ relations. Thus although *and* links together *John* and *Mary*, it is these dependents that determine that the resulting phrase is noun-like (an NP in phrase structure terminology) and sentient (and thus can occur as the subject of verbs like *ate*). Another common example of transparent relations are the relations connecting certain nouns and the prepositional objects under them, e.g., *the box of cookies* is edible, because cookies are edible even though boxes are not. These features are marked in the NOMLEX-PLUS dictionary (Meyers et al., 2004b). In Figure 4, we represent transparent relations, by prefixing the LOGIC1 label with asterisks.

The above description most accurately describes English GLARF. However, Chinese GLARF has most of the same properties, the main exception being that PDTB arguments are not currently marked. For Japanese, we have only a preliminary representation of LOGIC2 relations and they are not derived from PropBank/NomBank/PDTB.

### 2.1 Scoring the LOGIC1 Structure

For purposes of scoring, we chose to focus on LOGIC1 relations, our proposed high-performance level of semantics. We scored with respect to: the LOGIC1 relational label, the identity of the functor and the argument, and whether the relation is transparent or not. If the system output differs in any of these respects, the relation is marked wrong. The following sections will briefly describe each system and present an evaluation of its results.

The answer keys for each language were created by native speakers editing system output, as represented similarly to the examples in this paper, although part of speech is included for added clarity. In addition, as we attempted to evaluate logical relation (or dependency) accuracy independent of sentence splitting. We obtained sentence divisions from data providers and treebank annotation for all the Japanese and most of the English data, but used automatic sentence divisions for the English BLOG data. For the Chinese, we omitted several sentences from our evaluation set due to incorrect sentence splits. The English and Japanese answer keys were annotated by single native speakers expert in GLARF. The Chinese data was annotated by several native speakers and may have been subject to some interannotator agreement difficulties, which we intend to resolve in future work. Currently, correcting system output is the best way to create answer keys due to certain ambiguities in the framework, some of which we hope to incorporate into future scoring procedures. For example, consider the interpretation of the phrase *five acres of land in England* with respect to PP attachment. The difference in meaning between attaching the PP *in England* to *acres* or to *land* is too subtle for these authors– we have difficulty imagining situations where one statement would be accurate and the other would not. This ambiguity is completely predictable because *acres* is a transparent noun and similar ambiguities hold for all such cases where a transparent noun takes a complement and is followed by a PP attachment. We believe that a more complex scoring program could account for most of these cases.

Similar complexities arise for coordination and several other phenomena.

## 3 English GLARF

We generate English GLARF output by applying a procedure that combines:

1. The output of the 2005 version of the Charniak parser described in (Charniak, 2001), which label precision and recall scores in the 85% range. The updated version of the parser seems to perform closer to 90% on News data and perform lower on other genres. That performance would reflect reports on other versions of the Charniak parser for which statistics are available (Foster and van Genabith, 2008).

2. Named entity (NE) tags from the JET NE system (Ji and Grishman, 2006), which achieves F-scores ranging 86%-91% on newswire for both English and Chinese (depending on Epoch). The JET system identifies seven classes of NEs: Person, GPE, Location, Organization, Facility, Weapon and Vehicle.

3. Machine Readable dictionaries: COMLEX (Macleod et al., 1998), NOMBANK dictionaries (from `http://nlp.cs.nyu.edu/meyers/nombank/`) and others.

4. A sequence of hand-written rules (citations omitted) such that: (1) the first set of rules convert the Penn Treebank into a Feature Structure representation; and (2) each rule $N$ after the first rule is applied to an entire Feature Structure that is the output of rule $N-1$.

For this paper, we evaluated the English output for several different genres, all of which approximately track parsing results for that genre. For written genres, we chose between 40 and 50 sentences. For speech transcripts, we chose 100 sentences–we chose this larger number because a lot of so-called sentences contained text with empty logical descriptions, e.g., single word utterances contain no relations between pairs of words. Each text comes from a different genre. For NEWS text, we used 50 sentences from the aligned Japanese-English data created as part of the JENAAD corpus (Utiyama

| Genre | Prec | Rec | F |
|---|---|---|---|
| NEWS | $\frac{731}{815}$ = 89.7% | $\frac{715}{812}$ = 90.0% | 89.9% |
| BLOG | $\frac{704}{844}$ = 83.4% | $\frac{704}{899}$ = 78.3% | 80.8% |
| LETT | $\frac{392}{434}$ = 90.3% | $\frac{392}{449}$ = 87.3% | 88.8% |
| TELE | $\frac{472}{604}$ = 78.1% | $\frac{472}{610}$ = 77.4% | 77.8% |
| NARR | $\frac{732}{959}$ = 76.3% | $\frac{732}{964}$ = 75.9% | 76.1% |

Table 1: English Aggregate Scores

| Corpus | Prec | Rec | F | Sents |
|---|---|---|---|---|
| NEWS | 90.5% | 90.8% | 90.6% | 50 |
| BLOG | 84.1% | 79.6% | 81.7% | 46 |
| LETT | 93.9% | 89.2% | 91.4% | 46 |
| TELE | 81.4% | 83.2% | 84.9% | 103 |
| NARR | 77.1% | 78.1% | 79.5% | 100 |

Table 2: English Score per Sentence

and Isahara, 2003); the web text (BLOGs) was taken from some corpora provided by the Linguistic Data Consortium through the GALE (`http://projects.ldc.upenn.edu/gale/`) program; the LETTer genre (a letter from Good Will) was taken from the ICIC Corpus of Fundraising Texts (Indiana Center for Intercultural Communication); Finally, we chose two spoken language transcripts: a TELEphone conversation from the Switchboard Corpus (`http://www.ldc.upenn.edu/Catalog/readme_files/switchboard.readme.html`) and one NARRative from the Charlotte Narrative and Conversation Collection (`http://newsouthvoices.uncc.edu/cncc.php`). In both cases, we assumed perfect sentence splitting (based on Penn Treebank annotation). The ICIC, Switchboard and Charlotte texts that we used are part of the Open American National Corpus (OANC), in particular, the SIGANN shared subcorpus of the OANC (`http://nlp.cs.nyu.edu/wiki/corpuswg/ULA-OANC-1`) (Meyers et al., 2007).

Comparable work for English includes: (1) (Gabbard et al., 2006), a system which reproduces the function tags of the Penn Treebank with 89% accuracy and empty categories (and their antecedents) with varying accuracies ranging from 82.2% to 96.3%, excluding null complementizers, as these are theory-internal and have no value for filling gaps. (2) Current systems that generate LFG F-structure such as (Wagner et al., 2007) which achieve an F score of 91.1 on the F-structure PRED relations, which are similar to our LOGIC1 relations.

## 4 Chinese GLARF

The Chinese GLARF program takes a Chinese Treebank-style syntactic parse and the output of a Chinese PropBanker (Xue, 2008) as input, and attempts to determine the relations between the head and its dependents within each constituent. It does this by first exploiting the structural information and detecting six broad categories of syntactic relations that hold between the head and its dependents. These are *predication*, *modification*, *complementation*, *coordination*, *auxiliary*, and *flat*. Predication holds at the clause level between the subject and the predicate, where the predicate is considered to be the head and the subject is considered to the dependent. Modification can also hold mainly within NPs and VPs, where the dependents are modifiers of the NP head or adjuncts to the head verb. Coordination holds almost for all phrasal categories where each non-punctuation child within this constituent is either conjunction or a conjunct. The head in a coordination structure is underspecified and can be either a conjunct or a conjunction depending on the grammatical framework. Complementation holds between a head and its complement, with the complement usually being a core argument of the head. For example, inside a PP, the preposition is the head and the phrase or clause it takes is the dependent. An auxiliary structure is one where the auxiliary takes a VP as its complement. This structure is identified so that the auxiliary and the verb it modifies can form a verb group in the GLARF framework. Flat structures are structures where a constituent has no meaningful internal structure, which is possible in a small number of cases. After these six broad categories of relations are identified, more fine-grained relation can be detected with additional information. Figure 5 is a sample 4-tuple for a Chinese translation of the sentence in figure 3.

| L1 | Surf | L2 | Func | Arg |
|---|---|---|---|---|
| SBJ | SBJ | ARG0 | 说<br>claims | 代理<br>agency |
| COMP | COMP | NIL | 说<br>claims | 是<br>is |
| NIL | SBJ | ARG1 | 是<br>is | 酱<br>ketchup |
| N-POS | N-POS | NIL | 酱<br>ketchup | 香蕉<br>banana |
| PRD | PRD | ARG2 | 是<br>is | 有<br>have |
| ADV | ADV | NIL | 有<br>have | 很<br>very |
| OBJ | OBJ | ARG2 | 有<br>have | 营养<br>nutrition |
| SBJ | NIL | ARG1 | 有<br>have | 酱<br>ketchup |
| SENT | NIL | NIL | 的<br>DE | 有<br>have |

代理说，香蕉酱是很有营养的。

Figure 5: Agency claims, Banana Ketchup is very have nutrition DE.

For the results reported in Table 3, we used the Harper and Huang parser described in (Harper and Huang, Forthcoming) which can achieve F-scores as high as 85.2%, in combination with information about named entities from the output of the JET Named Entity tagger for Chinese (86%-91% F-measure as per section 3). We used the NE tags to adjust the parts of speech and the phrasal boundaries of named entities (we do the same with English). As shown in Table 3, we tried two versions of the Harper and Huang parser, one which adds function tags to the output and one that does not. The Chinese GLARF system scores significantly (13.9% F-score) higher given function tagged input, than parser output without function tags. Our current score is about 10 points lower than the parser score. Our initial error analysis suggests that the most common forms of errors involve: (1) the processing of long NPs; (2) segmentation and POS errors; (3) conjunction scope; and (4) modifier attachment.

## 5 Japanese GLARF

For Japanese, we process text with the KNP parser (Kurohashi and Nagao, 1998) and convert the output into the GLARF framework. The KNP/Kyoto Corpus framework is a Japanese-specific Dependency framework, very different from the Penn Treebank framework used for the other systems. Processing in Japanese proceeds as follows: (1) we process the Japanese with the Juman segmenter (Kuro-

| Type | Prec | Rec | F |
|---|---|---|---|
| **No Function Tags Version** | | | |
| Aggr | $\frac{843}{1374} = 61.4\%$ | $\frac{843}{1352} = 62.4\%$ | 61.8% |
| Aver | 62.3% | 63.5% | 63.6% |
| **Function Tags Version** | | | |
| Aggr | $\frac{1031}{1415} = 72.9\%$ | $\frac{1031}{1352} = 76.3\%$ | 74.5% |
| Aver | 73.0% | 75.3% | 74.9% |

Table 3: 53 Chinese Newswire Sentences: Aggregate and Average Sentence Scores

hashi et al., 1994) and KNP parser 2.0 (Kurohashi and Nagao, 1998), which has reported accuracy of 91.32% F score for dependency accuracy, as reported in (Noro et al., 2005). As is standard in Japanese linguistics, the KNP/Kyoto Corpus (K) framework uses a dependency analysis that has some features of a phrase structure analysis. In particular, the dependency relations are between *bunsetsu*, small constituents which include a head word and some number of modifiers which are typically function words (particles, auxiliaries, etc.), but can also be prenominal noun modifiers. Bunsetsu can also include multiple words in the case of names. The K framework differentiates types of dependencies into: the normal head-argument variety, coordination (or parallel) and apposition. We convert the head-argument variety of dependency straightforwardly into a phrase consisting of the head and all the arguments. In a similar way, appositive relations could be represented using an APPOSITIVE relation (as is currently done with English). In the case of bunsetsu, the task is to choose a head and label the other constituents–This is very similar to our task of labeling and subdividing the flat noun phrases of the English Penn Treebank. Conjunction is a little different because the K analysis assumes that the final conjunct is the functor, rather than a conjunction. We automatically changed this analysis to be the same as it is for English and Chinese. When there was no actual conjunction, we created a theory-internal NULL conjunction. The final stages include: (1) processing conjunction and apposition, including recognizing cases that the parser does not recognize; (2) correcting parts of speech; (3) labeling all relations between arguments and heads; (4) recognizing and labeling special constituent types such as Named Entities, double quote constituents and number phrases (*twenty one*); (5) handling common idioms; and (6) processing light verb and copula constructions.

| L1 | Surf | L2 | Func | Arg |
|---|---|---|---|---|
| PRD | PRD | NIL | だ | 責務 |
| | | | is | duty |
| NIL | SBJ | NIL | だ | こと |
| | | | is | fact |
| SBJ | NIL | NIL | 責務 | こと |
| | | | duty | fact |
| COMP | COMP | NIL | 責務 | 国家 |
| | | | duty | state |
| PRT | PRT | NIL | 国家 | の |
| COMP | COMP | NIL | こと | 守る |
| | | | fact | protect |
| PRT | PRT | NIL | こと | は |
| OBJ | OBJ | NIL | 守る | NULL |
| | | | protect | CONJ |
| *CONJ | CONJ | NIL | NULL | 財産 |
| | | | CONJ | assets |
| PRT | PRT | NIL | 財産 | を |
| *CONJ | CONJ | NIL | NULL | 生命 |
| | | | CONJ | lives |

生命・財産を守ることは国家の責務だ。

Figure 6: It is the state's duty to protect lives and assets.

| Type | Prec | Rec | F |
|---|---|---|---|
| Aggr | $\frac{764}{843} = 91.0\%$ | $\frac{764}{840} = 90.6\%$ | 90.8% |
| Aver | 90.7% | 90.6% | 90.6% |

Table 4: 40 Japanese Sentences from JENAA Corpus: Aggregate and Average Sentence Scores

Figure 6 is a sample 4-tuple for a Japanese sentence meaning *It is the state's duty to protect lives and assets.* Conjunction is handled as discussed above, using an invisible NULL conjunction and transparent (asterisked) logical CONJ relations. Copulas in all three languages take surface subjects, which are the LOGIC1 subjects of the PRD argument of the copula. We have left out glosses for the particles, which act solely as case markers and help us identify the grammatical relation.

We scored Japanese GLARF on forty sentences of the Japanese side of the JENAA data (25 of which are parallel with the English sentences scored). Like the English, the F score is very close to the parsing scores achieved by the parser.

## 6 Concluding Remarks and Future Work

In this paper, we have described three systems for generating GLARF representations automatically from text, each system combines the output of a parser and possibly some other processor (segmenter, Named Entity Recognizer, PropBanker, etc.) and creates a logical representation of the sentence. Dictionaries, word lists, and various other resources are used, in conjunction with hand written rules. In each case, the results are very close to parsing accuracy. These logical structures are in the same annotation framework, using the same labeling scheme and the same analysis for key types of constructions. There are several advantages to our approach over other characterizations of logical structure: (1) our representation is among the most accurate and reliable; (2) our representation connects all the words in the sentence; and (3) having the same representation for multiple languages facilitates running the same procedures in multiple languages and creating multilingual applications.

The English system was developed for the News genre, specifically the Penn Treebank Wall Street Journal Corpus. We are therefore considering adding rules to better handle constructions that appear in other genres, but not news. The experiments describe here should go a long way towards achieving this goal. We are also considering experiments with parsers tailored to particular genres and/or parsers that add function tags (Harper et al., 2005). In addition, our current GLARF system uses internal Propbank/NomBank rules, which have good precision, but low recall. We expect that we achieve better results if we incorporate the output of state of the art SRL systems, although we would have to conduct experiments as to whether or not we can improve such results with additional rules.

We developed the English system over the course of eight years or so. In contrast, the Chinese and Japanese systems are newer and considerably less time was spent developing them. Thus they currently do not represent as many regularizations. One obstacle is that we do not currently use subcategorization dictionaries for either language, while we have several for English. In particular, these would be helpful in predicting and filling relative clause and others gaps. We are considering automatically acquiring simple dictionaries by recording frequently occurring argument types of verbs over a larger corpus, e.g., along the lines of (Kawahara and Kurohashi, 2002). In addition, existing Japanese dictionaries such as the IPAL (monolingual) dictionary (technology Promotion Agency, 1987) or previously acquired case information reported in (Kawahara and Kurohashi, 2002).

Finally, we are investigating several avenues for using this system output for Machine Translation (MT) including: (1) aiding word alignment for other MT system (Wang et al., 2007); and (2) aiding the creation various MT models involving analyzed text, e.g., (Gildea, 2004; Shen et al., 2008).

## Acknowledgments

This work was supported by NSF Grant IIS-0534700 Structure Alignment-based MT.

## References

C. F. Baker, C. J. Fillmore, and J. B. Lowe. 1998. The Berkeley FrameNet Project. In *Coling-ACL98*, pages 86–90.

E. Charniak. 2001. Immediate-head parsing for language models. In *ACL 2001*, pages 116–123.

N. Chomsky. 1957. *Syntactic Structures*. Mouton, The Hague.

M. Collins. 1999. *Head-Driven Statistical Models for Natural Language Parsing*. Ph.D. thesis, University of Pennsylvania.

J. Foster and J. van Genabith. 2008. Parser Evaluation and the BNC: 4 Parsers and 3 Evaluation Metrics. In *LREC 2008*, Marrakech, Morocco.

R. Gabbard, M. Marcus, and S. Kulick. 2006. Fully parsing the penn treebank. In *NAACL/HLT*, pages 184–191.

D. Gildea. 2004. Dependencies vs. Constituents for Tree-Based Alignment. In *EMNLP*, Barcelona.

J. Hajič, M. Ciaramita, R. Johansson, D. Kawahara, M. A. Martí, L. Màrquez, A. Meyers, J. Nivre, S. Padó, J. Štěpánek, P. Straňák, M. Surdeanu, N. Xue, and Y. Zhang. 2009. The CoNLL-2009 shared task: Syntactic and semantic dependencies in multiple languages. In *CoNLL-2009*, Boulder, Colorado, USA.

M. Harper and Z. Huang. Forthcoming. Chinese Statistical Parsing. In J. Olive, editor, *Global Autonomous Language Exploitation*. Publisher to be Announced.

M. Harper, B. Dorr, J. Hale, B. Roark, I. Shafran, M. Lease, Y. Liu, M. Snover, L. Yung, A. Krasnyanskaya, and R. Stewart. 2005. Parsing and Spoken

Structural Event. Technical Report, The John-Hopkins University, 2005 Summer Research Workshop.

Z. Harris. 1968. *Mathematical Structures of Language*. Wiley-Interscience, New York.

J. R. Hobbs and R. Grishman. 1976. The Automatic Transformational Analysis of English Sentences: An Implementation. *International Journal of Computer Mathematics*, 5:267–283.

H. Ji and R. Grishman. 2006. Analysis and Repair of Name Tagger Errors. In *COLING/ACL 2006*, Sydney, Australia.

K. Parton and K. R. McKeown and R. Coyne and M. Diab and R. Grishman and D. Hakkani-Tür and M. Harper and H. Ji and W. Y. Ma and A. Meyers and S. Stolbach and A. Sun and G. Tür and W. Xu and S. Yarman. 2009. Who, What, When, Where, Why? Comparing Multiple Approaches to the Cross-Lingual 5W Task. In *ACL 2009*.

D. Kawahara and S. Kurohashi. 2002. Fertilization of Case Frame Dictionary for Robust Japanese Case Analysis. In *Proc. of COLING 2002*.

S. Kurohashi and M. Nagao. 1998. Building a Japanese parsed corpus while improving the parsing system. In *Proceedings of The 1st International Conference on Language Resources & Evaluation*, pages 719–724.

S. Kurohashi, T. Nakamura, Y. Matsumoto, and M. Nagao. 1994. Improvements of Japanese Morphological Analyzer JUMAN. In *Proc. of International Workshop on Sharable Natural Language Resources (SNLR)*, pages 22–28.

C. Macleod, R. Grishman, and A. Meyers. 1998. COMLEX Syntax. *Computers and the Humanities*, 31:459–481.

M. P. Marcus, B. Santorini, and M. A. Marcinkiewicz. 1994. Building a large annotated corpus of english: The penn treebank. *Computational Linguistics*, 19(2):313–330.

A. Meyers, M. Kosaka, S. Sekine, R. Grishman, and S. Zhao. 2001. Parsing and GLARFing. In *Proceedings of RANLP-2001*, Tzigov Chark, Bulgaria.

A. Meyers, R. Reeves, C. Macleod, R. Szekely, V. Zielinska, B. Young, and R. Grishman. 2004a. The NomBank Project: An Interim Report. In *NAACL/HLT 2004 Workshop Frontiers in Corpus Annotation*, Boston.

A. Meyers, R. Reeves, Catherine Macleod, Rachel Szekeley, Veronkia Zielinska, and Brian Young. 2004b. The Cross-Breeding of Dictionaries. In *Proceedings of LREC-2004*, Lisbon, Portugal.

A. Meyers, N. Ide, L. Denoyer, and Y. Shinyama. 2007. The shared corpora working group report. In *Proceedings of The Linguistic Annotation Workshop, ACL 2007*, pages 184–190, Prague, Czech Republic.

A. Meyers. 2008. Using treebank, dictionaries and glarf to improve nombank annotation. In *Proceedings of The Linguistic Annotation Workshop, LREC 2008*, Marrakesh, Morocco.

E. Miltsakaki, A. Joshi, R. Prasad, and B. Webber. 2004. Annotating discourse connectives and their arguments. In A. Meyers, editor, *NAACL/HLT 2004 Workshop: Frontiers in Corpus Annotation*, pages 9–16, Boston, Massachusetts, USA, May 2 - May 7. Association for Computational Linguistics.

T. Noro, C. Koike, T. Hashimoto, T. Tokunaga, and Hozumi Tanaka. 2005. Evaluation of a Japanese CFG Derived from a Syntactically Annotated corpus with Respect to Dependency Measures. In *2005 Workshop on Treebanks and Linguistic theories*, pages 115–126.

M. Palmer, D. Gildea, and P. Kingsbury. 2005. The Proposition Bank: An annotated corpus of semantic roles. *Computational Linguistics*, 31(1):71–106.

J. Pustejovsky, A. Meyers, M. Palmer, and M. Poesio. 2005. Merging PropBank, NomBank, TimeBank, Penn Discourse Treebank and Coreference. In *ACL 2005 Workshop: Frontiers in Corpus Annotation II: Pie in the Sky*.

L. Shen, J. Xu, and R. Weischedel. 2008. A New String-to-Dependency Machine Translation Algorithm with a Target Dependency Language Model. In *ACL 2008*.

Y. Shinyama. 2007. *Being Lazy and Preemptive at Learning toward Information Extraction*. Ph.D. thesis, NYU.

M. Surdeanu, R. Johansson, A. Meyers, Ll. Màrquez, and J. Nivre. 2008. The CoNLL-2008 Shared Task on Joint Parsing of Syntactic and Semantic Dependencies. In *Proceedings of the CoNLL-2008 Shared Task*, Manchester, GB.

Information technology Promotion Agency. 1987. IPA Lexicon of the Japanese Language for Computers IPAL (Basic Verbs). (in Japanese).

M. Utiyama and H. Isahara. 2003. Reliable Measures for Aligning Japanese-English News Articles and Sentences. In *ACL-2003*, pages 72–79.

J. Wagner, D. Seddah, J. Foster, and J. van Genabith. 2007. C-Structures and F-Structures for the British National Corpus. In *Proceedings of the Twelfth International Lexical Functional Grammar Conference*, Stanford. CSLI Publications.

C. Wang, M. Collins, and P. Koehn. 2007. Chinese syntactic reordering for statistical machine translation. In *EMNLP-CoNLL 2007*, pages 737–745.

N. Xue, F. Xia, F. Chiou, and M. Palmer. 2005. The Penn Chinese TreeBank: Phrase Structure Annotation of a Large Corpus. *Natural Language Engineering*, 11:207–238.

N. Xue. 2008. Labeling Chinese Predicates with Semantic roles. *Computational Linguistics*, 34:225–255.

# Author Index

**Association for Computational Linguistics**
209 N. Eighth Street
Stroudsburg, Pennsylvania 18360

CURRAN ASSOCIATES INC
proceedings
.com